"Extraordinarily practical . . . This book is a must-read for all stakeholders in high-needs schools. The cases and findings would also be beneficial for educators seeking to resolve digital inequity and enhance digital learning, especially in the post-pandemic era."

—**Jongpil Cheon,** *Associate Professor of Instructional Technology,*
College of Education, Texas Tech University, USA

"In arguing that digital equity is school equity and analyzing the issue as one that involves both intersectional identities and an undergirding sociopolitical context, Heejung An and David Fuentes, professors and scholars of teacher education with expertise in preparing educators to serve diverse communities, provide a deep and nuanced exploration that broadens understanding. Chapters written by interdisciplinary scholars offer examples of equitable leadership of digital learning in high-needs schools that range from the use of social media in professional development to the role of school librarians to address the needs of all learners. There is something in this text for everyone who works in schools and cares about making needed change to provide children with more equitable learning environments."

—**Amy Ginsberg**, *Dean of the College of Education,*
William Paterson University, USA

"Where will education go next? The authors tackle this colossal question to embrace this era of uncertainty. This book covers a diverse array of perspectives and will add great value in high-needs schools."

—**Keol Lim**, *Professor, Department of Educational Technology,*
Konkuk University, South Korea

"The COVID-19 pandemic presented unprecedented challenges for K-12 schools while heightening the effects of unequal access to educational resources, particularly online digital technologies. An and Fuentes have gathered a fine group of experts that consider the complexity of these issues from a variety of angles. Rather than envisioning digital technologies as a panacea, the grounded approach generally shared by the authors focuses their concerns on funding and wrap-around resources, with new technologies as pieces of a much larger puzzle. Each chapter is framed with guiding questions and concluded with key takeaways and recommended resources, making it an eminently practical tool for both teachers and researchers."

—**Lance E. Mason**, *Associate Professor of Education,*
Indiana University Kokomo, USA

"Grounded in research and real school experiences, this essential and thought-provoking book challenges the reader to rethink and transform PreK-12 classroom teaching, administration, and schools, especially in high-needs communities. An and Fuentes have gathered varied respected individuals with expertise in working in schools in challenging times and communities to share their research, knowings, encounters, and strategies for addressing digital equity and student learning. By defining and examining the intertwined layers that impact student learning in high-needs communities, this book begins by laying a foundation for exploring student, family, and school needs to inform and support educational systems with an equity and digital lens. While inspired by the disruption and impact of the COVID-19 pandemic on schools and learning, the authors provide practical supports and guidance for PreK-12 teachers, administrators, undergraduate and graduate students in teacher preparation and education programs to renovate and reinvigorate student learning and family supports. With a focus on digital learning, equity, and best pedagogical practices, the authors provide guiding questions in each chapter to frame discussion, inspire action, and effect change in the best interests of students and schools. A must-have book with new and engaging information for anyone interested in impacting high-needs communities."

—**Holly Seplocha**, *Professor Emeritus in the Department of Teacher Education: PreK-12, College of Education, William Paterson University, USA*

"This edited book provides a unique collection of critical perspectives, policy analyses, organizational innovations, tools and strategies, and valuable lessons on digital learning in high-needs P-12 schools. A wide range of readers, such as policymakers, educators, administrators, educational researchers, and anyone interested in addressing the digital divide will find extremely relevant insights in this book to achieve accessible and equitable learning in high-needs schools. The contributions from 25 authors also demonstrate the vision and commitment of the editors to diversity, inclusion, innovation, and collaboration in this timely and needed publication."

—**Ke Zhang,** *Professor, Learning Design and Technology, College of Education, Wayne State University, USA*

DIGITAL LEARNING IN HIGH-NEEDS SCHOOLS

Digital Learning in High-Needs Schools examines the challenges and affordances that arise when high-needs school communities integrate educational technologies into their unique settings. Although remote, blended, and networked learning are ubiquitous today, a number of cultural, economic, and political realities—from the digital divide and digital literacy to poverty and language barriers—affect our most vulnerable and underresourced teachers and students. This book uses critical theory to compassionately scrutinize and unpack the systemic issues that impact high-needs schools' implementation of digital learning tools. Incisive sociocultural analyses across fifteen original chapters explore the intersection of society, technology, people, politics, and education in high-needs school contexts. Informed by real-world cases pertaining to technology infrastructure, formative feedback, Universal Design for Learning, and more, these chapters illuminate how best practices emerge from culturally responsive and context-specific foundations.

Heejung An is Professor in the Department of Educational Leadership and Professional Studies in the College of Education at William Paterson University of New Jersey, USA.

David A. Fuentes is Interim Associate Dean and Professor in the College of Education at William Paterson University of New Jersey, USA.

DIGITAL LEARNING IN HIGH-NEEDS SCHOOLS

A Critical Approach to Technology Access and Equity in PreK-12

Edited by
Heejung An and David A. Fuentes

Designed cover image: © Shutterstock

First published 2023

by Routledge
605 Third Avenue, New York, NY 10158

and by Routledge
4 Park Square, Milton Park, Abingdon, Oxon, OX14 4RN

Routledge is an imprint of the Taylor & Francis Group, an informa business

© 2023 selection and editorial matter, Heejung An and David A. Fuentes; individual chapters, the contributors

The right of Heejung An and David A. Fuentes to be identified as the authors of the editorial material, and of the authors for their individual chapters, has been asserted in accordance with sections 77 and 78 of the Copyright, Designs and Patents Act 1988.

All rights reserved. No part of this book may be reprinted or reproduced or utilised in any form or by any electronic, mechanical, or other means, now known or hereafter invented, including photocopying and recording, or in any information storage or retrieval system, without permission in writing from the publishers.

Trademark notice: Product or corporate names may be trademarks or registered trademarks, and are used only for identification and explanation without intent to infringe.

Library of Congress Cataloging-in-Publication Data
Names: An, Heejung, 1970– editor. | Fuentes, David, 1978– editor.
Title: Digital learning in high-needs schools : a critical approach to technology access and equity in preK-12 / edited by Heejung An and David A. Fuentes.
Description: New York, NY : Routledge, 2023. | Includes bibliographical references and index.
Identifiers: LCCN 2022060534 (print) | LCCN 2022060535 (ebook) | ISBN 9781032226408 (hardback) | ISBN 9781032228600 (paperback) | ISBN 9781003274537 (ebook)
Subjects: LCSH: Children with social disabilities—Education—United States. | Computer-assisted instruction—Social aspects—United States. | Web-based instruction—Social aspects—United States. | Educational technology—Social aspects.—United States. | Education—United States—Regional disparities. | Educational equalization—United States.
Classification: LCC LC4091 .D45 2023 (print) | LCC LC4091 (ebook) | DDC 371.33/44678—dc23/eng/20230221
LC record available at https://lccn.loc.gov/2022060534
LC ebook record available at https://lccn.loc.gov/2022060535

ISBN: 978-1-032-22640-8 (hbk)
ISBN: 978-1-032-22860-0 (pbk)
ISBN: 978-1-003-27453-7 (ebk)

DOI: 10.4324/9781003274537

Typeset in Bembo
by Apex CoVantage, LLC

CONTENTS

Foreword: It's Time to Finally Make All the World a School	*x*
Curtis J. Bonk	
Preface	*xx*
Acknowledgments	*xxv*

SECTION I
Understanding the Intersection of Students, Families, and Schooling in High-Needs Communities   **1**

1 Understanding the Sociocultural and Sociopolitical
   Contexts of U.S. High-Needs Public Schools Before,
   During, and After the COVID-19 Pandemic   3
   David Fuentes and Heejung An

2 Ramifications of the Digital Divide on Cognitive
   Development and School Preparedness   17
   Joshua L. DeVincenzo, Geryel Osorio-Godoy,
   and Thomas Chandler

3 Strategies to Help Administrators, Teachers, and
   Parents to Achieve Equitable Digital Learning in U.S.
   High-Needs School Communities   28
   Heejung An and Woonhee Sung

viii Contents

SECTION II
Vision and Leadership for Digital Learning in High-Needs Communities
41

4 Bridging the Digital Divide: An Analysis of Federal, State, and Local Policies in U.S. Schools
Thomas Chandler and Joshua L. DeVincenzo
43

5 Twitter for Professional Development and Learning in High-Needs Schools: Considerations for School Leaders
Samuel F. Fancera
54

6 Feedback, Evaluation, and Grading: The Unique Considerations Distance Learning Poses to the Evaluation Cycle and the Task of Ensuring Equitable Practices
Kimberly Moreno
69

7 Students' Informational Needs: Applying the Principles of Universal Design to Address Inequity in High-Needs Schools During Virtual Learning
Gihan Mohamad and Ellen Pozzi
83

SECTION III
Pedagogical Strategies and Digital Tools Across the Curriculum
97

8 Content-Neutral Technologies as a Pedagogical Response in High-Needs Schools and Communities: Design Thinking, Making, and Learning
Diallo Sessoms
99

9 Strategies to Facilitate Digital Learning in Urban High-Needs Social Studies Classrooms
Erik Kormos and Joe Sherman
118

10 Designing a Culturally Responsive Multilingual Arts-Integration Program: Read-Aloud and Book-Inspired Art-Making Videos
Heejung An, Triada Samaras, Maria Lanni, and Nisreen Rajab
130

Contents **ix**

11 The Impact of an Online Mathematics Activity on Elementary School Students' Engagement and Learning in a High-Needs Context 157
August Howerton and Drew Polly

12 Digital Learning for Students With Disabilities 167
Pei-Lin Weng

13 Using Bitmoji® and Google Classroom® to Support Remote Literacy Instruction in High-Needs Schools 179
Neil Grimes and Alicia Burchell

14 A Whole New World: Virtual Excursions for Learners From Urban Settings 199
Renee Whelan and Michael Salvatore

15 Rural Social Studies Teachers' Postpandemic Use of Technology Tools 209
Scott W. DeWitt and Ethan Podwojski

Contributors *219*
Index *225*

FOREWORD

It's Time to Finally Make All the World a School

Curtis J. Bonk, Indiana University

Anytime I am asked to write the foreword to a book, the first thing that comes to mind is what can I possibly say that will do justice to that particular book and the authors or editors who have worked extremely hard for months, sometimes years, on such a project? I know the routine and the many nights lacking significant sleep since I have had several large-scale edited book projects of my own. By the time someone can sit down to write the foreword, much blood and sweat and perhaps a few tears have gone into completing the beast. So when I sat down to read *Digital Learning in High-Needs Schools: A Critical Approach to Technology Access and Equity in PreK-12*, I was looking for some themes, patterns, and interesting vignettes. I soon noted several aspects of this book that deeply resonated with me. I elaborate on them in the paragraphs below.

Remembering the Early Years of Innovative Online Education

Extending Minds Online

As I read this book, I was delighted with the extensive learning resources and progressive educational ideas provided in each chapter. There is a "nowness" to the book and an ever-present "can do" mindset. As I turned the pages, I kept thinking about what others have written or suggested in the past. In the first few chapters, I was thinking about ideas advocated by my late friend Glenn Jones from Denver. Trained to be an attorney, Glenn Jones became the founder of a cable television giant, and then he moved into the field of education with such entities as Jones International University (JIU), Jones Knowledge, and Mind Extension University. Jones had spent much time pondering and promoting new forms of distance and

Foreword: It's Time to Finally Make All the World a School   **xi**

alternative education, primarily for adult learners but also technology-enhanced innovations in K-12 education; in particular, he had a distinct advantage of being able to deliver education to those who were living in remote areas through his cable TV network empire. According to Pamela Pease, the former president of JIU who was responsible for initially implementing the Web-based model eventually utilized at JIU and helping it gain accreditation status, the extensive client base and distribution network placed Jones on the cutting-edge of what was possible in the 1990s in terms of electronically delivered education en masse.

One way Jones helped cement his status as an early innovator in online education was to write a couple of books about K-12 distance education, which I am fortunate to possess with his signature. Fast-forward two or three decades and I am wondering what types of educational ideas and potential solutions he would have offered during the pandemic had he not passed away in 2015 at the age of 85 (Rusch & Chuang, 2015). Would he have been among the many who offered significantly discounted or free education to K-12 students in the United States or, more impressively, to those around the world? Or might Glenn Jones have held online forums on what education and learning actually mean in the 21st century? Might he have lobbied Congress for new laws and forms of funding that could benefit K-12 and higher education students and instructors? Equally important, might Jones have been able to change the conversation about learning loss into learning gains?

The last time I met with Glenn Jones was in April 2010 during the American Educational Research Association (AERA) conference in Denver. When I had the chance to visit him in his office that week, he gave me a personally signed copy of his book *Make All America a School: Mind Extension University* (Jones, 1991). As I recall, it was the last spare copy he had in his massive library of books. That library was situated next to his "war room," from which he monitored the Jones Empire in cable networks, e-commerce, mobile communication, entertainment, education, radio networks, music production and distribution, software development, and digital compression and encryption. But it was in the education sphere that Glenn Jones made a huge societal contribution since he was able to provide education to people in their homes and workplaces through his cable television network instead of having those same people make their way to an educational institution or organization. No longer was education constrained to those who could arrive early and find an open seat. Launched in 1995 and later known as the University of the Web, JIU became the first fully online university to obtain accreditation from a nationally recognized regional accrediting agency in 1999 (Baumgartner, 2015; Bonk, 2009b).

Glenn Jones was a distance education pioneer and visionary. In his 1991 book, he argued,

> Make all America a school. A school available to all regardless of their station in life. A school where equality of educational opportunity exists.

A school that is a place of excitement. Where hope is alive. A place where the clash of technologies and the maelstrom of ideas are orchestrated to the service of education. A place that sees the wilderness of information as our new frontier.

Make all America a school. We can do it, now. (p. iii)

Just one month earlier, in fact, Glen Jones had sent me his follow-up book, *Cyberschools: An Education Renaissance* (Jones, 2010). Once again, he accurately predicted the importance of online learning to learners worldwide. Today, I am left wondering what learning would have been like during the pandemic if America, and all the world for that matter, had, in fact, attempted to make every place a school as Glenn Jones had recommended three decades prior. Would COVID-19 have caused so much devastation and destruction to the hopes and dreams of millions of young people in their prime years of learning? You see, as Pamela Pease reminded me, his world of cable TV, which had started in the 1960s, had extended education to homes, businesses, schools, and even bars and restaurants. With Web-based instruction today, every place actually is a school, whether you are in a(n) cafe, prison, hospital bed, airport concourse, grocery store, boat at sea, back patio at home, or national forest (Bonk et al., 2016). The educational world has opened up during the past few decades to enable anyone to learn anything from anyone else at any time (Bonk, 2009a, 2009b). In fact, no matter your age or life goals, with mobile, online, and open education, you are likely to be learning; I bet you are learning all the time.

If Only We Had Opted for NotSchool

As I read *Digital Learning in High-Needs Schools*, I was also thinking about Stephen Heppell and his widely acclaimed project in the UK from two decades ago called "NotSchool" (Bonk, 2009b; Heppell, 2000). NotSchool, which ran from 1998–2016, enabled those who did not fare well in traditional schools due to situations such as being bullied, becoming pregnant, being committed to heavy travel schedules (e.g., athletes and musicians), suffering from phobias or other illnesses, or experiencing significant challenges or issues interfering with success in their educational pursuits.

In the NotSchool system, learners were given the title of researchers, and teachers were known as mentors. Internet connections provided access to free and open educational resources as well as the means for sharing their creative artifacts and expressions. Importantly, the NotSchool curriculum was extremely flexible and student driven, which were the key pillars of boosting learner confidence with each success. According to a conversation I had with Heppell in early December 2022, "it was widely commended both for good value—it needed no additional marginal funding—but also for remarkable outcomes."

He also noted that NotSchool worked impressively for the 3,500 children per year that were enrolled.

With success often comes opportunities as well as conundrums since people fail to fully grasp the inherent meanings and associated possibilities behind those successes. In fact, near the end of its life, NotSchool found its' way into the latter category. In 2016, just four short years before COVID-19 struck, Heppell decided to write to the UK government and tell them about the successes of NotSchool. In that letter, he implored them to embrace the NotSchool model or concept as a potential fallback strategy for school systems in case of a terrorist attack on schools or a major public health crisis or pandemic. As Heppell predicted, his warning was swiftly ignored. Imagine if instead he had received an encouraging letter back from the UK government and his ideas were substantively embraced. Let's take it a step further; imagine if thousands of NotSchools or entities like them had been established prior to the COVID-19 pandemic, not just in the UK but encircling the planet. Those wanting additional information about the NotSchool project might explore www.NotSchool.net or watch a few interviews of NotSchool students (see https://rubble.heppell.net/media_forum/notschool.mp4).

Certainly, young people during the pandemic experienced some aspects of the NotSchool experience anyway. As detailed in this book, they were often directing their own learning. However, self-directed learning (SDL) and forms of various creative expression within it occurred due to a deadly public health issue; as such, they were typically not preplanned or found in the school curriculum at the start of the year. For some young people, this was a highly successful experience; at the same time, for countless others, it definitely was not. And for many educators who previously had resisted online and blended forms of instruction, the quick ramp-up of their courses during the pandemic and newfound monies for professional development provided skills and competencies for thoughtful technology integration. Importantly, it also offered timely ideas and examples, often shared among colleagues, about how to create engaging online learning that will still exist far beyond the forced quarantine days and learn-at-home semesters of the pandemic.

Simply put, society currently fails to do an adequate job of preparing young learners for a later lifetime of SDL pursuits, a large majority of which might be classified as informal in nature. In response, my colleagues and I have been studying SDL in a series of studies and have recently offered 15 guidelines and strategies for fostering SDL (Bonk & Zhu, in press; Zhu & Bonk, 2022). In addition, we have just published a meta-analysis of the prevailing research on SDL during the past 12 years (Doo et al., 2023). As this study shows, SDL is becoming increasingly researched and discussed; there is even an alliance for those interested in participating in and perhaps making a contribution to SDL (see www.self-directed.org/). Similar to NotSchool, some educators refer to this movement as "unschooling" and emphasize the passion, purpose, and play that often occur in SDL situations (Mishra, 2021).

Embedding Engagement, Encouragement, and Empathy

The second aspect of *Digital Learning in High-Needs Schools* that struck me was how many times the word "engagement" was mentioned in the 15 chapters of this timely book. By the time I was halfway through the book, "engagement" was a mantra being replayed in my head. It was evident that there was a significant struggle to provide learning environments that were engaging, interactive, and responsive to learner needs during the pandemic.

As Kimberly Moreno points out in Chapter 6, most school districts in the United States settled for operating in survival mode during the pandemic, with most or all classes taking place in real time on Zoom or some other such synchronous technology platform. However, as I have documented elsewhere, there were other viable options to such survivor-mode mentalities (Bonk, 2020; Bonk & Wiley, 2020) and emergency remote forms of instruction (Hodges et al., 2020). It was like someone was a carnival barker insisting that the show must go on in the shift to online learning despite the fact that learning was not taking place in a physical showhouse; instead, it would be more of a magic show in the cloud. Somehow, teachers and schools were still expected to provide the same level of engagement and sense of feedback that these same children had previously experienced in in-person schooling. Anything less was deemed inferior and a step backward for the world of education as we knew it.

Myriad learning technologies documented in *Digital Learning in High-Needs Schools* proved to be of value in different degrees during the transition to online learning and emergency remote teaching (Hodges et al., 2020). For example, Erik Kormos and Joe Sherman, in fact, explicitly begin Chapter 9 by pointing out that in 2010, the United States Department of Education stated that since technology was at the core of everything we did in our daily work and home lives, it was incumbent on educators to use it to create powerfully engaging learning environments (United States Department of Education, 2010). Unfortunately, such technology dreams have too often resulted in severe migraine headaches and persistent nightmares rather than meaningful learning.

Sure, we can leverage learning technology to create environments that are more engaging and interactive for learners; however, that typically only occurs when married to innovative pedagogy and a whole range of learning principles that build an entire ecology of learning (Kim & Chung, 2015). Near the end of their chapter, Kormos and Sherman point to the need for establishing learning environments during such a pandemic that are encouraging and filled with compassion for teachers who were now forced to teach from their dining rooms, extra bedrooms, and basements. Everyone in the new educational ecosystem needed such encouragement. Encouragement to start over when lessons or activities were not working as planned. Encouragement to push on when there was limited feedback and support for teachers and students compared to what they previously encountered in physical classroom settings. And encouragement when students were seemingly lost or not participating.

Various chapters mention the need for learner autonomy and choice as well as creating a flexible and supportive learning environment. In Chapter 10, Heejung An and her colleagues point out how vital it was to develop empathy and mutual respect among the learners, most of whom were likely struggling with some aspects of the transition from physical classroom settings to virtual ones. They add that teachers now must engage in purposeful efforts to elicit active participation from their learners stranded at home. For them, a robust ecology of learning needs to foster a sense of belongingness and comfort as well as a meaningful learning that effectively incorporates the cultural diversity of the classroom and the community. The rich funds of knowledge in the community provide a key entry point for that to happen. According to An et al., to successfully travel down the road toward educational equity and inclusivity, teachers should celebrate diversity in all shapes and forms while finding ways to create positive interactions among community members and expose them to multiple perspectives and differing views whenever and wherever possible.

Learning Principles for the 21st Century

Across the 15 chapters, it is apparent that effective learning environments of the 21st century are multifaceted and complex, with an emphasis on skills related to critical and creative thinking, collaboration, and communication. Specifically, as you will discover in the pages of this book, the learning principles that educators should consider putting in place include the following:

1. The Principle of Comfort and Belongingness
2. The Principle of Learner and Instructor Well-Being
3. The Principle of Encouragement and Feedback
4. The Principle of Scaffolded Instruction and Support
5. The Principle of Flexibility in Learning and Thinking
6. The Principle of Fostering a Growth Mindset
7. The Principle of Learner Autonomy and Choice
8. The Principle of Engagement and Involvement
9. The Principle of Multiple Means of Representation
10. The Principle of Diversity Celebrations
11. The Principle of Learning by Doing
12. The Principle of Learner and Instructor Collaboration and Sharing
13. The Principle of Opening Opportunities (Not Detailing Constraints)
14. The Principle of Culturally Responsive Instruction
15. The Principle of Respect and Empathy
16. The Principle of Inquiry- and Problem-Based Learning
17. The Principle of Technology-Enhanced Learning

xvi Foreword: It's Time to Finally Make All the World a School

18. The Principle of Self-Reflection and Metacognition
19. The Principle of Interconnected, Integrative, and Interdisciplinary Instruction
20. The Principle of Whole Person–Centered Instruction

As you explore this book, you will have to decide on the learning principles that make the most sense for your learning situation or context. I hope that the list above can provide you with a solid starting point for designing effective learning environments in your school or other type of organization or institution. Interestingly, most of these principles are also a part of my TEC-VARIETY framework for motivating and engaging online learners. This framework is detailed in two books that are free to download and in an associated free course (Bonk & Khoo, 2014; Khoo & Bonk, 2022).

While these 20 principles of effective and engaging learning environments are detailed throughout the 15 chapters of *Digital Learning in High-Needs Schools*, David Fuentes and Heejung An introduce many of them in Chapter 1, as do Neil Grimes and Alicia Burchell in Chapter 13. Several principles are also embedded in Chapter 2 from Joshua DeVincenzo and his colleagues who remind us that standardized testing too often results in a failure to appreciate the "(un)standardized ways of learning" that take place informally at home and in local neighborhoods. If we want to make all the world a school, we educators must begin to account for the alternative, informal, and nontraditional forms of learning (Wedemeyer, 1981).

Perhaps we need to start paying attention to such forms of nontraditional and informal learning in equal doses to classroom-based learning. It is conceivable that learner stress would be reduced and overall wellness increased if the education system recognized and promoted the learning that takes place in the streets, not just in classroom seats. When this happens, the notion of expanded learning time that DeVincenzo et al. discuss will be modified to connote expanded learning time and space. There are seemingly infinite implications for learner equity, diversity, and inclusion with such mindsets. However, in Chapter 8, Diallo Sessoms reminds us that teachers will need significant professional development to prepare them for alternative learning environments in which learners are more often in charge of their own learning and are constantly building and making artifacts that matter to them.

Let's Make All the World a School

A third noteworthy aspect of *Digital Learning in High-Needs Schools* is that the scenarios described are familiar. As we all know, hundreds of millions of children around the world were forced to learn online during the pandemic, and those living in less privileged parts of the world without the internet relied on radio, television, and correspondence course packets for their education (Kanwar & Daniel, 2020; Miks & McIlwaine, 2020; Theirworld, 2020). Nearly four

Foreword: It's Time to Finally Make All the World a School **xvii**

decades ago, I was personally forced to learn using such seemingly primitive technology as television and correspondence courses when preparing to qualify for graduate school. Primitive as they were, those forms of distance education changed my life.

I fully realize that my learning could have been richer and more engaging in a face-to-face setting; nevertheless, I was passionately responding to the instructors moderating my correspondence courses and looking forward to the packets I received in the mail every week or so. Learners during the pandemic faced a similar dilemma. And many politicians and media outlets made the situation worse by constantly referring to learning losses as measured by controversial and problematic standardized assessments instead of highlighting new learning possibilities like the ones that Renee Whelan and Michael Salvatore detail in Chapter 14 when discussing all the engaging and potentially transformative forms of learning that await learners in visits to virtual museums, zoos, rainforests, and other online excursions around the planet. While Chapter 14 focuses on how such opportunities can enrich and enhance instruction in urban locations, they conceivably could have an equally powerful imprint on the minds of those in rural settings.

As you read through this book, I hope you reminisce about mentors and teachers you have had in the past and the alternative educational journeys that you pursued. I recommend that you do a thought experiment about what those mentors might have advised during the COVID-19 pandemic and beyond.

As Glenn Jones (1991) passionately argued, "It is time now to fuse our electronic tools of the information age with our great teaching institutions and repositories of information . . . Make all America a school. Working together, we can do it, now" (p. 76). However, I suggest that we extend Jones's hopes and vision by establishing a new goal or marker for this age, and that is to make all the world a school. With the acceleration of learning technologies, expansion of freely available content, and experimentation with innovative pedagogies, we can and must do it now before the next pandemic or climate catastrophe arises to perplex and isolate us once again.

References

Baumgartner, J. (2015, July 7). Glenn Jones dies at 85. *Multichannel.com*. https://www.nexttv.com/news/glenn-jones-dies-85-142366

Bonk, C. J. (2009a, October 19). The wide open learning world: Sea, land, and ice views. *Association for Learning Technology (ALT) Online Newsletter*, Issue 17. https://publicationshare.com/wide-open-learning-world_Sea-Land-and-Ice.pdf

Bonk, C. J. (2009b). *The world is open: How web technology is revolutionizing education.* Jossey-Bass.

Bonk, C. J. (2020). Pandemic ponderings, 30 years to today: Synchronous signals, saviors, or survivors? *Distance Education, 41*(4), 589–599. https://doi.org/10.1080/01587919.2020.1821610

Bonk, C. J., & Khoo, E. (2014). *Adding some TEC-VARIETY: 100+ activities for motivating and retaining learners online.* OpenWorldBooks.com and Amazon Kindle. http://tec-variety.com/

Bonk, C. J., Kim, M., & Xu, S. (2016). Do you have a SOLE? Research on informal and self-directed online learning environments. In J. M. Spector, B. B. Lockee, & M. D. Childress (Eds.), *Learning, design, and technology: An international compendium of theory, research, practice, and policy. Section: Informal resources and tools for self-directed online learning environments* (pp. 1–32). Springer International Publishing. https://doi.org/10.1007/978-3-319-17727-4_35-1

Bonk, C. J., & Wiley, D. (2020). Preface: Reflections on the waves of emerging learning technology. *Educational Technology Research and Development, 68*(4), 1595–1612. https://doi.org/10.1007/s11423-020-09809-x. https://link.springer.com/content/pdf/10.1007/s11423-020-09809-x.pdf

Bonk, C. J., & Zhu, M. (in press). On the trail of self-directed learners. *ECNU Review of Education.*

Doo, M. Y., Zhu, M., & Bonk, C. J. (2023). Influences of self-directed learning on learning outcomes in MOOCs: A meta-analysis. *Distance Education, 44.* https://doi.org/10.1080/01587919.2022.2155618

Heppell, S. (2000, December). NotSchool.net. *Literacy Today, 25.*

Hodges, C., Moore, S., Lockee, B., Trust, T., & Bond, A. (2020, March 27). The difference between emergency remote teaching and online learning. *EDUCAUSE Review.* https://er.educause.edu/articles/2020/3/the-difference-between-emergency-remote-teaching-and-online-learning

Jones, G. R. (1991). *Make all America a school: Mind Extension University* (2nd ed.). Jones 21st Century.

Jones, G. R. (2010). *Cyberschools: An education renaissance* (2nd ed.). Jones International Ltd.

Kanwar, A., & Daniel, J. (2020). *Report to Commonwealth education ministers: From response to resilience.* Commonwealth of Learning. http://oasis.col.org/handle/11599/3592

Khoo, E., & Bonk, C. J. (2022). *Motivating and supporting online learners.* Commonwealth of Learning. http://hdl.handle.net/11599/4481 and free course available: https://colcommons.org/welcome/coursedetails/8; www.colvee.org/

Kim, P., & Chung, C. (2015). Creating a temporary spontaneous mini-ecosystem through a MOOC. In C. J. Bonk, M. M. Lee, T. C. Reeves, & T. H. Reynolds (Eds.), *MOOCs and open education around the world* (pp. 157–168). Routledge.

Miks, J., & McIlwaine, J. (2020, April 20). Keeping the world's children learning through COVID-19. *UNICEF.* www.unicef.org/coronavirus/keeping-worlds-children-learning-through-covid-19

Mishra, P. (2021, June 19). Episode 64 | Self-directed learning with Peter Gray and Bria Bloom. *Silver Lining for Learning.* https://silverliningforlearning.org/episode-64-self-directed-learning-with-peter-gray-and-bria-bloom/

Rusch, E., & Chuang, T. (2015, July 7). Cable television pioneer Glenn R. Jones dies at age 85. *The Denver Post.* www.denverpost.com/2015/07/07/cable-television-pioneer-glenn-r-jones-dies-at-age-85/

Theirworld. (2020, March 20). Hundreds of millions of students now learning from home after coronavirus crisis shuts their schools. *ReliefWeb.* https://reliefweb.int/report/world/hundreds-millions-students-now-learning-home-after-coronavirus-crisis-shuts-their

United States Department of Education. (2010). *Transforming American education: Learning powered by technology.* www.ed.gov/sites/default/files/netp2010.pdf

Wedemeyer, C. (1981). *Learning at the back door: Reflections on nontraditional learning in the lifespan* (Reissued: September 2010). University of Wisconsin Press.

Zhu, M., & Bonk, C. J. (2022, online first). Guidelines and strategies for fostering and enhancing self-directed online learning. *Open Learning: The Journal of Open, Distance and e-Learning*. https://doi.org/10.1080/02680513.2022.2141105

PREFACE

The COVID-19 pandemic, which began in March 2020, has been a time of enormous upheaval for U.S. PreK-12 schools. After several decades of an expanding digital divide in student access to technology, the detrimental nature of this problem has grown exponentially for high-needs schools, resulting in thousands of low-income schools failing to provide adequate educational learning opportunities for their students. It should come as no surprise that student learning processes and outcomes, which were disparate largely based on race and socioeconomic status prior to the pandemic, worsened during this disaster. Historic issues of equity and injustice in schools also took on renewed prominence, with *Brown v. Board of Education* (Fenwick, 2022) and even Jim Crow laws and segregated schools becoming key points of discussion.

Prior to the pandemic, many education reforms focused on serving the needs of children while structuring schools as a one-size-fits-all system toward the goal of achieving a level playing field. During the pandemic, however, it became abundantly clear that in order to thrive in schools, students' basic needs must be met, and in order for them to flourish, they must progress through a series of hierarchical needs on their way to higher-order learning and thinking. The basic idea here is that in order to Bloom, students must first Maslow, a reference to the intrinsic needs of learners and our desires for higher-order learning outcomes. As a result of the pandemic, the general public has also now seen a glimpse of the inequities and negative impacts on student learning.

We witnessed these challenges firsthand before and during the pandemic surges and continue to witness them now, although in varying degrees. While doing grant work in the Paterson, New Jersey, Public Schools District, in a high-needs community, for example, we saw hundreds of paper-based instructional packets that the schools had prepared for the students never being picked up because

Preface **xxi**

families were not properly informed and encouraged to pick them up. We also saw hundreds of students waiting in line outside of schools for lunch, even though the schools were closed. These issues underscore the lack of communication and preparedness in our schools along with long-standing sociocultural and economic challenges in the wake of the abrupt move to online learning at the onset of the pandemic.

Nevertheless, we have also observed acts of heroism on the part of PreK-12 teachers and administrators. In particular, one elementary school principal, Dr. Jorge Ventura, working in the Paterson Public Schools District, noted that when the pandemic first struck, his school experienced few challenges transitioning to online learning. While the rest of the schools in the same high-needs district were printing out all of the instructional materials for pick-up, as they were not prepared for the transition to remote learning, his school was moving along efficiently and effectively. To probe these differences further, in January 2021, we interviewed Dr. Ventura and learned that what set him apart and enabled his success was that (a) he was a lifelong learner who was constantly implementing new digital programs and fostering digital management; (b) he understood his school as a community—his students, their parents/guardians, their teachers, and their sociocultural and economic contexts; (c) he engaged in digital leadership, defined as "using instructional technology, including digital devices, services, and resources, to inspire and lead school digital transformation, create and sustain digital learning culture, support and enhance technology-based professional development, provide and maintain digital organization management, and facilitate and manage digital citizenship" (Zhong, 2017, p. 28); and (d) he focused on digital learning not for the sake of technology itself but to help Generation Z students learn more effectively with emergent technologies that were adapted to their learning trends and styles. In short, he authentically understood what was needed in a cost-effective manner for teachers to design, develop, and teach lessons for online learning modalities. In addition, he offered targeted professional development for teachers, along with workshops for parents and students. Taken together, his school community was ready to move smoothly toward online learning during the first months of COVID-19 in 2020.

While the efforts of many teachers and administrators should be commended, it is also important to note the tremendous need for systemic change in how PreK-12 high-needs schools approach digital learning. In short, how can we enable more schools to meet the aforementioned benchmarks of success?

To formulate the outline for this book, we drew from firsthand experiences as documented during the COVID-19 pandemic (see An et al., 2022) as well as previously (see Fuentes, 2022). We have included three foundational sections to foster a deeper understanding of the various factors that contribute to high-needs school communities' ability to successfully provide digital learning for students in high-needs schools and to gain a more in-depth understanding of the whole phenomenon rather than merely generalizing.

xxii Preface

To that end, we invited authors who have a deep understanding of high-needs schools to share their knowledge in the 15 chapters of this book, organized into three sections. The chapters contribute to the emerging body of literature seeking to understand the specific and contextualized digital learning needs of high-needs school communities. They are also likely to contribute to our understanding of best practices and the trials and tribulations related to effective use of technology and integration of teaching and learning with technology in high-needs school communities.

Section I. Understanding the Intersection of Students, Families, and Schooling in High-Needs Communities

This section provides a foundation for the book, discussing the complex and multilayered components that impact students' learning in high-needs schools.

In Chapter 1, Fuentes and An explore the impact of the pandemic through a critical, sociocultural lens that perceives learning and schooling as political acts that unfold within the context and sociopolitical framework that guide U.S. public education. This lens offers us a glimpse of how we can conceptualize *digital equity* as school equity and the *digital divide* as, first and foremost, a school equity divide.

In Chapter 2, DeVincenzo, Osorio-Godoy, and Chandler analyze the school ecosystem of stakeholders, students, educators, parents/guardians/caregivers, administrators, and support staff, with a specific focus on the negative cognitive impacts on each group attributed to digital divides. As the impacts of COVID-19 are global in nature, the chapter draws upon research and examples worldwide.

In Chapter 3, An and Sung provide suggestions for administrators, teachers, and parents to consider derived from interviews conducted during COVID-19, based on four factors—accessibility, usability, wellness, and support—with the aim of establishing equitable digital learning environments.

Section II. Vision and Leadership for Digital Learning in High-Needs Communities

This section addresses digital learning from a leadership perspective and presents an analysis of policies that have been generated at the federal, state, and local levels, along with considerations for policy and/or practice that could improve school equity and outcomes.

In Chapter 4, Chandler and DeVincenzo analyze the ways U.S. federal, state, and local policies have helped and hindered decision-making capabilities in various local schools during the COVID-19 pandemic, with a particular focus on the impacts of distance learning efforts. The ramifications of the ongoing digital divide on learning outcomes, along with potential positive steps that can be undertaken by fostering continuity-of-operations planning, are also addressed.

In Chapter 5, Fancera discusses how school leaders in high-needs schools can use Twitter to overcome some of the common obstacles to traditional forms of PDL—time, money, and teacher absence from the classroom—to lead with continuous growth and development of staff as a priority.

In Chapter 6, Moreno describes the strategic implementation of the formative feedback process and identifies strategies that can be utilized across content areas, including evaluation strategies that address disproportionality and create more equitable evaluation practices within an urban preK-12 school district.

In Chapter 7, Mohamad and Pozzi share how librarians can apply the principles of Universal Design for Learning (UDL) to meet students' needs for digital learning with recommendations for using UDL to address the educational needs of students of all abilities.

Section III. Pedagogical Strategies and Digital Tools Across the Curriculum

This section provides pedagogical strategies and digital tools that can be used by teachers across the curriculum in high-needs schools.

In Chapter 8, Sessoms discusses the impact on high-needs schools of teachers not being prepared to infuse technology to enhance teaching and learning and offers suggestions for how to become better prepared.

In Chapter 9, Kormos and Sherman explore the impact of the digital divide on digital learning in high-needs urban schools and suggest teaching strategies and technologies that can be implemented as part of social studies teaching practices.

In Chapter 10, An, Samaras, Lanni, and Rajab describe the impetus for the creation of the "Learning Arts at Home" program, a culturally responsive multilingual arts-integration program that includes read-aloud and book-inspired art-making videos. They also describe its instructional design and various pedagogical strategies employed.

In Chapter 11, Howerton and Polly present the findings of an exploratory research study, framed with equity-based mathematics teaching, on the use of an online mathematics program called Math Playground with fourth graders in a high-needs school. The authors also share the implications for the use of this online mathematics program in schools where students are experiencing poverty and where a high percentage of students may not have demonstrated proficiency in math standards from previous grade levels.

In Chapter 12, Weng provides a review of effective affordances and accessibility features in digital learning for students with disabilities.

In Chapter 13, Grimes and Burchell detail how elementary school teachers used Bitmojis to create digital classrooms and how these digital learning environments provided opportunities for engaging remote literacy instruction in high-needs rural areas. The chapter also details how moving forward, whether with in-person or remote instruction, digital classrooms will continue to offer teachers and students alike increased opportunities to achieve and possibly surpass the outcomes experienced in traditional modes of instruction.

In Chapter 14, Whelan and Salvatore discuss the perceptions of educators and learners as they explore scientific concepts and provide examples of learning in specific areas such as the complexities of real-time medical triage, engineering, life sciences, and solving environmental problems in their high-needs school communities, all through a digital lens.

In Chapter 15, DeWitt and Podwojski explore the experiences of social studies teachers in high-needs rural schools as they navigate the challenges of online teaching.

Audience

The intended audience for this book consists of four groups: (a) professors, educational researchers, and undergraduate and graduate students in programs of teacher education and educational technology in higher education; (b) administrators, supervisors, and teachers in preK-12 schools; (c) readers interested in learning more about perspectives and best practices pertaining to digital learning in high-needs schools; and (d) diversity, equity, and inclusion experts interested in issues surrounding the digital divide. To support and guide readers, each chapter includes guiding questions at the beginning, along with key takeaways and recommended resources at the end of the chapter. In many instances, suggestions and recommendations pertaining to the given chapter's topic are also offered. It is the aim of this book to provide readers with a more holistic understanding of digital learning in high-needs settings, as well as steps that can be taken to bridge existing gaps.

As you read the chapters, we hope that you will take time to answer the guiding questions. Be sure to engage, reflect, and aspire to become a change agent for digital equity.

Heejung An and David Fuentes, From New Jersey, United States

References

An, H., Mongillo, G., Sung, W., & Fuentes, D. (2022). Factors affecting online learning during the COVID-19 pandemic: The lived experiences of parents, teachers, and administrators in U.S. high-needs K-12 schools. *The Journal of Online Learning Research (JOLR)*, 8(2), 203–234. www.learntechlib.org/primary/p/220404/

Fenwick, L. (2022). *Jim Crow's pink slip: The untold story of Black principal and teacher leadership*. Harvard Education Press.

Fuentes, D. (2022). Profoundly antiracist questions about schools. *Teachers College Record*. www.tcrecord.org/Content.asp?ContentID=23978

Zhong, L. (2017). Indicators of digital leadership in the context of K-12 education. *Journal of Educational Technology Development and Exchange (JETDE)*, 10(1), Article 3. https://aquila.usm.edu/jetde/vol10/iss1/3

ACKNOWLEDGMENTS

We offer our sincere thanks and gratitude to all of the chapter authors who contributed to this book. We are grateful that they have shared their knowledge, experience, wisdom, and beliefs about digital equity.

We thank Daniel Schwartz, our Routledge editor, for his rapid and thorough responses for all of the questions throughout the publishing process.

We also would like to acknowledge the countless families who ensured their children persisted; the countless teachers who worked day and night, often sacrificing time with their own children and families to support other people's children, and to the countless children who experienced a disruption to their lives, safety, well-being, and learning during some of the most daunting and debilitating times ever experienced in public education in the United States. Let us learn from your experiences so that we can be better prepared to position schools to teach the *whole child*.

We also express our gratitude to our dear friend, Dr. Holly Seplocha, Professor Emeritus at William Paterson University, for her long-lasting support. Holly, you are a true scholar, leader, and mentor. Please know how much we admire and appreciate you.

Finally, we express our thankfulness to our families, who have always stood by us, and for their endless support.

SECTION I

Understanding the Intersection of Students, Families, and Schooling in High-Needs Communities

1

UNDERSTANDING THE SOCIOCULTURAL AND SOCIOPOLITICAL CONTEXTS OF U.S. HIGH-NEEDS PUBLIC SCHOOLS BEFORE, DURING, AND AFTER THE COVID-19 PANDEMIC

David Fuentes and Heejung An

Guiding Questions:

- What are the sociocultural and sociopolitical contexts that undergirded the impact of COVID-19 on U.S. high-needs public schools?
- How do these contexts contribute to our understanding of digital and equity divides in U.S. high-needs K-12 schools?
- How can we better support students in order to make school outcomes post-COVID more equitable?

Introduction

The impact of the COVID-19 pandemic on U.S. high-needs public schools has been catastrophic (Kuhfield et al., 2022; Pokhrel & Chhetri, 2021). At the onset of the pandemic, schools, teachers, students, administrators, and families encountered school shutdowns, loss of instructional time, and quarantines—in other words, severe disruptions of academic normalcy. As the pandemic progressed, many school districts relied heavily on digital tools to maintain a semblance of schooling, whereas all the while, parents, students, administrators, teachers, and society grappled with shutdowns, the role of essential workers, and remote learning, among other abrupt life changes, not to mention experiencing loss of the highest magnitude: life.

Amidst all this peril and chaos, patterns emerged that sharpened society's insights into disparities experienced during the pandemic based on race and class.

DOI:10.4324/9781003274537-2

4 David Fuentes and Heejung An

To better understand these disparities, the authors turn to a critical theory analysis to provide a framework for understanding the sociocultural and sociopolitical contexts of schools and the impact of COVID-19 on U.S. public schools during the mass transition to remote learning as a result of the pandemic and beyond.

The pandemic necessitated a continuation of schooling in America that placed a strain on the structure of how schools are run, how teaching is planned, and how learning is administered. Based largely on the public health needs of society, coupled with mandated quarantines, schools were forced to shutter and reimagine themselves digitally to the best of their abilities. No blueprint existed to guide this transition. In fact, it had been 100 years since public education in America had experienced a closure as a result of a worldwide health crisis.

Schools have a long history of incorporating digital tools in learning and an even longer history of investing in digital technology with a desire to enhance learning and student outcomes (Cuban, 2001). Nevertheless, everybody was unprepared for the sudden task of ensuring students' learning outcomes amid the pandemic. Schools were even less prepared to ensure those outcomes remained equitable. This comes as little surprise, though, as we look closer and are reminded that schools have never had a level playing field despite an espoused desire for them to function as such within a perceived meritocracy. Thus, the digital divide, digital equity, and the disparities in school outcomes experienced as a result of the pandemic should be viewed as a continuation of the existing disparities, exacerbated, not created, during the COVID-19 pandemic.

In this chapter, the authors explore the impact of the pandemic through a critical, sociocultural (Nieto, 2005) lens that perceives learning and schooling as political acts that unfold within the context and sociopolitical framework that guides schools. Such a lens offers us a glimpse of how we can conceptualize digital equity as school equity using digital tools and well-trained teachers who can utilize these digital tools for teaching and learning—a view we consider, important as it rests on the interconnected nature of schooling, society, and politics and does not place social inequities as a result of learning ecology alone. Such a view further supports the notion that the digital divide is, first and foremost, an equity divide, as evidenced in continued disparate school outcomes based on race and gender.

School Equity, Digital Equity, and Digital-Use Divide

In 2022, the United States Department of Education (USDOE) introduced executive Order 13985, an equity plan that infused $122 billion into U.S. education to "help K-12 schools safely reopen, stay open, and address the academic, social, and emotional needs of all students" (USDOE, 2022, p. 1). Importantly, the bill noted and acknowledged long-standing issues related to unequal outcomes in U.S. schools and offered as part of the solution an increase in resources to address the academic, social, and emotional impediments that some children experience and that contributes to the overall inequality seen in U.S. schools. Thus, school equity is concerned with the kinds of academic, social, and emotional experiences students encounter and creating support(s) for students to enable them to achieve successful learning outcomes.

Our view of school equity is based on the notion that all people are created equal and that explanations that account for disparate school outcomes can only point to the problematic nature and systematic processes inherent in schools and society rather than the individual deficits of students or groups (Kendi, 2019). School equity, in general, seeks to find explanations for school outcomes, focusing more on access than the value of the individuals who experience unequal access. This stands in direct contrast to notions of equality, which espouse that all people must be treated the same and given the same level of support and intervention regardless of their lived experiences and known challenges. Achieving equity of outcomes in schools is the goal. Decreasing disparate outcomes based on race and class is an essential component of democratic education.

In this chapter, *digital divide* is defined as "a division between people who have access and use of digital media and those who do not (van Dijk, 2020, p. 1); *digital equity*, on the other hand, is defined as "making sure students have equal access to technology like devices, software and the internet, and that they have trained educators to help them navigate those tools" (International Society for Technology in Education [ISTE], 2021, p. 2). Despite the ease with which the term *digital equity* is defined, what makes it a problem to achieve in practice is that the students we serve in public education occupy such different spaces on a continuum of opportunities afforded in schools and in life. Thus, a lack of access to quality experiences learning with digital tools represents an issue related to digital equity. Moreover, "a lack of digital access is a lack of access to education (school equity) period" (ISTE, 2021, p. 1).

Similarly, we use the term *digital divide* to describe what happens when K–12 students have access to digital tools and yet differences remain in their use and understanding of the use of digital tools. Our discussion of the digital divide falls closer to the field's understanding of a *digital-use divide* than one that focuses entirely on access disparities. With growing frequency, schools have managed to address access issues related to inequity of personal experience and preparedness for use of digital tools, yet disparities still exist, since the broader impediments that give rise to high-needs have not been addressed. As such, we define the *digital-use divide* as the divide between students whose use of digital tools is transformative and contributes to novel ways of thinking and being versus students who use digital tools in less meaningful ways, perhaps, limiting the impact of the digital tools to a means of task completion (USDOE, 2017, p. 7).

Regardless of the nature of the divide, digital use, digital equity, or school equity, they all render the results of student assessments difficult to decipher in terms of what students know and are capable of and what they are prepared to evidence because their basic needs have been met. That is, when students' basic needs have not been met, we have tremendous difficulty determining if student motivation, aptitude, comprehension, and acquisition of new knowledge are taking place or if the rigors of life are impeding students' ability to evidence what they know.

The Sociocultural and Sociopolitical Contexts of High-Needs Schools

Public education in the United States operates within a social and political framework that guides its structure, application, and function within our pluralistic democracy. The structure and design of schools have a direct connection to capitalism and serve as the basis of a system of societal and social stratification (Labaree, 1997). Thus, schools determine who gets to become a doctor and who may become an essential worker, serving others in our society. Schools also determine who will occupy certain spaces in our economy, as the direct correlations between degree attainment and salary have long been depicted (NCES, 2019). A high school diploma, on average, earns far less than a college degree, which earns less than advanced degrees. As we are reminded through things like the college admissions scandal at Stanford University (Camera, 2019) in recent years, our belief that schools operate as meritocracies often supports societal beliefs that school outcomes are valid and justified. However, the notion that the outcomes of schools are valid becomes questioned when the connection between merit and privilege becomes obfuscated, as was the case in the aforementioned college admissions scandal. The general notion of schools serving as meritocracies, rewarding the achievements of students, connecting certain social stratospheres through accomplishment as a result of schooling is largely based on the idea of a level playing field. Within capitalistic democracies, our belief that equal opportunity exists in schools goes beyond our shared common belief, as it has been venerated in our legal system. Today, we continue to grapple with notions of equality versus equity in U.S. schools, as the systemic outcomes of schools raise questions about fairness, access, funding, resources, and pedagogy while threatening to expose the meritocracy we believe exists with the realization that things are indeed far less egalitarian and far more structurally reciprocal than disruptive to the status quo and maintenance of power and wealth.

The Social (Academic) Development of Learners

One of the key functions of school is to socialize students into being able to know and communicate with others who they might otherwise not encounter. Thus, a component of the social context of schools rests in its ability to socialize youth to take part in society, including but not limited to socializing within different sectors or jobs within the economy. In this regard, schools emulate an aspect of communication needed to function at work and provide a site for students to practice the kind of socialization needed to participate in the economy by design. The focus of schools on the social development of learners promotes students interacting in a variety of ways with a cross-section of peers and adults. An emphasis on social development rests in the academic and social development of academic communication and ways of knowing and being. Much less attention is paid to the equally important development of learners' social and emotional development and the important roles both play in learner development and understanding school outcomes. Various aspects of social understanding about ways to connect with others, expression of emotion, emotional regulation, impulse control, and empathy development relate to desired increase in school equity, with a focus outside the academic reality to extend into understanding the intersection of academic, social, and emotional development and learning.

The Sociocultural (Social and Emotional) Development of Learners

The act of learning occurs within social contexts. Learning has been defined as "a social activity, involving the individual's use of shared language, tools, norms and practices in interaction with his or her social context" (Shepard et al., 2018, p. 23). As a social construct developed through interaction, the results of learning are often dependent on the socialization practices of the learner and are valued in different ways. This understanding, in turn, has led to certain realizations of the role of privileging certain types of ways of knowing, discourses, and communication patterns. In fact, many critics of standardized testing, for example, assert that these tests are favoring students from upper-middle-class backgrounds and whose parents have achieved certain levels of educational attainment (Knoester & Au, 2017). This does not represent that level playing field that meritocracies necessitate.

The Political Contexts That Give Rise to High-Needs Schools

Schools in the United States were developed as a structure prior to the integration of American society and began operating with a direct connection to justifying the unequal distribution of wealth and rights based largely on race and gender. Many universities in the United States are older than many of the states that make up the Union. Many have direct ties to the cultivation of past presidents and Supreme Court justices and the production of university faculty. Schools were used in the landmark Supreme Court decision *Brown v. Board of Education*, overturning the "separate but equal" clause used during Jim Crow to justify unequal opportunities in access to education. Given the deep structural history of schools tied to social stratification and unequal rights, it is difficult to imagine how this same system can seamlessly and effectively transition into one that ushers in equitable and equal outcomes.

School (In)Equity

Despite increased attention, funding, awareness, and numerous policy initiatives, there continues to be a gap in school outcomes in the United States based on several protected classes, including but not limited to race and class. For example, Asian Pacific Islander, Black, and Latino students continue to be underserved in the U.S. public education system, and several troubling patterns emerge when we look at the disparate outcomes of schools (Fuentes, 2022). While we collect data on school performance and standardized testing in reading and mathematics, a number of intersecting agencies guide different social realities related to the outcomes we see in schools. Specifically, public housing, welfare, social services, health departments, and family planning each contribute to the manner in which society operates to ensure citizens' basic needs are met. When these services fall short, the outcome is often captured in a variety of ways, including school outcomes.

Thus, the failure of U.S. schools to undo the damage caused by large numbers of people not having their basic needs met shows that we are suffering from long-standing societal inequities related to housing, access to medical care, and quality education, among other widespread disparities. That is, the intersection of schooling in American society points to a large number of failures that cut across agencies designed to ensure a basic quality of life and, eventually, the pursuit of life, liberty, and happiness. What happens when children whose basic needs have not been met are sent to school may account for aspects of gaps in learning outcomes that do not reflect an achievement gap but rather a gap in equity.

Social Reproduction and Schools

Schools are sites that reproduce and recreate societal inequities. Simultaneously, they are sites well poised to change those same inequities by enacting critical pedagogies that intentionally disrupt the reproduction of societal inequities. Critical pedagogy may be defined as pedagogies designed to go beneath the surface in order to understand the social contexts that give rise to unjust phenomena in an effort to make them more just. This is a justice-oriented view of critical pedagogy. Schools can be sites of liberation if they actively, intentionally ensure that students succeed by leveling the playing field for learners whose experiences and opportunities have not rendered them ready to learn to their full potential.

Increasing School Outcomes in a Post-COVID Learning Ecology

By design, schools function on the basis of a one-size-fits-all structure. Curriculum is often defined independent of students. Developmental norms guide placement of students into grades. And once assigned to grades, students progress in groups. Such progression is thought to be independent of social factors such as class and wealth and instead is believed to be a product of hard work, intellect, and aptitude. However, a sociocultural approach, one that embraces the social and political contexts of schools in the United States, reveals the thinly veiled reality that schools operate as meritocracies and point to the ways in which schools reproduce rather than disrupt social inequities. Similarly, using the same critical approach allows us to see that the solution to the vast inequities experienced by generations in America's schools rests in the notion of schools teaching to the *whole child* and embracing social and emotional health alongside and at the intersection of the academic. A view that separates the academic from the social and emotional and political is incomplete, decontextualized, ahistorical, and deeply flawed because it ignores or fails to consider the contexts that give rise to the school outcomes we have in U.S. high-needs schools. A critical approach, on the other hand, centers the lived experience of the learner—the notion that the subjectivity of the learner is deeply and profoundly connected to the way in which the learner sees the world. A central premise of critical pedagogy, then, is that reading the word is reading the world. That is, objective meaning does not exist outside of the interpretation of the subject. Thus, to learn more about the world, one must learn more about oneself, and to learn more about oneself is to learn more about the world. The notion that learners play a significant role in knowledge creation is essential to the belief that pedagogy must center the lived experiences of learners and that learners' readiness and preparedness, their affect, each contribute greatly to learning outcomes.

With this realization, we begin to plan instruction in ways that teach students about themselves and help them acquire skills to positively impact themselves, as we are aware of the interconnectedness of academic, social, emotional and political contexts as contributing factors to school outcomes. Our increased understanding of the social, emotional, and political contexts of high-needs schools has pushed us to understand more about how we can teach the whole child and has reminded us that the science of learning tells us that children are always learning as they interact with their environment. The gap between what children know and what schools value is not an achievement gap; it is a cultural mismatch. Understanding when we have learning gaps versus cultural mismatches is challenging and can be elusive; however, the distinction is imperative, as the necessary interventions can be vastly different.

A Whole-Child Approach

Recent research has shown that "student learning and development depend on affirming relationships operating within a positive school climate" (Darling-Hammond et al., 2021, p. 1). This growing body of evidence reinforces the importance of "affect" as it relates to learning and development and the basic needs of children (Maslow, 1943) as they prepare to become ready to learn. This has several implications for pedagogy and understanding students' outcomes by helping us understand why gaps persist in student outcomes. In fact, much of what has been derided as the failures of education points more to the replication of the inequities seen in society and an inability to disrupt societal inequities. Regardless of the origin of inequities, whether they come before schools or are created within them, they point to the solution being focused on the social and emotional as a means to improve the academic.

The Science of Learning

There has been and will continue to be a great deal of emphasis placed on "learning loss" as a result of school shutdowns, the move to remote instruction, and the general disruption to schooling following the COVID-19 pandemic. In fact, billions of dollars were reserved in the American Rescue Plan enacted by the U.S. Congress to address learning loss as a result of the pandemic (Edsource, 2022). Despite the loss of learning, aspects of the science of learning inform us about the possible learning gains that did take place during the pandemic and, in turn, inform our understanding of the speedy recovery of the learning lost, as evidenced by reading and math scores as seen in the elementary grades, for example (Edsource, 2022). This shift from loss to gain illustrates, conceptually, the foundational needs of learners and their ability to adapt to shifting landscapes. It also helps educators understand self-actualized learning. The importance of autonomy and self-reflection as part of the learning process has increased as a result of our understanding of the science of learning. The principles of the science of learning will be described and connected to digital and remote learning environments in the section that follows.

According to the Learning Policy Institute (LPI), several design principles derived from the science of learning can and should be put into practice as foundational principles of educators' knowledge. These principles (Darling-Hammond et al., 2021, p. 6), when taken together, represent a blueprint for healthy development, learning, and thriving. These principles have been adapted and are summarized as the following:

1. positive developmental relationships
2. environments filled with safety and belonging
3. rich learning experiences and knowledge development
4. development of skills, habits, and mindsets
5. integrated support systems

Teaching the Whole Child and Digital Equity Pedagogical Approaches

Equity issues in schools were well documented prior to the COVID-19 pandemic (Nieto, 2002). The pandemic had such a pervasive impact on schooling that it likely will not return to prepandemic routines and practices. Specifically, the context around schooling has changed in a variety of ways, including the mediums and delivery of instruction. Digital learning had emerged prior to the pandemic and showed great promise to guide schooling in the United States; however, no one could have predicted the extent to which remote learning, Zoom, and Teams would become as ubiquitous in schools as chalk and number 2 pencils in generations past. A holistic view of learning, one that encompasses equity and strives to provide students the support they need in order to succeed, must focus on the learner and the learning environment while seeking to build supportive learning environments that build learners' academic, social, and emotional skills and capacities. This imperative is largely based on the recognition that equity, rather than equality, is what is needed to create a level playing field.

A key component of teaching the whole child (Darling-Hammond & Cook-Harvey, 2018) involves building space and ensuring that positive social interactions and relationships are created and maintained. Within the classroom post-COVID-19, we must build spaces to form relationships between learners and adults and between learners as a necessary means to creating the conditions needed to exchange information—strong relationships. Building secure, positive, and sustainable relationships requires sustained interactions and time to create trust. In building trusting relationships, it is important to include all aspects of the child, such as culture, identity, and any other aspect that may be important to a given student. Developing supportive relationships is also a preemptive strategy, as it strengthens students' ability to overcome adversity and maintain well-being in the face of hardship.

Structures within digital environments that promote **building positive relationships**:

1. Create small learning groups and small class sizes to maximize interaction.
2. Create advisory teams that focus on specific themes of wellness.
3. Consider keeping groups together for longer periods of time to build trust/ relationships.
4. Create opportunities for shared decision-making.
5. Encourage behaviors that communicate respect.
6. Use pedagogies that promote teachers getting to know their students' lived experiences.

Another key component of teaching the whole child involves creating and maintaining positive **learning environments filled with safety and belonging**. A positive learning environment is one that supports students' growth across all domains of learning and understands that all domains intersect in the academic area. A learning environment that focuses on the social and emotional as well as the academic offers students the opportunity to experience an increased sense of belonging and demonstrates that their perceptions matter and that they play an active role in their learning.

Educators can focus on these actions to ensure **safety and belonging**:

1. Create a safe environment and learning community that has the same rules and guidelines and that allows students to comfortably participate, knowing the expectations.
2. Develop and build restorative practices that promote trauma-informed and healing-oriented practices.
3. Support culturally responsive and inclusive learning experiences through which all students feel welcomed, valued, and supported to succeed.

When we think about teaching the whole child, we are also referring to educators creating **rich learning experiences and knowledge development**. The science of learning tells us a great deal about how children acquire new knowledge. Children actively construct knowledge based on their existing understanding of the world around them, and they do so through social contexts and interactions. Since learners connect new information to what they already know, educators must be able to assess students' prior knowledge and leverage experiences that are most likely to assist learners in adding to what they know. Effective teachers guide students in using what they know and applying it to both new and familiar situations to develop new ideas to test. Since learning is personalized, this also means that variability in student learning is the norm, not the exception. As a result, the prevailing one-size-fits-all approach must be individualized to what is most relevant, engaging, and developmentally appropriate for the individual learner. Similarly, from this perspective, student engagement and motivation are situational, so we are best able to meet desired learning outcomes when students meaningfully connect the material with their own experiences.

Educators can support **rich learning experiences and knowledge development** by:

1. providing learning experiences that promote student inquiry and problem-solving related to real-world problems, tasks, and solutions.
2. providing performance assessments that facilitate metacognition and awareness of student performance.
3. building careful scaffolds to ensure student development of knowledge and access to experiences that include cognitive supports that ensure student success.

A fourth design principle focuses on ensuring that structures and practices develop cognitive, emotional, and social skills such as a growth mindset, social awareness, and self-direction that promote academic development. Since learning is social, emotional, cognitive, and academic, an integrated approach is needed, because the parts of the brain that guide academics are not the same parts of the brain that guide the social and vice versa. These skill sets are interrelated and develop one another as one is nurtured and progresses.

We offer the following pedagogical considerations for educators concerned with the **development of skills, habits, and mindsets**:

1. Place social and emotional (SEL) learning at the center of the integrated learning experience.
2. Teach explicitly about the interconnected parts of SEL (self-awareness, self-management, responsible decision-making, relationship skills, and social awareness).
3. Encourage adaptability and flexibility of thinking.

Finally, the fifth design principle involves a focus on **integrated support systems**. We want to build autonomy and resiliency in learners, knowing that at some point, they will need the skills to persevere and overcome life obstacles while building agency and resilience. Successful human development depends on a nurturing environment, and the brain develops nimbly and in experientially dependent ways (Jackson, 2011). As such, the context of development becomes important. Adverse stress caused by the environment is one of the most common factors impeding growth and development. Relational trust can combat the causes of adverse stress, and since stress is everywhere, relational trust must also be easily found by the developing learner.

We recommend the following pedagogical considerations for educators seeking to create **integrated support systems**:

1. Create assessments and practices that help educators understand student wellness.
2. Enable access to high-quality tutoring and extracurricular support.
3. Create approaches that are culturally competent, carefully integrated, and age appropriate.

Conclusion

Issues related to digital equity and the digital divide are, first and foremost, issues of school equity and represent iterations of disparity that cut across several U.S. institutions: education, health, housing, and criminal justice among others. Despite our desire for schools to become sites that disrupt social inequities, schools, like other institutions, remain more likely to reproduce social inequities and norms rather than undo them. U.S. public schools were originally structured to serve as a basis for social stratification in a capitalist, slave-based society. Nonetheless, they also represent the possibility of serving as "the great equalizer" for other people's children (Delpit, 1995).

From a sociocultural perspective, one that views schools as political sites that reflect rather than produce the status quo, it behooves educators to address the root cause of school inequity even while pursuing all of its tentacles, digital or otherwise. As educators who seek to provide equitable opportunities for students to succeed, we must teach the whole child and build curriculum and pedagogy that addresses students' well-being and lived experiences as valued components of teaching and learning.

According to the science of learning, in order for K-12 students to learn to their full potential, their basic needs must be met. When constructing digital learning environments, when teaching with digital tools to leverage students' critical thinking, when preparing students for citizenship in a pluralistic democracy driven by the use of digital tools, it behooves educators to think about the five principles of the science of learning in order to address the needs of the whole child. While each of the five principles is designed to apply to pedagogy more broadly, digital teaching and learning must encompass each of them if the future of schooling, one inextricably linked with digital tools and learning, can begin to fulfill the promise of education and schooling to undo rather reproduce societal inequities.

Much like a whole-child approach offers the potential to address long-standing disparities, a whole-systems approach is one that views all social institutions, not just education, as responsible for school outcomes. Yet despite this realization, many continue to find schooling in America to be equitable. Whether you view equitable schooling as equality or whether you view equal opportunity as equity, nobody can deny the duality of public education in the United States: It is home to both the best and the worst. It works for many families yet fails so many more. Little has changed in this regard since its inception.

We must continue to grapple with notions of equity as we individualize learning to ensure student success, especially as we prepare a learning ecology that leverages digital tools. Until policies, schools, and practitioners place the full spectrum of learners' needs at the center of the structure of schooling, we will continue to have disparate outcomes. While it is not solely an educational imperative, educators can empower learners and equip them with strategies and a digital learning environment designed to ensure success by teaching the whole child.

Key Takeaways:

1. In order for K-12 students to learn to their full potential, their basic needs must be met.
2. We must continue to grapple with notions of equity as we individualize learning to ensure students' success, especially as we prepare a learning ecology that leverages digital tools.

3. Until policies, schools, and practitioners place the full spectrum of learners' needs at the center of the structure of schooling in the United States, we will continue to have disparate outcomes. While it is not solely an educational imperative, educators can empower learners and equip them with strategies and a learning ecology designed to ensure success by teaching the whole child.

4. When constructing digital learning environments, when teaching with digital tools to leverage students' critical thinking, when preparing students for citizenship in a pluralistic democracy driven by the use of digital tools, it behooves educators to think about the five principles of the science of learning in order to address the needs of the whole child.

Recommended Resources

Books:

- Rafalow, M. (2020). *Digital divisions: How schools create inequality in the tech era.* The University of Chicago Press.
- Schaffer, R., Howard, N. R., & Thomas, S. (2019). *Closing the gap: Digital equity strategies for the K-12 classroom.* The International Society for Technology in Education (ISTE).

Websites:

- COVID-19: Impact on Education Equity Resources and Responses: https://edtrust.org/covid-19-impact-on-education-equity-resources-responding/
- Department of Education Equity Action Plan: www.ed.gov/equity
- The Learning Policy Institute (LPI): https://learningpolicyinstitute.org/
- The Science of Learning National Education Association (NEA): www.nea.org/advocating-for-change/new-from-nea/science-learning
- United States Department of Education (USDOE). (2022). *Education in a Pandemic: The Disparate Impacts of COVID-19 on America's Students*: https://www2.ed.gov/about/offices/list/ocr/docs/20210608-impacts-of-covid19.pdf
- Whole Child Approach to Education Chan Zuckerberg Initiative: https://chanzuckerberg.com/education/whole-child-approach-to-education/

References

Camera, L. (2019). White privilege and the college admissions scandal. *U.S. News & World Report.* www.usnews.com/news/education-news/articles/2019-03-13/white-privilege-and-the-college-admissions-scandal

Cuban, L. (2001). *Oversold and underused: Computers in the classroom.* Harvard University Press.

Darling-Hammond, L., & Cook-Harvey, C. M. (2018). *Educating the whole child: Improving school climate to support student success* (research brief). Learning Policy Institute.

Darling-Hammond, L., Flook, L., Schachner, A., & Wojcikiewicz, S. (with P. Cantor & D. Osher). (2021). *Educator learning to enact the science of learning and development.* Learning Policy Institute. https://doi.org/10.54300/859.776

Delpit, L. D. (1995). *Other people's children: Cultural conflict in the classroom.* New Press. Distributed by W. W. Norton.

Edsource. (2022). *Elementary students are recovering faster from Covid learning loss, research shows.* https://edsource.org/2022/elementary-students-are-recovering-faster-from-covid-learning-loss-research-shows/675811

Fuentes, D. (2022). Profoundly antiracist questions about schools. *Teachers College Record.* www.tcrecord.org/Content.asp?ContentID=23978

International Society for Technology in Education (ISTE). (2021). *6 things every educator should know about digital equity.* www.iste.org/explore/Lead-the-way/5-things-every-educator-should-know-about-digital-equity

Jackson, Y. (2011). *The pedagogy of confidence: Inspiring high intellectual performance in urban schools.* Teachers College Press.

Kendi, I. (2019). *How to be an antiracist.* Bodley Head.

Knoester, M., & Au, W. (2017) Standardized testing and school segregation: Like tinder for fire? *Race Ethnicity and Education, 20*(1), 1–14. https://doi.org/10.1080/13613324.2015.1121474

Kuhfield, M., Soland, J., Lewis, K., & Morton, E. (2022). The pandemic has had devastating impacts on learning. What will it take to help students catch up? *Brookings.* www.brookings.edu/blog/brown-center-chalkboard/2022/03/03/the-pandemic-has-had-devastating-impacts-on-learning-what-will-it-take-to-help-students-catch-up/

Labaree, D. (1997). Public goods, private goods: The American struggle over educational goals. *American Educational Research Journal, 34*(1), 39–81.

Maslow, A. H. (1943). A theory of human motivation. *Psychological Review, 50*(4), 370–396. https://doi.org/10.1037/h0054346

National Center for Education Statistics (NCES). (2019). *Employment and unemployment rates based on educational attainment, 2019.* U.S. Department of Education, Office of Educational Research and Improvement.

Nieto, S. (2002). Profoundly multicultural questions. *Educational Leadership, 60*(4), 610.

Nieto, S. (2005). Public education in the twentieth century and beyond: High hopes, broken promises, and an uncertain future. *Harvard Educational Review, 75*(1), 57–78.

Pokhrel, S., & Chhetri, R. (2021). A literature review on impact of COVID-19 pandemic on teaching and learning. *Higher Education for the Future, 8*(1), 133–141. https://doi.org/10.1177/2347631120983481

Shepard, L. A., Penuel, W. R., & Pellegrino, J. W. (2018). Using learning and motivation theories to coherently link formative assessment, grading practices, and large-scale assessment. *Educational Measurement: Issues and Practice, 37*(1), 21–34.

United States Department of Education (USDOE). (2017). *Reimagining the role of technology in education.* Author. https://tech.ed.gov/files/2017/01/NETP17.pdf

United States Department of Education (USDOE). (2022). *Secretary Cardona lays out vision for education in America.* Author. www.ed.gov/news/press-releases/secretary-cardona-lays-out-vision-education-america/

van Dijk, J. (2020). *The digital divide.* Polity Press.

2

RAMIFICATIONS OF THE DIGITAL DIVIDE ON COGNITIVE DEVELOPMENT AND SCHOOL PREPAREDNESS

Joshua L. DeVincenzo, Geryel Osorio-Godoy, and Thomas Chandler

---

Guiding Questions:

- In what ways did the ecosystem of school stakeholders respond to digital divides present in COVID-19 distance learning?
- What have been some of the early cognitive impacts of distance learning during COVID-19 across stakeholders identified from the literature?
- How did distributive justice play a role in the cognitive impacts of digital learning for each stakeholder?

Introduction

The conceptualization of the digital divide—or, as some scholars have pointed out (Jung et al., 2001), digital divides—began multiple decades prior to the focal themes of this chapter as well as the implications of the COVID-19 pandemic on education. As has been widely discussed in the literature as well as the popular press, numerous existing and long-standing inequities were accentuated throughout the pandemic, not the least of them the digital divide.

Burbules et al. (2006) defined the digital divide as access to information and communication technologies that is important for educational, employment, and life opportunities. This definition underscores the importance of public concern for digital resources on the grounds of its centrality to life chances and the relationship between digital access and the social dimensions of advantage and disadvantage.

Inextricably linked to the socially rooted ramifications presented by the digital divide are the impacts on the cognitive well-being and development of all human

DOI:10.4324/9781003274537-3

stakeholders within an education system. Bavel et al. (2020) emphasized that the pandemic exhausted many so-called cognitive and behavioral vehicles, including emotion and risk perception, trust, identity, social norms, social inequality, culture, polarization, stress, and coping. Not surprisingly, the cognitive load for the entire learning ecosystem present in a student's life, encompassing the mental well-being of parents/guardians, family members, teachers, and administrators, increased to alarming levels during the pandemic with potential long-term impacts on future learning, school operations, and social capital. For example, the mental health and social supports of children who lost loved ones or experienced their parental figures lose employment are both critical considerations to a student's learning outcomes that must be accounted for in unprecedented ways (Iyengar, 2020).

This chapter focuses on the school ecosystem of stakeholders, students, educators, parents/guardians/caregivers, administrators, and support staff, with a narrow focus on the themes of the cognitive impacts on each group attributed to digital divides. Because the impacts of COVID-19 are global in nature, the chapter will draw upon research and examples worldwide.

Students

Focusing on students' cognitive development during the pandemic, McCoy et al. (2021) noted that at least 167 million children worldwide have lost access to early educational supports, with the lapse in childhood care and education potentially derailing early childhood development for tens of millions of children. In the United States alone, kindergarten enrollment dropped by 16% in 2020 (Dorn et al., 2020). This is particularly critical as it is well documented (Berens & Nelson, 2019; Black et al., 2017; Shonkoff & Garner, 2011) that early childhood involves a developmental period in which the brain is susceptible to environmental inputs or a lack thereof. The cognitive development of children who have experienced this interruption in early childhood care and education requires extensive research to fully understand the extent to which their overall human development has been affected. In addition, at the time of this writing, the long-term health impacts of those who have suffered from a case(s) of COVID-19 termed "long COVID" are still being investigated.

In terms of practical implications, the development of children should be a key focus area for research, practice, and new educational recovery programs moving forward. Following a disaster, in this case, a global pandemic, children have limited capacities to mobilize and advocate for themselves and often depend on social support to help them adapt to the stress of a disaster event and its long-term impacts (Abramson et al., 2010). In fact, an essential indicator of the larger community-level recovery process is the stabilization of the social supports that children depend on in the community. Consequently, the needs of children should be prioritized at all levels of disaster recovery (Abramson et al., 2010).

Digital Divide, Cognitive Development, & School Preparedness **19**

The role of technology permeates both the challenges and solutions when it comes to the disaster impacts and the road to recovery for students and their cognitive development. For example, Amro and Dabbagh (2020) investigated the unique needs of English language learners (ELLs) and successfully employed technology to deliver linguistic scaffolding. Herrmann et al. (2021) found improved levels of social-emotional skills during education under pandemic conditions despite the challenges and high levels of stress felt by all actors within the education system.

However, although certain outcomes were indeed positive, it is important to note the challenges that accompanied the new dependency on technology as a conduit for continuity of learning. Specifically, research from the Adolescent Brain Cognitive Development (ABCD) study observed poorer mental health and higher perceived stress associated with higher screen use, while coping behaviors and more social support were associated with lower levels of screen use (Nagata et al., 2022). Continued analysis of the relationship between extended screen use brought about as a result of distance learning specific to the COVID-19 context and the mental well-being of adolescents should inform future planning for remote learning under emergency situations.

Findings from a longitudinal study of 1,600 caregiver–child dyads in Providence, Rhode Island, showed that young infants born since the onset of the pandemic demonstrated a significantly lower overall level of cognitive performance than children born before the pandemic (Deoni et al., 2021). These results are indicative of how environmental conditions shape early development. Similar studies on older youth in 2022 have found reduced social interaction, increased media consumption, and reduced physical activity (Bezerra et al., 2020; Calbi et al., 2021; Fiorillo & Gorwood, 2020). These trends may be associated with impaired motor development/coordination, language development, and socioemotional processing. Although the permanency of observed declines or impairments remains unclear as prepandemic levels of interactions return, Deoni et al. (2021) calls on further research for the primary factors underlying these trends and on social programs like SNAP (Supplemental Nutritional Assistance Program) and WIC (Special Supplemental Nutrition Program for Women, Infants, and Children), which can help mitigate the impact of the pandemic on the most vulnerable populations.

Dorn et al. (2020) pointed to the likely compounding effects on learning losses over time, as evidenced in other types of long-term disasters. To address the needs of students, therefore, it will be imperative to account not only for the learning losses in the short term but also for the complex long-term impacts on social and human development that have yet to be actualized.

Educators

The role of educators in crisis tends to be understated. Teachers are often left to their own ingenuity when working with the community and translating current needs to children of all ages. The COVID-19 pandemic was no exception.

Educators and schools responded in myriad creative ways to the challenges presented by the pandemic, ranging from hi-tech to no-tech. Some schools provided Wi-Fi hotspots from their parking lots, while others provided Wi-Fi-enabled devices or hotspots to their students. In other situations, teachers relied on postal mail or private tutoring or even stopped by their students' homes and taught from the driveway (Correia, 2020).

The technological demands of shifting curricula online resulted in rapid professional development and investments on all scales. For example, Bozkurt et al. (2020) documented the success of incorporating specialists for online learning as well as instructional designers. At the same time, however, the authors also underlined a series of issues in the digital transition process, as teachers cited lack of time to prepare, lack of support in the process, and loss of personal connection with students.

Many of the initial short-term solutions will likely have long-term academic implications for online learning. Prior to the pandemic, the most marginalized and underperforming schools, predominantly in low-income and communities of color, were unprepared for asynchronous learning (Hammond, 2021). Current research related to the digital divide across different countries has primarily looked through a deficit-based lens on the learning that took place at the height of the pandemic and school closures. However, this narrative of learning loss disregards what students have learned in their own contexts, neighborhoods, and homes and fails to recognize the (un)standardized ways of learning that fail to be captured in standardized testing and delivery of instruction. By contrast, the ability to build on the strong foundation youth may already possess means adopting a vision in which the education system provides the space and tools for children and their educators to heal simultaneously.

Sosa Díaz (2021) summarized that educators approached the new and sudden educational conditions positively, with many showing an ability to adapt to the changing nature of the situation and policies. However, Sosa Díaz also noted that such adaptability often comes at a cost, with educators having to balance family, stress, and the need to quickly develop digital competencies. Sosa Díaz (2021) further highlighted the importance of collaboration among educators as a means of support, as collaboration and adaptability are key when educators are also confronted with social and cognitive challenges of all magnitudes. When conceptualizing future directions to support educators, Price-Dennis and Sealey-Ruiz (2021) pointed to the weight social protest movements via social media have on both students and teacher educators, calling on the need for teacher education programs to develop racial literacy as a necessary means to increase their capacity and agency to better respond to inequities in the system.

Parents, Guardians, and Caregivers

Parents, guardians, and caregivers (PGCs) play a fundamental role in educational attainment and performance as well as in early childhood development. During infancy and childhood, these figures in a child's life can provide the most intimate setting to nurture and protect children as they grow, develop, and mature (American Psychological Association [APA], 2009). Findings from the APA (2009) emphasize that relationships between PGC and youth that are communicative, respectful of boundaries, and open to explaining the rules behind behaviors are associated with a higher level of student self-esteem and academic achievement. However, from household to household, the extent to which PGCs are able to be involved in a student's education varies widely. While this variability can be due to several factors, it often stems from structural inequality. For example, Goudeau et al. (2021) found working-class students and parents shared lower levels of academic self-efficacy than their counterparts from the upper/middle class. The researchers surmise that the addition of COVID-19-elicited distance learning has only exacerbated the disparity of academic self-efficacy based on class (Goudeau et al., 2021). Despite an existing understanding of the variability in household involvement and perceived academic self-efficacy in students' education, COVID-19 brought unprecedented expectations of PGCs, and even more than before, their involvement was a key indicator of the extent to which students had access to and engaged in learning from early in the COVID-19 pandemic (2020) to the present.

In the context of PGCs and the digital divide, it is important to note that the digital divide goes beyond access to devices and competency to maneuver hardware and software, extending to how effective and accessible support to operationalize the technology is. Sosa Díaz (2021) highlighted the dependence of students' academic success on their families' digital competency. Further, the study found that during the academic lockdown across Spain, students' academic results depended heavily on strategies such as motivation, attention, attitude, and parental skills. Additionally, having older siblings was found to serve as a protective factor by reducing the difficulties families experienced while supporting their child's learning. Varela et al. (2021), in a study of 622 heads of households from different towns in Spain, noted that the level of priority given to homework before the pandemic in private-school households was far greater than that of families whose children attended public schools. This phenomenon continued after the quarantine period ended and schools reopened.

For parents and caregivers who were able to work from home during the pandemic and did not experience a loss of employment, the dual role of childcare and work increased stress and anxiety (Deoni et al., 2021). Furthermore, maternal education was found to be associated with improved cognitive function and seemed to have a buffering effect against the impact of the pandemic. This finding is pertinent given the overrepresentation of families of lower socioeconomic status in essential-service positions, who faced a heightened level of financial insecurity, job loss, and COVID illnesses.

Future policies and plans for continuity of learning must integrate the perspectives and realities of PGCs. Identifying early indicators of digital divides is an important first step. For example, it is imperative to develop plans that take into account the 41% of working-class families in the U.S. who do not possess a laptop or desktop computer and the 43% who do not have broadband access in comparison to upper-/middle-class American families, who are far better equipped in terms of devices, broadband, and familiarity with digital tools and resources (Goudeau et al., 2021). When future plans fail to take into consideration the unique circumstances and unmet needs of families that are most heavily impacted by digital divides, the result is continued social vulnerability.

Administrators and Support Staff

School leadership and support staff experienced their share of challenges when navigating distance learning and the cognitive impacts elicited by administrative decision-making throughout the COVID-19 pandemic. Herrmann et al. (2021) categorized the conditions faced by school leadership as volatile, unpredictable, complex, and ambiguous (VUCA). Under VUCA conditions, school leaders emerged as crisis and safety managers (Herrmann et al., 2021). The ways in which leaders responded to these challenges and new demands varied significantly, with some leaders discovering newfound conflicts with faculty and difficulty adjusting to new communication styles while others experienced an increase in confidence and competence in safety procedures and excelled in the extension of their roles and responsibilities (Herrmann et al., 2021). In addition to extended responsibilities and new cognitive demands to be able to successfully lead in times of crisis, Beauchamp et al. (202 1) observed that throughout the pandemic, a blurring of professional boundaries took place that impacted stakeholders within the educational system.

In addition to the shifts in people management for school leaders, the technological challenges were also significant. For example, school leaders at the district level not only had to address many of the aforementioned challenges experienced by all the stakeholder vignettes in this chapter but also had to respond to challenges related to shifts in traditional educational paradigms. One extreme example is the reconfiguration of learning time. Thus, some school districts shifted to expanded learning time (ELT) strategies that extend their academic school year calendar and run into the summer months (Dorn et al., 2020). The consequences of ELT can impact all stakeholders, including the school leaders and support staff themselves.

A study from 2020 to 2021 from the National Association of Elementary School Principals (NAESP) among 860 rural, suburban, and urban schools found that nearly 70% of the participating principals reported not being able to meet their students' mental health needs with the staffing shortages they were facing (NAESP, 2021). One principal from Maine stated, "all employees in public schools need support, not just teachers. We need help for our bus drivers, custodians, secretaries, and paraprofessionals" (NAESP, 2021, p. 3). This disproportionately affected districts' and schools' efforts to serve ELLs through virtual instruction and exacerbated a problem that predated COVID-19, whereby many schools had only one or very few teachers with certification or licensing to teach ELLs. These support staff members typically collaborate with content-area teachers while also delivering small-group or full-class instruction (U.S. Department of Education, 2021).

Digital Divides From the Perspective of Distributive Justice

Digital divides across each stakeholder group can be conceptualized from a distributive justice framework (Hendrix, 2005). A distributive justice framework examines the scarcity of a personal or public good and begins to ask critical questions about (a) who are the recipients of this good and in what amounts? and (b) by which criterion is this good distributed? (Hendrix, 2005). In the context of COVID-19, the distributive justice framework offers multiple dimensions of analysis, focusing on equity as well as procedural fairness.

In examining the inequities of education under COVID-19, it is important to illustrate the existing distributive (in)justices of education in society. Educational attainment becomes a good in a society that is accepted (implicitly and explicitly) with a certain degree of inequality even under "blue sky" (i.e., "normal") conditions (Burbules et al., 2006). The degree of inequality, as well as its acceptance, originates from merit-based criteria that span perceived talent, ability, and level of effort.

Arnove (2020) noted that the pre-COVID-19 status quo of the education system was far from satisfactory and that, therefore, this moment in time should be seen as an opportunity to reimagine an educational system in which all students have the opportunity for success. The discussion of each stakeholder group in this chapter is an exemplar of the challenges of distributive justice (Hendrix, 2005) experienced in the process of digital learning as a "good" that was distributed or not distributed in response to COVID-19. When we examined the distribution of digital learning across each group, it became evident that how effectively and justly the distribution of digital learning was implemented had immediate and long-term implications for overall cognitive development and mental well-being.

Conclusion

This chapter has presented several stakeholder groups that, together, create a broader education system with a focus on the impacts of the COVID-19 pandemic on how each group navigated shifts to digital learning both socially and cognitively. As such, this chapter helps to identify both direct and indirect digital divides experienced across the educational ecosystem. The review and discussion of the digital divides were not intended to bemoan or restate issues throughout the educational system but to provide key areas of focus for future planning and disaster preparedness. It is important to note that many of the most innovative solutions generated were "just in time" and adaptive, as the authors of this chapter recognize the time delays between what is needed immediately in the classroom and the time it may take to generate a policy, procedure, or practice or to garner the necessary resources to influence an educational response. In addition, this chapter aimed not only to focus on the deficits or learning losses but also to incorporate examples of advancements and progress in both educational operations and cognition experienced across major educational stakeholder groups during the COVID-19 pandemic. As pointed out, future planning can address both the positive and negative themes identified as a result of multiple years of education under global pandemic conditions to strengthen school, community, family, and student preparedness.

Key Takeaways:

1. For the purposes of this chapter, the authors analyzed the following stakeholder groups: students, educators, parents/guardians/caregivers, administrators, and support staff. Each group warrants a more localized investigation to further understand cognitive impacts, digital divides, and solutions for a given school system moving forward.
2. Human development in general and early childhood development in particular in relation to COVID-19 should be key focus areas for research, practice, and new educational recovery programs.
3. To address the needs of students, it is imperative to account not only for the learning losses in the short term but also for the potential complex social and human developmental long-term impacts that have yet to materialize.
4. The distribution and effectiveness of digital learning and the extent to which they were implemented equitably resulted in immediate and long-term implications for overall cognitive functioning and mental well-being across each stakeholder group and must be factored into future preparedness plans.

Recommended Resources

- Federal Communications Commission (FCC)—Homework Gap and Connectivity Divide (www.fcc.gov/about-fcc/fcc-initiatives/homework-gap-and-connectivity-divide): This website offers resources on the Emergency Broadband Benefit, the Affordable Connectivity Program, and news and updates on helping close the homework gap along with further issues of the digital divide.

- Intercultural Development Research Association (IDRA)—Educator and Student Support (www.idra.org/support/): IDRA offers a searchable webpage for materials, webinars, and other information and resources generated throughout COVID-19 school closures to assist educators and families in supporting students as they continue learning.
- Resilient Children Resilient Communities (RCRC) Tool Box (https://rcrc toolbox.org/toolbox_cat/child-serving-organizations/): The Resilient Children Resilient Communities (RCRC) Tool Box is a collection of resources developed and curated to benefit those working to make communities and children more resilient to all kinds of disasters. The toolbox is available in both English and Spanish.
- U.S. Department of Education (DOE)—Guiding Principles for Use of Technology with Early Learners (https://tech.ed.gov/earlylearning/principles/): This resource from the U.S. Department of Education (DOE) offers and outlines the department's four guiding principles for the use of technology with early learners.

References

Abramson, D. M., Park, Y. S., Stehling-Ariza, T., & Redlener, I. (2010). Children as bellwethers of recovery: Dysfunctional systems and the effects of parents, households, and neighborhoods on serious emotional disturbance in children after Hurricane Katrina. *Disaster Medicine and Public Health Preparedness, 4*(S1), S17–S27.

American Psychological Association. (2009, April). *Parents and caregivers are essential to children's healthy development.* www.apa.org/pi/families/resources/parents-caregivers

Amro, F., & Dabbagh, N. (2020). Using primary language support in a computer-based intervention to Scaffold second language learners. *Journal of Online Learning Research, 6*(1), 57–76.

Arnove, R. F. (2020). Imagining what education can be post-COVID-19. *Prospects, 49*(1), 43–46. https://doi.org/10.1007/s11125-020-09474-1

Bavel, J. J. V., Baicker, K., Boggio, P. S., Capraro, V., Cichocka, A., Cikara, M., Crockett, M. J., Crum, A. J., Douglas, K. M., Druckman, J. N., Drury, J., Dube, O., Ellemers, N., Finkel, E. J., Fowler, J. H., Gelfand, M., Han, S., Alexander Haslam, S., Jetten, J., . . . Willer, R. (2020). Using social and behavioural science to support COVID-19 pandemic response. *Nature Human Behaviour, 4*(5), 460–471.

Beauchamp, G., Hulme, M., Clarke, L., Hamilton, L., & Harvey, J. A. (2021). "People miss people": A study of school leadership and management in the four nations of the United Kingdom in the early stage of the COVID-19 pandemic. *Educational Management Administration & Leadership, 49*(3), 375–392.

Berens, A. E., & Nelson, C. A. (2019). Neurobiology of fetal and infant development. In C. H. Zeanah (Ed.), *Handbook of infant mental health* (4th ed., pp. 41–62). The Guilford Press.

Bezerra, A. C. V., Menezes Da Silva, C. E., Soares, F. R. G., & Menezes Da Silva, J. A. (2020). Factors associated with people's behavior in social isolation during the COVID-19 pandemic. *Ciência & Saúde Coletiva, 25*(1), 2411–2421. https://doi.org/10.1590/1413-81232020256.1.10792020

Black, M. M., Walker, S. P., Fernald, L. C. H., Andersen, C. T., DiGirolamo, A. M., Lu, C., McCoy, D. C., Fink, G., Shawar, Y. R., Shiffman, J., Devercelli, A. E., Wodon, Q. T., Vargas-Barón, E., & Grantham-McGregor, S. (2017). Early childhood development coming of age: Science through the life course. *The Lancet, 389*(10064), 77–90. https://doi.org/10.1016/s0140-6736(16)31389-7

Bozkurt, A., Jung, I., Xiao, J., Vladimirschi, V., Schuwer, R., Egorov, G., Lambert, S. R., Al-Freih, M., Pete, J., Olcott, Jr., D., Rodes, V., Aranciaga, I., Bali, M., Alvarez, Jr., A. V., Roberts, J., Pazurek, A., Raffaghelli, J. E., Panagiotou, N., de Coëtlogon, P., . . . Paskevicius, M. (2020). A global outlook to the interruption of education due to COVID-19 pandemic: Navigating in a time of uncertainty and crisis. *Asian Journal of Distance Education, 15*(1), 11–26. https://doi.org/10.5281/zenodo.3878572

Burbules, N. C., Callister, T. A., & Taaffe, C. (2006). Beyond the digital divide. *Technology and Education: Issues in Administration, Policy, and Applications in K12 Schools, 8*, 85–99. https://doi.org/10.1016/s1479-3660(05)08007-8

Calbi, M., Langiulli, N., Ferroni, F., Montalti, M., Kolesnikov, A., Gallese, V., & Alessandra Umiltà, M. (2021). The consequences of COVID-19 on social interactions: An online study on face covering. *Scientific Reports, 11*, 2601. https://doi.org/10.1038/s41598-021-81780-w

Correia, A. (2020). Healing the digital divide during the COVID-19 pandemic. *Quarterly Review of Distance Education, 21*(1), 13–22.

Deoni, S. C., Beauchemin, J., Volpe, A., D'Sa, V., & The Resonance Consortium. (2021). Impact of the COVID-19 Pandemic on early child cognitive development: Initial findings in a longitudinal observational study of child health. *MedRxiv*. Preprints. https://doi.org/10.1101/2021.08.10.21261846

Dorn, E., Hancock, B., Sarakatsannis, J., & Viruleg, E. (2020). *COVID-19 and learning loss—Disparities grow and students need help.* McKinsey & Company. www.mckinsey.com/industries/public-and-social-sector/our-insights/covid-19-and-learning-loss-disparities-grow-and-students-need-help

Fiorillo, A., & Gorwood, P. (2020). The consequences of the COVID-19 pandemic on mental health and implications for clinical practice. *European Psychiatry, 63*(1), E32. https://doi.org/10.1192/j.eurpsy.2020.35

Goudeau, S., Sanrey, C., Stanczak, A., Manstead, A., & Darnon, C. (2021). Why lockdown and distance learning during the COVID-19 pandemic are likely to increase the social class achievement gap. *Nature Human Behaviour, 5*(10), 1273–1281. https://doi.org/10.1038/s41562-021-01212-7

Hammond, Z. (2021). Integrating the science of learning and culturally responsive practice. *American Educator, 45*(2), 4–11. www.aft.org/ae/summer2021/hammond

Hendrix, E. (2005). Permanent injustice: Rawls' theory of justice and the digital divide. *Journal of Educational Technology & Society, 8*(1), 63–68. www.jstor.org/stable/jeductechsoci.8.1.63

Herrmann, L., Nielsen, B. L., & Aguilar-Raab, C. (2021). The impact of COVID-19 on interpersonal aspects in elementary school. *Frontiers in Education, 6*. https://doi.org/10.3389/feduc.2021.635180

Iyengar, R. (2020). Education as the path to a sustainable recovery from COVID-19. *Prospects, 49*, 77–80. https://doi.org/10.1007/s11125-020-09488-9

Jung, J. Y., Qiu, J. L., & Kim, Y. C. (2001). Internet connectedness and inequality: Beyond the divide. *Communication Research, 28*(4), 507–535. https://doi.org/10.1177/009365001028004006

McCoy, D. C., Cuartas, J., Behrman, J., Cappa, C., Heymann, J., López Bóo, F., Lu, C., Raikes, A., Richter, L., Stein, A., & Fink, G. (2021). Global estimates of the implications of COVID-19 related preprimary school closures for children's instructional access, development, learning, and economic wellbeing. *Child Development, 92*(5), e883–e899. https://doi.org/10.1111/cdev.13658

Nagata, J. M., Cortez, C. A., Cattle, C. J., Ganson, K. T., Iyer, P., Bibbins-Domingo, K., & Baker, F. C. (2022). Screen time use among US adolescents during the COVID-19 pandemic: Findings from the Adolescent Brain Cognitive Development (ABCD) study. *JAMA Pediatrics, 176*(1), 94–96. https://doi.org/10.1001/jamapediatrics.2021.4334

National Association of Elementary School Principals. (2021, January 13). *NAESP releases results of midyear national principal survey on Covid-19 in schools* [Press release]. www.naesp.org/news/naesp-releases-results-of-midyear-national-principal-survey-on-covid-19-in-schools/

Price-Dennis, D., & Sealey-Ruiz, Y. (2021). *Advancing racial literacies in teacher education: Activism for equity in digital spaces.* Teachers College Press.

Shonkoff, J. P., Garner, A. S., Siegel, B. S., Dobbins, M. I., Earls, M. F., Garner, A. S., McGuinn, L., Pascoe, J., & Wood, D. L. (2011). The lifelong effects of early childhood adversity and toxic stress. *Pediatrics, 129*(1), e232–e246. https://doi.org/10.1542/peds.2011-2663

Sosa Díaz, M. J. (2021). Emergency remote education, family support and the digital divide in the context of the COVID-19 lockdown. *International Journal of Environmental Research and Public Health, 18*(15), 7956. https://doi.org/10.3390/ijerph18157956

U.S. Department of Education. (2021). *Education in a pandemic: The disparate impacts of COVID-19 on America's students.* https://www2.ed.gov/about/offices/list/ocr/docs/20210608-impacts-of-covid19.pdf

Varela, A., Fraguela-Vale, R., & López Gómez, S. (2021). Juego y tareas escolares: El papel de la escuela y la familia en tiempos de confinamiento por la COVID-19. *Estudios sobre Educación, 41*, 27–47. https://doi.org/10.15581/004.41.001

3

STRATEGIES TO HELP ADMINISTRATORS, TEACHERS, AND PARENTS TO ACHIEVE EQUITABLE DIGITAL LEARNING IN U.S. HIGH-NEEDS SCHOOL COMMUNITIES

Heejung An and Woonhee Sung

Guiding Questions:

- What strategies can be used to foster equitable digital learning in U.S. high-needs schools?
- How can these strategies be implemented by administrators, teachers, and parents?
- What exemplary actions can support strategies based on the lived experiences of interviewees?

Introduction

The COVID-19 pandemic forced K-12 communities to experiment with and implement online learning while attempting to move forward without proper preparation and training for administrators, teachers, parents, and learners. While this sudden urgency resulted in many frustrations and failures, success stories and opportunities have also arisen. To describe what transpired during the COVID-19 pandemic in high-needs school communities in the United States, An et al. (2022) conducted in-depth individual online interviews with parents, teachers, and administrators in high-needs schools from the fall 2020 through the spring 2021, employing phenomenology as a methodological approach. Four factors that impacted online learning in U.S. high-needs schools were identified: accessibility, usability, wellness, and support (hereinafter referred to as AUWS) (see An et al., 2022). The study also found that some

DOI:10.4324/9781003274537-4

high-needs schools managed to adapt to online learning more effectively than others despite the challenges they all faced.

As the pandemic continues to dissipate, it is time to reflect upon our collective experiences. This prompted the authors to examine why some high-needs schools were able to carry out online learning relatively effectively while others fell behind. Even though almost all public schools have returned to in-person schooling at the time of this writing, some strategies and tools that were implemented during COVID-19 continue to be used in many classrooms to enhance in-person schooling. Rather than *online learning*, in this chapter, we will use the term *digital learning*, defined as "any instructional practice that effectively uses technology to strengthen a student's learning experience and encompasses a wide spectrum of tools and practices" (New Jersey Department of Education [NJDOE], n.d.). We do not want to confine the scope of our suggestions to online schools. Rather, the suggestions we have derived can be applied to any K-12 school but, particularly, high-needs schools with the overarching goal of achieving digital equity, as described in Chapter 1.

Online and Blended Learning in U.S. K-12 High-Needs Schools

Online learning in K-12 education has been carried out in different formats from fully online schools to blended programs or brick-and-mortar schools with some online elements (Schwirzke et al., 2018). That said, the problems inherent in K-12 education in terms of online learning have not been on the radar of policymakers, online learning designers, instructional designers, or researchers (Lokey-Vega et al., 2018), including a lack of teacher- and administrator-level training, certification, and funding for integrating digital learning (Cavanaugh, 2013). More importantly, there are issues related to equitable access and resources, internet safety, different developmental levels and physical ability to work with digital tools, parental involvement, and curriculum mandates (Cavanaugh, 2013; Rice, 2014).

These issues revealed in previous studies share similarities with the findings of a recent study conducted in U.S. high-needs schools during COVID-19 (An et al., 2022): (a) accessibility, (b) usability, (c) wellness, and (d) support. Some of the subcategories of these four themes include digital equity, parental involvement, safety, and physical accessibility to tools that appeared in studies previously. An et al.'s findings (2022) confirmed several unsolved issues in K-12 online education.

The transition to online platforms during the COVID-19 pandemic worsened the issues of access, equity, students' capabilities, teachers' preparedness, and parents' understanding because K-12 schools had no well-established standards to turn to as they attempted to address the unique needs of K-12 classrooms, especially for online classrooms. Blended learning often used by K-12 teachers contains a mixture of online meetings or online assignments and in-person classroom meetings. However, teachers do not always demonstrate a good understanding of the various types of blended learning or the ability to design lessons based on these models (Sung et al., 2022). In the case of high-needs schools, the decision to deliver materials on- or offline can only be made based on availability and affordability. Thus, stakeholders in these communities cannot make informed decisions. In addition, studies published during the COVID-19 pandemic have pointed to parental contributions as one essential component in the success of online learning (Novianti & Garzia, 2020). Although these studies were not conducted in high-needs schools, the importance of parental engagement in online learning and parents' awareness of information and communications technology (ICT) clearly apply across the board (Novianti & Garzia, 2020).

So far, no systemic research has explored the authentic concerns of K-12 high-needs schools. Thus, the four AUWS shown in Figure 3.1, addressing the basic needs for access, space, and tools have become the guiding themes for us. The following strategies and practices were derived from interviews conducted pertaining to the four factors that affected online learning in high-needs schools during the COVID-19 pandemic. That is, when these factors were sufficiently present in high-needs communities, they played a facilitating role in making online learning successful. As a result, when these factors are not present and considered to meet specific needs in high-needs classrooms, online learning may face fundamental challenges.

FIGURE 3.1 Four Factors Affecting Online Learning During the COVID-19 Pandemic in U.S. High-Needs Schools

Suggested Strategies and Example Practices for Equitable Digital Learning to Support High-Needs School Communities

By repetitively reviewing the interview transcripts conducted with the stakeholders—administrators, teachers, and parents—we were able to distill what the participants mentioned as effective strategies, thus enabling online learning to be successful in their high-needs schools. We have listed these ideas in separate tables for each group: administrators (see Table 3.1), teachers (see Table 3.2), and parents (see Table 3.3). The strategies listed in Tables 3.1 through 3.3 are action items that must be taken into consideration for each group. The tables also include so-called practice examples—that is, what the interviewees suggested as being effective and useful. Some of the items apply to a given group, while others were suggested as a means of supporting other groups in improving their experiences and practices. In other words, the roles and responsibilities in each table are a list of what should be accomplished as a dynamic learning system. In addition, the strategies that appear in all three tables are applicable to all three groups, and thus are critically important.

For administrators in high-needs schools, it is critical to consider external funding to be able to implement one-to-one computing for all teachers, staff members, and students and foster the usage of free hardware and software. A large number of high-quality open-access textbooks and multimedia programs are available. In addition, digital and culturally responsive leadership is critical. In order to develop digital leadership, administrators must keep abreast of current trends and be knowledgeable about educational technology by attending conferences such as the International Society for Technology in Education (ISTE) conference or other local educational technology conferences or webinars. This will help them gain a vision of appropriate professional development (PD) training, including basic technology skills, instructional design, and the benefits and limitations of various modalities.

Faculty and administrator diversity has also gained increasing attention in recent years as policy reports and studies continue to show the added benefit of diversity in the school workforce (Carver-Thomas, 2018). This study brought about similar realizations (An et al., 2022). That is, we found that teachers and staff who came from ethnic backgrounds and cultures similar to those of the parents and students were able to navigate through challenging situations better than less experienced staff. Much of this came down to sharing the same language as a means to quickly rectify urgent problems. Further, it was also evident that there were only a few staff in each school who had the time, linguistic ability, and cultural understanding to deal with hundreds of parents and students each day. Consequently, hiring a diverse workforce and providing ready-to-go digital lessons and resources in bilingual form should be a priority in high-needs schools. In addition, providing professional development for teachers is critical.

The strategies suggested in this chapter address not only the instructional needs in online teaching environments, but also the design of activities for physical,

32 Heejung An and Woonhee Sung

emotional, and learning domains that may ultimately benefit learners. In addition to pedagogical strategies and content knowledge delivery, incorporation of technical skills, the ability to choose effective tools, and the preparation of materials for both parents and students were found to be important teacher strategies. However, these strategies require increased time and effort on the part of teachers and, therefore, require support from administrators in this regard.

For parents, the strategies include actions that could benefit students but require teachers' efforts. Specifically, parents of students who attend high-needs schools have experienced issues related to inaccessible and unusable digital tools, space, and instructional resources. The suggested strategies include the importance of bilingual resources, visual guidelines, and the use of low to medium technologies, such as applications and software that can function in handheld devices or that do not require high-capacity devices. Parents are closer than teachers to students when they take online classes and, therefore, experience and observe firsthand their child's physical fatigue, changes in emotions, and confusion from the lack of communication. Strategies for the support and wellness category not only include training or resources that provide technical guidelines for parents but also highlight activities students can do at home with their parents. These activities involve physical education and arts-integrated work at home, which, in turn, requires that teachers develop lesson activities that provide guidelines for creating hands-on or digital products with family members at home. As a result, the extensive burden on such teachers should be acknowledged and addressed by the school administration.

TABLE 3.1 Suggested Strategies With Practice Examples for Administrators Based on the AUWS Factors

For Administrators		
Four Factors	*Strategies*	*Practice Examples*
Accessibility	• Establish one-to-one computing for teachers, staff, and students. • Establish relationships in the local and regional communities for fundraising. • Foster a culture of using open-source technology for both hardware and software.	→ Provide hardware (e.g., computers, tablets) and software that teachers need or want. → Seek out nonprofit organizations that offer technology in high-needs schools (e.g., OLPC). → Develop a relationship with the community leaders in the town and county who have a similar vision. → Create a working group to research free learning management systems (LMSs) such as Google Classroom and open educational resources (OERs) for possible adoption.

(Continued)

Achieving Equitable Digital Learning in High-Needs Schools **33**

TABLE 3.1 (Continued)

For Administrators		
Four Factors	*Strategies*	*Practice Examples*
Usability	• Keep abreast of the latest trends, research, and ideas in the field of educational technology.	→ Regularly attend educational technology conferences or take webinars to keep abreast of digital learning trends and needs. → Be familiar with the ISTE standards for administrators to develop digital leadership capacity and skills.
Wellness	• Maintain physical, social, and emotional health by providing activities and strategies to ensure physical, social, and emotional balance and health.	→ Provide nonmandatory mindful yoga sessions for administrators, teachers, and students. → Offer synchronous lunch and snack times via videoconferencing programs.
Support	• Develop hiring policies that foster diverse teachers and staff members. • Proactively seek out and communicate with teachers, staff, parents, and students in their native and/or home languages. • Create a peer online support network system for teachers and parents.	→ Focus on diversity in teacher and staff hiring by communicating with human resources and reviewing best practices for hiring teachers and other staff from different jurisdictions. → Disseminate information, instructions, and announcements for parents/guardians in bilingual formats. → Create an online support network space by using social media (e.g., Facebook, Twitter, Dojo) or chatting programs (e.g., Slack) that teachers and parents can easily access with their phones, so everyone in the building has somebody to turn to for support when needed. This is necessary since immigrant parents often don't have time or feel comfortable reaching out to teachers or forming lasting friendships with native English speakers.

TABLE 3.2 Suggested Strategies With Practice Examples for Teachers Based on the AUWS Factors

For Teachers		
Four Factors	*Strategies*	*Practice Examples*
Accessibility	• Establish a flexible policy on the use of software or videos that teachers want to use.	→ Enable teachers to access and open educational videos and software online using school networks.

(Continued)

34 Heejung An and Woonhee Sung

TABLE 3.2 (Continued)

For Teachers		
Four Factors	*Strategies*	*Practice Examples*
		→ Consider installing separate internet connections for teachers/administrators to allow widened access.
Usability	• Provide ready-to-go digital lessons by grade level and by subject. • Use free (bilingual) instructional materials and resources. • Use digital applications for translation.	→ Subscribe to programs that include ready-to-go digital lessons for the district (e.g., Gizmos, PhET, Newsela, Discover Education). → Use free open educational resources (OERs) (e.g., Common Sense Education). → Find or create bilingual resources, especially for parents/guardians. → Dub or use caption functions for video-based resources. → Use reliable translation apps (e.g., Google Translate) or software to disseminate information, instructions, and announcements for parents/guardians.
Wellness	• Promote sharing noncurricular strategies for wellness.	→ Share fun activities such as playing games, singing, and dancing to provide social and emotional support among teachers and students.
Support	• Provide nonmandatory and constant professional development (PD) opportunities about technical learning to gain skills and technological pedagogical content knowledge (TPACK). • Promote modifications of existing templates that align with digital learning contexts.	→ Design and implement just-in-time sessions to assist "help ticket" requests for technology-related questions instantly. → Provide PD on the following topics in multiple modalities, in-person, online, and blended. This may be a one-time PD or a series of PDs on the same topic. o Technology skills o Instructional design o Technology integration across the curriculum o Digital equity

Achieving Equitable Digital Learning in High-Needs Schools **35**

TABLE 3.2 (Continued)

For Teachers		
Four Factors	Strategies	Practice Examples
		Allow teachers to showcase their teaching practices using technology informally, such as at a professional learning community (PLC) meeting.
		→ Modify existing or open-source lesson plan templates to minimize efforts and time for creating various new tasks and activities to carry out digital learning.

TABLE 3.3 Suggested Strategies With Practice Examples for Parents Based on the AUWS Factors

For Parents		
Four Factors	Strategies	Practice Examples
Accessibility	• Provide fundamental tools for accessing online content. • Utilize and develop lessons that require a minimum level of technology skills.	→ Utilize existing devices such as Google Chromebooks that the school already possesses for student usage. → Use apps that are available via handheld devices and any technology that can be easily installed and function on small devices. → When selecting tools, applications, and online lessons, check if the selected tools are available on the device(s) that can be provided or are available for students and parents at home.
Usability	• Use bilingual digital resources and tools (software). • Use applications that can be shared with family devices. • Use clear communication channels.	→ Develop guidelines in different languages for tools or other digital resources that parents can use at home. If the tool or digital resources support bilingual students, create guidelines for parents to utilize bilingual support. → For applications or course management systems, set up a family-sharing functionality so that parents, guardians, and students can receive information together. → Use one unified, consistent, and clear communication channel with parents.

(Continued)

36 Heejung An and Woonhee Sung

TABLE 3.3 (Continued)

For Parents

Four Factors	Strategies	Practice Examples
Wellness	• Recommend activities and time for physical activity.	→ Provide suggested time and physical activities or hold synchronous workout sessions for parents to do at home with students.
	• Recommend activities and strategies to ensure social and emotional balance.	→ Consider designing the physical activities to focus on improving the relationship between parents and students and allow time to talk about concerns students may have.
	• Introduce physical education lessons, music, and arts-related work appropriate for doing at home.	→ Consider designing the physical education lessons, music, and art classes to include hands-on work that students can produce with their parents, siblings, or guardians at home.
	• Provide open talks or check-ins for students and with parents, if available.	→ Online classrooms can allow time to do open talks with students and family members and to check in with family members regularly when available.
	• Create a classroom-like environment at home.	→ Allow online meeting time to share and appreciate students' and parents' collaborative work at home.
		→ Create separate working/studying stations for students at home.
Support	• Provide skills and function-focused workshops in parents' native/home language.	→ Create supplemental videos for any new tools used in the online classroom and include problem-solving steps for frequent problems.
	• Provide printable guidelines or handouts to each home.	→ Provide basic skill-focused or technique-focused training sessions for the given tool that requires parents' support at home.
	• Create online peer/parents/guardian support systems (e.g., social media Facebook group).	→ Make available printable guidelines with visual images and clear directions for troubleshooting for parents to use at home.
		→ Set up an online social media group where students and parents can participate and share their ideas and information.

Conclusion

As Bonk and Wiley (2020) have noted about online learning, we must start by falling "in love with the problem, not the solution" (p. 1606), especially when the same problems have persisted in high-needs public school communities for decades. That is, through an authentic understanding of front-line workers' deep-rooted problems, we can uncover obstacles that impede progress for digital learning in high-needs communities and, therefore, be able to identify what to prioritize and how to precisely support communities in high-needs schools. Listening to all the stakeholders and educators in high-needs schools could provide real-world problem-solving ideas that do not require tremendous changes to the existing resources or capabilities. Rather, the solution could include low-floor strategies that promote simpler starting points for making positive impacts. The strategies and examples reported in this chapter focus on the feasibility and flexibility to promote immediate and necessary changes in real-world classrooms.

It is important to note that these strategies were driven by interviews conducted in high-needs schools, taking into account the unique sociocultural and socioeconomic themes, such as the digital divide, digital literacy, cultural barriers, language barriers, and a lack of skilled faculty and staff, thus making digital learning and teaching efforts in these communities much more difficult for many students and their families than in other K-12 school environments. The same may be said for teachers. As such, these findings may help high-needs school communities to develop more pragmatically effective practices, leading to a more sustainable digital learning environment.

Key Takeaways:

1. Having a comprehensive understanding of administrators, teachers, and parents in high-needs schools could lead to the development of a more precise and effective implementation of digital learning in high-needs schools.
2. When considering equitable digital learning for high-needs schools, it is important to embrace strategies drawn from the AUWS factors.
3. These strategies should be addressed by all groups, including administrators, parents, teachers, and students, not just one group.
4. Understanding the strategies that can benefit specific populations will lead to the development of applicable and practical ideas that can be implemented in high-needs classrooms.

Recommended Resources

Books and Articles:

Gamrat, C., Tiwari, S., & Ozkan Bekiroglu, S. (2022). Inclusive ADDIE: Initial considerations for DEI pedagogy. *EDUCAUSE Review*. https://er.educause.edu/articles/2022/3/inclusive-addie-initial-considerations-for-dei-pedagogy

Morin, H., & Curry, J. (2022). Open educational resources for K-12 teachers: A sustainable plan. *TechTrends*, *66*, 938–944. https://doi.org/10.1007/s11528-022-00799-6

Sheninger, E. C. (2014). *Digital leadership: Changing paradigms for changing times*. Corwin.

Turner, P. (2022). Revisiting camera use in live remote teaching: Considerations for learning and equity. *EDUCAUSE Review*. https://er.educause.edu/articles/2022/3/revisiting-camera-use-in-live-remote-teaching-considerations-for-learning-and-equity

West Island College. (2020). *Online learning framework for students & parents*. https://resources.finalsite.net/images/v1606256208/westislandcollege-abca/dglr3pefhviqo5pybm9s/OnlineLearningFrameworkV2.pdf

Websites:

- MERLOT: https://merlot.org/: The MERLOT system provides access to curated online learning and support materials and content-creation tools led by an international community of educators, learners, and researchers.
- OER Commons: www.oercommons.org/: This is a public digital library of open free educational resources for a variety of subjects.
- UNICEF for Every Child: www.unicef.org/serbia/en/open-digital-educational-tools-interactive-online-teaching-and-learning/: Open digital educational tools for interactive online teaching and learning for teachers and students.

References

An, H., Mongillo, G., Sung, W., & Fuentes, D. (2022). Factors affecting online learning during the COVID-19 pandemic: The lived experiences of parents, teachers, and administrators in U.S. high-needs K-12 schools. *The Journal of Online Learning Research (JOLR)*, *8*(2), 203–234. www.learntechlib.org/primary/p/220404/

Bonk, C. J., & Wiley, D. (2020). Preface: Reflections on the waves of emerging learning technology. *Educational Technology Research and Development (ETR&D)*, *68*(4), 1595–1612. https://doi.org/10.1007/s11423-020-09809-x

Carver-Thomas, D. (2018). *Diversifying the teaching profession: How to recruit and retain teachers of color*. Learning Policy Institute. https://doi.org/10.54300/559.310

Cavanaugh, C. (2013). Student achievement in elementary and high school. In M. G. Moore (Ed.), *Handbook of distance education* (3rd Edn., pp. 170–184). Routledge.

Lokey-Vega, A., Jorrín-Abellán, I. M., & Pourreau, L. (2018). Theoretical perspectives in K-12 online learning. In K. Kennedy & R. E. Ferdig (Eds.), *Handbook of research on K-12 online and blended learning* (pp. 65–90). ETC Press.

New Jersey Department of Education [NJDOE]. (n.d.). *Educational technology: Digital learning glossary of terms*. www.nj.gov/education/techno/glossary/

Novianti, R., & Garzia, M. (2020). Parental engagement in children's online learning during COVID-19 pandemic. *Journal of Teaching and Learning in Elementary Education*, *3*(2), 9–23.

Rice, K. (2014). Research and history of policies in K-12 online and blended Learning. In R. Ferdig & K. Kennedy (Eds.), *Handbook of research on K-12 online and blended learning* (pp. 51–82). ETC Press.

Schwirzke, K., Vashaw, L., & Watson, J. (2018). A history of K-12 online and blended instruction in the United States. In K. Kennedy & R. E. Ferdig (Eds.), *Handbook of research on K-12 online and blended learning* (2nd Edn., pp. 7–20). ETC Press.

Sung, W., An, H., & Thomas, C. L. (2022). *A comparison between primary and secondary teachers' online teaching experiences in U.S. K-12 schools* [Online presentation]. SITE Interactive Conference, Association for the Advancement of Computing in Education (AACE).

SECTION II

Vision and Leadership for Digital Learning in High-Needs Communities

4

BRIDGING THE DIGITAL DIVIDE

An Analysis of Federal, State, and Local Policies in U.S. Schools

Thomas Chandler and Joshua L. DeVincenzo

Guiding Questions:

- In what ways have U.S. federal, state, and local efforts to address the digital divide during the H1N1 and COVID-19 pandemics been successful? In what ways have they failed?
- How can continuity-of-operations planning benefit K-12 distance learning efforts?
- What can the U.S. Department of Education do to be more proactive in guiding pandemic responses?

Introduction

The COVID-19 pandemic has brought about a number of extreme challenges for U.S. K-12 public schools. Starting on March 15, 2020, a U.S. Presidential Disaster Declaration was issued for all 50 states, bringing about unprecedented school closings and an immediate expectation to pivot to distance learning. More than 76 million students were suddenly required to learn from home, with many of the nation's most vulnerable schools provided with little to no guidance on how to adequately proceed beyond the confines of the physical classroom and with only existing resources and ingenuity to depend on (Psacharopoulos et al., 2020). Likewise, thousands of schools, in both urban and rural regions, began this transition without adequate internet bandwidth or laptops and portable devices that could be distributed to students. Further, many school faculty did not have basic competency in using new videoconferencing technologies to adequately

DOI:10.4324/9781003274537-6

teach various types of subject matter. Even worse, some schools lacked the network infrastructure, software licenses, or plans to continue operations of crucial technologies needed for online learning, such as secure servers, learning management systems, and associated staff training. Given these realities, the COVID-19 pandemic clearly exacerbated an existing digital divide, with the most extreme declines in learning occurring in low-income, minority communities that have faced economic, social, and political oppression throughout U.S. history (Lee, 2020).

This chapter provides an analysis of the highly fragmented disaster response that took place in U.S. schools from March through December 2020 as efforts were made to continue instruction for the nation's students remotely. Various initiatives conducted at the federal, state, and local level are evaluated, with a particular emphasis on the U.S. Department of Education's failure to adhere to its own previous objectives for pandemic planning and distance learning. Also addressed are the ramifications of this ongoing digital divide on learning outcomes, as well as potential mitigation measures that educational organizations can adopt by fostering continuity-of-operations planning.

Historical Background

As noted by former U.S. Secretaries of Education Rod Paige, Margaret Spellings, and Arne Duncan, it wasn't supposed to be this way. During the presidential administrations of both George W. Bush and Barack Obama, federally led continuity-of-operations plans were developed to prepare for a major pandemic and culminating K-12 school closures (Treene, 2020). Specifically, the U.S. Department of Education noted in 2004 that schools should be prepared to support home learning activities, such as web-based lessons and instructional phone calls, as well as the distribution of textbooks, workbooks, and homework packets to be available at students' residences. Further, the 2006 National Strategy for Pandemic Influenza noted that "sustaining the operations of critical infrastructure under conditions of pandemic influenza would depend largely on (1) each individual organization's development and implementation of plans for business continuity under conditions of staffing shortages and (2) to protect the health of their workforces" (U.S. Homeland Security Council, 2006, p. 169). However, planning did not end there. The U.S. Department of Education was responsible for verifying and ensuring that every public K-12 school had an emergency response plan on file, including elements of distance learning or traditional correspondence courses. Many schools that did not meet required benchmarks were not eligible to apply for or receive federal funding (U.S. Government Accountability Office, 2007).

During the H1N1 pandemic in 2009 and the school closures that occurred in response to it, the U.S. Department of Education recommended that school districts use websites to share information with staff, students, and families in the event schools had to close. The department also said schools should incorporate radio, public-broadcast television stations, telephone conference calls, phone tutoring, and educational packets to support students (Keierleber, 2020). Again, more pandemic planning guidance documents were developed, and more large-scale funding efforts were implemented to ensure that school operations could continue remotely.

Unfortunately, many of the aforementioned plans were largely aspirational. Although specific needs for digital technologies were identified and included in plans after the H1N1 pandemic, little was done to rectify decades of discriminatory policies and procedures that were holding thousands of schools back in terms of both technology infrastructure and training. As with most disasters, unfavorable predisaster conditions would determine not only the impacts but also the response and recovery. Wealthy public and private schools throughout the U.S. continued to implement exorbitant technology plans, while low-income public schools in close proximity, with little technology investment, were left to languish. The 2007 subprime mortgage crisis and the resulting great recession dramatically increased unemployment by 2009, leaving millions of families living paycheck to paycheck and thus becoming less able to afford internet access or personal computers needed for many types of remote schoolwork.

As the H1N1 pandemic dissipated and faded from the headlines, pandemic preparedness and associated distance learning protocols became decreasing priorities. In a 2012 survey of nearly 2,000 school nurses across 26 states, fewer than half said their district updated emergency plans after the 2009 H1N1 pandemic despite major gaps in preparation. While nearly half of respondents said their schools had emergency plans that addressed pandemics, just 4% said they actually conducted drills over a two-year period. More often than not, the first casualty of these plans was a failure to include specific and actionable distance learning protocols and procedures (Rebmann et al., 2012).

The nomination of Betsy DeVos by President Donald J. Trump to be the Secretary of the U.S. Department of Education in 2017 was, in many ways, a further departure from several decades of support for pandemic planning and technology integration at a time when federal leadership was sorely needed. Although 11.6 million students in more than 19,000 schools still lacked the minimum connectivity necessary for digital learning, the U.S. Department of Education failed to incorporate digital divide inequalities into emergency planning or response or to review disaster planning efforts from past administrations. In many ways, there was little consideration for the needs of students in the most vulnerable communities in the U.S. (Treene, 2020). In large part, this was due to a belief that federal oversight of U.S. education policies was either unnecessary or counterproductive. Indeed, even as the COVID-19 pandemic began to result in mass school closures, Secretary DeVos stated that it was time for the U.S. Department of Education to be abolished. For instance, she noted, "I view this department as one that probably never should have been stood up. I think there are ample arguments for it having gotten more in the way of students and their futures than actually being any kind of value-add" (Soave, 2020).

Long gone was the belief that federal education policies could have a lasting positive impact on students' lives, particularly in terms of distance learning and the leadership required during crisis situations. As more than 1.1 million high school students chose to stop attending school altogether during the first year of the COVID-19 pandemic, often to care for dying loved ones or to enter the workforce to help financially support their families, the agency neglected to address these indirect impacts caused by an unprecedented disaster that has taken more than 1,000,000 American lives at the time of this writing. Further, cascading problems, such as food insecurity and deteriorating technology infrastructure in Title I schools, were not adequately addressed. So much so, in fact, that the U.S. Department of Education was unable to implement or even acknowledge key objectives that were once part of its core mission. Instead, regardless of the guidelines of the Centers for Disease Control and Prevention (CDC), by July 2020, Secretary DeVos placed an emphasis on reopening schools in the following fall by federal mandate, because distance learning efforts across the U.S. were, in her mind, colossal failures (Mansoor, 2020).

In fairness, it should be noted that U.S. policy has always placed education governance at the local and state rather than the federal level and that the digital divide is largely an issue impacted by municipal property tax expenditures and voting actions in local jurisdictions. That said, the COVID-19 pandemic was the first presidentially declared disaster in all 50 states to have resulted in more American deaths than World Wars I and II combined (U.S. White House, 2021). In fact, this was a disaster so large in scale that it has forever changed U.S. society in terms of how we prepare our school systems nationally. But at the same time, a pandemic of this magnitude presents opportunities to reconceive of U.S. federal response capabilities in the education sector, specifically in relation to distance learning continuity-of-operations efforts for historically underserved populations.

Future Mitigation Measures: Continuity-of-Operations Planning

Establishing and implementing a continuity-of-operations plan (COOP) is of crucial importance for large organizations, such as U.S. K-12 schools, so that they can mitigate, protect, respond to, and recover from various types of disasters, according to predefined essential functions. For K-12 schools, such efforts involve communication with students, staff, and associated communities, student transportation, prearrangement of food programs and medical services, and business functions, as well as emotional and psychological recovery. If a large-scale disaster occurs, schools should have processes and systems in place to ensure continuity of teaching and learning and supporting activities, even if this means that essential functions need to occur in other buildings or with different staff support mechanisms. To carry on educational activities following a major disaster, schools need to consider specific tasks or even programs that are essential while at the same time discontinuing those that do not add immediate value (U.S. Department of Homeland Security [DHS, 2015]). As an example, as thousands of Title I schools throughout the U.S. were required to close their doors during the COVID-19 pandemic, they were also being mandated to provide food to students in need. Addressing both conflicting demands simultaneously can be a formidable task, often requiring staff to go above and beyond their prescribed functional roles and to serve as emergent community organizers (Schlegelmilch et al., 2020).

Such a planning framework was expanded further as the COVID-19 pandemic disrupted school operations, to further include the capabilities of distance learning via new video-based telecommunication technologies such as Zoom. In turn, teachers and administrators began thinking more specifically about damage assessments needed to understand the magnitude of school absenteeism, digital divides, and the historical inequities in predisaster U.S. schooling (DeVincenzo, 2020). Few predicted that school responses would be required for years, not weeks or months. In terms of the damage assessments proposed in April of 2020, the extent of direct and indirect damages far exceeded anything imaginable at the time. UNESCO's Global Monitoring (UNESCO, 2022) of school closures estimates that schoolchildren around the globe have missed more than 2 trillion hours in the classroom (in-person learning). Additional impacts span interrupted learning, poor nutrition, a confused and stressed labor force, parents unprepared for homeschooling, challenges in creating and sustaining distance learning, gaps in childcare, economic costs, the unintended strain on health care systems and their loved ones, pressures on schools to remain open, increased dropout rates, increased exposure to violence and exploitation in and outside of the home, social isolation, and the challenges in learning measurement and validation (UNESCO, 2020).

At the district level in the U.S., the impacts are parallel to those highlighted in the global reports. That is, school districts are confronting issues including attendance problems, increased rates of childhood depression and anxiety, and the long-term socioemotional outcomes of students, especially those in low-performing and low-income schools (Gottfried et al., 2022). Districts are now investigating improvements in support for nonnative English-speaking students and families, transportation services, student health services, and virtual learning environments (Gottfried et al., 2022). Gottfried et al. (2022) also caution about the potential pitfalls that might arise from aiming for perfect attendance in planning as well as adopting strategies that rely too heavily on external organizations for support in addressing the identified challenges.

Much of the focus of education recovery efforts has been on performance-based/standardized measures of learning gaps as a result of students not being in the classroom; however, it might be beneficial for educators and administrators to also include attention to *what* is learned and *how* it is learned within this recovery period in contrast to ambiguous parameters of the amount of knowledge that is prescribed to students in a specific amount of time (Arnove, 2020). As a result of multifaceted priorities, new frameworks for long-term recovery have surfaced.

Suggested Frameworks for Long-Term Recovery

Table 4.1 lists essential pandemic planning tools needed by large organizations such as schools. As noted in this chapter, distance learning protocols should be included, particularly for disadvantaged student populations.

Although the indirect impacts from the COVID-19 pandemic have continued to cascade during the past two years, initial recovery reports published by leading organizations are beginning to define guiding principles for long-term recovery objectives. UNESCO/UNICEF/The World Bank (2022) advise that learning recovery programs should focus on actions that bring students back to school utilizing the RAPID Learning Recovery Framework. The RAPID Learning Recovery Framework shown in Figure 4.1 aims to support students' needs to stay in school (R, Reach and Retain), measure learning levels (A, Assess), prioritize fundamentals and content missed during school closures or remote learning (Prioritize), provide supplemental measures for increased learning efficiency (I, Increase), and important, offer psychosocial and well-being protection (P, Protection).

TABLE 4.1 Key Terms and Definitions

Key Term	Definition
Direct and indirect impacts	Direct impact refers to immediate changes as a result of the hazard, such as destruction of a building as a result of the force of high winds or flooding (FEMA).
	Indirect impact refers to subsequent changes given the direct impact, such as loss of housing if the building was inhabitable (FEMA).
Continuity-of-operations planning (COOP)	COOP aims to ensure critical school services, organizational functions, and programs continue to be operational or restored as quickly as possible following a disaster event lasting more than two years (National Center for Disaster Preparedness & Save the Children, 2020).
Emergency operations plan (EOP)	EOPs describe the plans a school or district has in place to provide for the continuation of essential services during prolonged impacts caused by emergencies (The Readiness and Emergency Management for Schools [REMS], 2020).

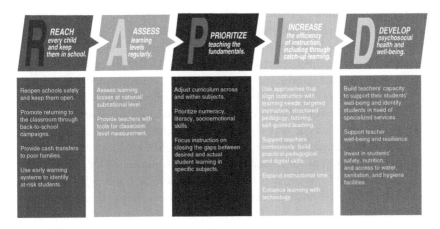

FIGURE 4.1 RAPID Learning Recovery Framework

Source: World Bank, the Bill & Melinda Gates Foundation, FCDO, UNESCO, UNICEF, and USAID. (2022). Guide for learning recovery and acceleration: Using the RAPID framework to address COVID-19 learning losses and build forward better. World Bank. www.worldbank.org/en/topic/education/publication/the-rapid-framework-and-a-guide-for-learning-recovery-and-acceleration

Another key tenet carried over from studies on long-term disaster recovery involves beginning with a coherent planning framework (Abramson et al., 2010). To understand the magnitude of the impact of the COVID-19 pandemic on U.S. schools, more attention is necessary at the federal, state, and local levels to the tried-and-true practice of continuity-of-operations planning (COOP) as a future mitigation strategy (U.S. Department of Homeland Security, FEMA, n.d.). COOP aims to ensure that critical services, organizational functions, and programs continue to be operational or are restored as quickly as possible following a disaster event lasting more than two years (National Center for Disaster Preparedness & Save the Children, 2020). At the school district level, the COOP plan is typically located in the "annex" within a school emergency operations plan (EOP), which describes the resources and capabilities a school or district has to provide for the continuation of essential services during prolonged impacts caused by emergencies (The Readiness and Emergency Management for Schools [REMS], 2020). According to the Federal Emergency Management Agency (FEMA), continuity planning is an important practice that is a fundamental responsibility of public and private entities engaging with community stakeholders. The agency expands the working definition of COOP in the context of pandemics to include considerations of the widely dispersed geographical footprint in a pandemic spread and the potential waves of pandemic surges that might last several years at a time. FEMA encourages organizations to develop and/or update the annex in existing or new continuity plans to include pandemic-related factors such as increased absenteeism, social distancing protocols, and the identification of interdependencies of an organization for their continuity of operations for several years rather than weeks or months.

Federal guidance for school emergency plans in the U.S. are often interagency byproducts between the Department of Education, U.S. Departments of Justice, DHS, and Health and Human Services (REMS, 2020). Interagency collaboration will also be necessary to ensure adequate updates are made to school district policies and plans for continuity of operations and pandemic planning. Many plans are no longer annexed but rather stand-alone documents in each district.

The National Center for Disaster Preparedness of the Columbia Climate School, Columbia University, in partnership with Save the Children, offers a free COOP tool kit designed specifically for child-serving organizations through their Resilient Children, Resilient Community (RCRC) initiative (https://rcrctoolbox.org/toolbox/coop-planning-tools/). The tool kit provides educators and administrators with template plans that can be customized to a school-specific COOP, including a presentation template for sharing long-term planning documents for school stakeholders, a facilitator's guide to provide pointers on leading COOP planning discussions, a how-to guide to assist in the formation of a steering committee, an essential functions worksheet to identify essential functions within the school ecosystem, and, finally, an essential functions table in the form of a spreadsheet to organize planning efforts (RCRC Initiative, 2020).

The Readiness and Emergency Management for School (REMS) Technical Assistance (TA) Center through the U.S. Department of Education also offers several resources for school preparedness across all hazards. Specific to pandemics, the technical assistance center provides a guidance report entitled *Continuity of Operations (COOP) Planning for Education Agencies: Ensuring Continuity of Feeding and Food Distribution During Prolonged Absences, Dismissals, and Closures*, dedicated to continuity of operations in the context of COVID-19 and the continuity of feeding and food distribution. In this example, REMS leverages a planning process that incorporates community partners as well as the various state models that involve traditional planning and the integration of private community partners, state education agencies, and local education agencies. This resource serves as a COVID-19-relevant example of the design and implementation of COOP for essential school and community function and a potential roadmap for future federal planning efforts.

Conclusion

The initial response to the COVID-19 pandemic in 2020 by the U.S. Department of Education was sometimes inadequate. Previous large-scale efforts from the Bush and Obama administrations in relation to pandemic planning were often ignored or disregarded, and schools and families were left to deal with a hodgepodge of educational efforts that often ignored the needs of society's most vulnerable. The conceptualization of the digital divide, or what some scholars (Jung et al., 2001) have referred to as digital divides (plural), originated multiple decades prior to the focal themes of this chapter as well as the implications of the COVID-19 pandemic. There are many ways to identify and describe existing and long-standing inequities that were spotlighted throughout the pandemic; the digital divide is no exception.

As a consequence of COVID-19, novel ideas to improve and support the U.S. education system continue to emerge, including text-based notifications to parents on student attendance, data systems that can identify students in need of increased support, home visits by nurses or teachers to build stronger relationships between schools and families, and mass tutoring campaigns supported by the federal government to assist students with coping and loss of learning (Gottfried et al., 2022; Iyengar, 2020). Amid both social and technological innovations, it is important to also focus on continuity-of-operations planning that encompasses pandemic considerations. Moreover, the COVID-19 pandemic has set a new precedent for education preparedness, response, and recovery in the U.S. The U.S. Department of Education would benefit from more research initiatives that integrate emerging technologies as well as new types of pandemic risks, including another variant of COVID-19, avian influenza, along with other emerging infectious diseases, into consideration for planning efforts. At the current juncture, the opportunity to ensure better outcomes begins with all involved focusing on how we prepare and how we confront the responsibility for addressing the inequities in the U.S. education system during major disruptions in in-person learning.

Recommended Resources

- National Center for Disaster Preparedness, Columbia University: *Continuity of operations plan (COOP) training presentation, guide, & plan templates.* https://rcrtoolbox.org/toolbox/coop-planning-tools
- UNESCO: *Adverse consequences of school closures.* https://en.unesco.org/covid19/educationresponse/consequences
- U.S. Department of Education: *The readiness and emergency management for schools (REMS) technical assistance center: Multiple resources.* https://rems.ed.gov/REMSPublications.aspx
- U.S. Federal Emergency Management Agency (FEMA): *What is continuity of operations planning?* www.fema.gov/pdf/about/org/ncp/coop_brochure.pdf
- U.S. Federal Emergency Management Agency (FEMA): *Continuity of operations considerations for pandemic influenza.* www.fema.gov/pdf/about/org/ncp/pan_brochure.pdf

References

Abramson, D. M., Park, Y. S., Stehling-Ariza, T., & Redlener, I. (2010). Children as bellwethers of recovery: Dysfunctional systems and the effects of parents, households, and neighborhoods on serious emotional disturbance in children after Hurricane Katrina. *Disaster Medicine and Public Health Preparedness, 4*(S1), S17–S27.

Arnove, R. F. (2020). Imagining what education can be post-COVID-19. *Prospects*, *49*(1), 43–46.

DeVincenzo, J. L. (2020, April 20). Absent: Prioritizing recovery for our nation's schools. *State of the Planet. Columbia Climate School.* https://blogs.ei.columbia.edu/2020/04/20/covid-19-recovery-schools/

Gottfried, M., Page, L., & Edwards, D. (2022). (Rep.). *District strategies to reduce student absenteeism* (pp. 1–7). EdResearch for Recovery.

Iyengar, R. (2020). Education as the path to a sustainable recovery from COVID-19. *Prospects*, *49*(1), 77–80.

Jung, J. Y., Qiu, J. L., & Kim, Y. C. (2001). Internet connectedness and inequality: Beyond the "divide." *Communication Research*, *28*(4), 507–535.

Keierleber, M. (2020). Most schools have long had pandemic plans. But a watchdog warned years ago that half of all districts had no real strategy for how to operate if classrooms remained closed. *The 74.* www.the74million.org/article/most-schools-have-long-had-pandemic-plans-but-a-watchdog-warned-years-ago-that-half-of-all-districts-had-no-real-strategy-for-how-to-operate-if-classrooms-remained-closed/

Lee, J. (2020, April 14). Mental health effects of school closures during COVID-19. *The Lancet: Child and Adolescent Health*, *4*(6), 421. https://doi.org/10.1016/S2352-4642(20)30109-7

Mansoor, S. (2020). Dismissing "flexible" CDC guidelines, Education Secretary Betsy DeVos doubles down on pushing schools to reopen. *Time.* https://time.com/5865987/betsy-devos-school-reopening-coronavirus/

National Center for Disaster Preparedness & Save the Children. (2020, March 10). Coop presentation, guides and templates. *RCRC Toolbox.* https://rcrctoolbox.org/toolbox/coop-planning-tools/

Psacharopoulos, G., Patrinos, H., Collis, V., & Vegas, E. (2020). The COVID-19 cost of school closures. *Brookings Institute.* www.brookings.edu/blog/education-plus-development/2020/04/29/the-covid-19-cost-of-school-closures/

RCRC Initiative. (2020, March 10). Coop presentation, guides and templates. *RCRC Toolbox.* https://rcrctoolbox.org/toolbox/coop-planning-tools/

Rebmann, T., Elliott, M. B, Reddick, D., & Swick, Z. D. (2012, September). U.S. school/academic institution disaster and pandemic preparedness and seasonal influenza vaccination among school nurses. *American Journal of Infectious Disease*, *40*(7), 584–589. https://doi.org/10.1016/j.ajic.2012.02.027

Schlegelmilch, J., Sury, J., Brooks, J., & Chandler, T. (2020). A philanthropic approach to supporting emergent disaster response and recovery. *Disaster Medicine and Public Health Preparedness*, *14*(1), 158–160.

Soave, R. (2020, November). This building has caused more problems than it solved. *Reason.* https://reason.com/2020/10/25/this-building-has-caused-more-problems-than-it-solved/

The Readiness and Emergency Management for Schools (REMS) Technical Assistance Center. (2020). *Publications & guidance documents. Continuity of operations (COOP) planning for education agencies: Ensuring continuity of feeding and food distribution during prolonged absences, dismissals, and closures.* https://rems.ed.gov/REMSPublications.aspx

Treene, A. (2020). Predecessors try to fill void left by DeVos. *Axios.* www.axios.com/2020/06/13/former-education-secretaries-schools-devos

U.S. Department of Homeland Security, FEMA. (2015). *National preparedness goal. https://www.fema.gov/sites/default/files/2020-06/national_preparedness_goal_2nd_edition.pdf*

Bridging the Digital Divide **53**

U.S. Department of Homeland Security, FEMA. (n.d.). What is continuity of operations—FEMA. In *Continuity of operations: An overview of continuity planning for pandemic influenza*. www.fema.gov/pdf/about/org/ncp/pan_brochure.pdf

U.S. Government Accountability Office. (2007). *Emergency management: Most school districts have developed emergency management plans, but would benefit from additional federal guidance*. GAO-07-609 https://www.gao.gov/products/gao-07-609a

U.S. Homeland Security Council. (2006). *National strategy for pandemic influenza*. www.google.com/books/edition/National_Strategy_for_Pandemic_Influenza/yF6O0xRa2oEC?hl=en&gbpv=0

U.S. White House. (2021, March 11). *Remarks by President Biden on the anniversary of the COVID-19 shutdown*. www.whitehouse.gov/briefing-room/speeches-remarks/2021/03/11/remarks-by-president-biden-on-the-anniversary-of-the-covid-19-shutdown/

UNESCO. (2020, May 13). *Adverse consequences of school closures*. https://en.unesco.org/covid19/educationresponse/consequences

UNESCO. (2022, February 28). *Education: From disruption to recovery*. https://en.unesco.org/covid19/educationresponse/

UNESCO/UNICEF/The World Bank. (2022, March 1). Where are we on education recovery? *UNICEF*. www.unicef.org/reports/where-are-we-education-recovery

World Bank, the Bill & Melinda Gates Foundation, FCDO, UNESCO, UNICEF, and USAID. (2022). *Guide for learning recovery and acceleration: Using the RAPID framework to address COVID-19 learning losses and build forward better*. World Bank.

5

TWITTER FOR PROFESSIONAL DEVELOPMENT AND LEARNING IN HIGH-NEEDS SCHOOLS

Considerations for School Leaders

Samuel F. Fancera

Guiding Questions:

- How do social media and social networking services differ? How can school leaders in high-needs schools use both types of services for professional development and learning (PDL)?
- How can school leaders in high-needs schools turn some of the common barriers to traditional PDL into opportunities to develop a Twitter-for-PDL initiative?
- Why is it important for school leaders in high-needs schools to consider using Twitter for PDL for the entire school?
- Why do school leaders in high-needs schools prefer Twitter for PDL as compared to other social media and networking services?
- How can school leaders in high-needs schools begin to use Twitter for PDL with both certified and noncertified staff?

Introduction

Social media and networking (SMN) have become ingrained in the lives of many for both personal and professional use. Nearly 3.6 billion people engaged in some SMN use in 2020, and the number of SMN users is likely to approach 4.5 billion by 2025 (Statista, 2022a). During summer 2022, the top 10 SMN services based on the number of monthly users included Facebook, Instagram, Facebook Messenger, Twitter, Pinterest, Reddit, Snapchat, WhatsApp, Messenger by Google, and Tumblr (Statista, 2022b). One of the reasons so many people use SMN is

DOI:10.4324/9781003274537-7

because the services are ubiquitous. That is, from personal computers to tablet devices and smartphones, users can access their personal SMN accounts from anywhere they are connected to the internet and at any time.

Given the number of active users, one can infer that educators already utilize several of the more popular services, so it is worthwhile to consider their value in serving as a professional development and learning (PDL) tool. Therefore, it is important for school leaders in high-needs school settings to gain a basic understanding of SMN and the potential utility of these services for use as PDL tools as a regular part of their overall leadership practice.

Differences Between Social Media and Social Networking

While the two terms are often used interchangeably, there are certain differences between social media and social networking that educators should understand before considering using these services for PDL. Briefly and in the most basic sense, *social media* permit users to share content, whereas *social networking* allows users to connect and interact with other users. This connected and interactive nature of social networking is valuable for educators who are interested in using these services for PDL. To clarify some differences between social media and social networking, consider the following school-level scenarios.

A principal might post a short article to their blog about the successful implementation of an inquiry-based instructional strategy to improve student outcomes in science. The post is on the internet for other users to consume through reading and reflection, but the post is unlikely to garner much interactive discussion. Some of the principal's regular blog readers, as well as other users who consume the post, might consider the instructional approach and decide whether it holds any value in other school settings or warrants trial implementation. Some of these readers and users might comment on the blog post, and the principal might reply to some of these comments. When using social media, the interactions typically end there.

Alternatively, rather than writing a blog post, the principal decides to ask members of their professional learning network (PLN), which the principal developed through social networking, if they observed student success when their teachers use this inquiry-based science approach by posting a question to a social networking service. In response to this question, the principal makes connections with other school leaders throughout the country, and perhaps around the world, who then engage in ongoing discussions about the value of inquiry-based science lessons. All educators involved contribute to and consume the discussions, and they make connections with others who might help them improve their practice.

56 Samuel F. Fancera

Researchers have reported on the utility of a variety of SMN services for PDL among teachers and school leaders (Carpenter et al., 2020; Carpenter & Green, 2017; Carpenter & Krutka, 2014, 2015; Nochumson, 2020); however, the focus of this chapter is specific to the role of Twitter for PDL in high-needs schools. The data presented in this chapter were collected for another project (Fancera, 2020).

Twitter for PDL

Founded on March 21, 2006, Twitter is a microblogging service that is limited to 280 characters per individual tweet to allow users to post content, connect with other users, and discuss and comment on a variety of topics. Twitter is a popular social networking service in the P-12 educational arena, with many teachers and school leaders using it to connect with others on an international scale. Building and district-level leaders find value in using Twitter to communicate with their greater school communities, and this practice was particularly evident during the COVID-19-related school closures that began in March 2020 (Michela et al., 2022). Twitter also emerged as an important tool for teachers and school leaders to share resources, as well as to support each other during the remote learning and teaching that occurred during these school closures (Carpenter et al., 2021). Although educators find value in using Twitter for a variety of reasons, school leaders agree that Twitter is in the lead of all currently available services when it comes to using SMN as a platform for delivering PDL to educators (Fancera, 2020, 2021). One of the more popular features of this service specific to educator PDL is Twitter education chats, which are scheduled discussions that take place using this social networking service (Hsieh, 2017; Kerr & Schmeichel, 2018; Sturm & Quaynor, 2020). Teachers and school leaders can find a variety of education-related Twitter chats throughout each day of the week (Chat Calendar, n.d.), which increases the importance of this service for PDL.

But despite the generally agreed-upon advantages, before fully embracing Twitter as a tool for PDL, school leaders need to consider the perceived benefits and limitations of SMN in general as well as the pros and cons associated with the different formats of traditional teacher PDL. As shown in Figure 5.1, some of the more common obstacles to traditional PDL include cost, time, and the need for teacher coverage. Findings from research involving building- and district-level school leaders who worked in high-needs schools throughout the Midwest and Northeast regions of the United States support the important role Twitter can play in PDL in high-needs schools, especially to overcome some of these obstacles (Fancera, 2020). Participants in the study represented nearly 14,000 students and more than 1,100 certified staff members in schools whose student population ranged from 25% to 65% economically disadvantaged students. The perspectives of these school leaders specific to using Twitter as a tool for PDL can help to inform the practice of school leaders in other high-needs schools.

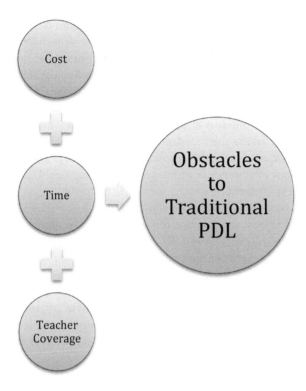

FIGURE 5.1 Obstacles to Traditional Professional Development and Learning (PDL)

Obstacles as Opportunities

The two barriers most often associated with PDL are money and time. High-quality PDL is costly to schools and districts, and the time required for teachers to attend traditional PDL settings takes them out of their classrooms. This is especially problematic for leaders of high-needs schools, which are typically under-resourced, further limiting the money and time that can be dedicated to PDL. It can cost schools several hundred dollars to send individual educators to workshops, conferences, or other training sessions held outside the school or district, while inviting thought leaders or keynote speakers to address a group of educators in-house can cost several thousand dollars for just a few hours. Most schools simply do not have the budget to adequately address PDL for all their educators.

The major benefits school leaders mention regarding the use of Twitter for PDL is that it can eliminate the cost associated with traditional PDL formats and can reduce the time required to initiate and sustain targeted or schoolwide PDL. School leaders and educators who embrace Twitter for PDL have the potential to eliminate these costs, because use of this SMN service is free. A major assumption here, of course, is that staff members have a device that can access the internet.

This may not always be the case for educators in high-needs schools. The pandemic-related school closures highlighted the lack of technology that often exists in high-needs schools. However, many schools have increased the amount of technology since early 2020. Therefore, given the technology initiatives in most schools throughout the last decade, and specifically since the COVID-19-related school closures, most educators likely have access to a school-owned device they can use to access the internet at school, home, or some other location. Additionally, as one considers the prevalence of personal ownership of smartphones, tablets, and other computing devices among educators, it is not unreasonable to assume that most educators can access Twitter at home for PDL during a time most convenient for them.

The time commitment associated with either sending teachers out of district or arranging for classroom coverage for in-house PDL is an ongoing challenge for school leaders. More traditional PDL formats require classroom teachers to be absent from teaching and learning opportunities with their students. Educators who use Twitter outside of the regular school day can eliminate absences due to PDL. Therefore, school leaders who focus on protecting instructional time find value in using Twitter for PDL. This is especially important in high-needs schools, because protecting instructional time is an important instructional leadership function that has a positive influence on student achievement (Fancera & Bliss, 2011).

School leaders can work with and encourage staff to use Twitter throughout the school day, before student arrival, after student dismissal, over lunch breaks, or during scheduled PDL days throughout the school year. Additionally, school leaders can encourage staff to participate in this type of PDL on their own time. These options provide many opportunities for school staff to engage in learning experiences that eliminate the need to hire substitute teachers or otherwise arrange for classroom coverage.

A final thought regarding the freedom of time associated with embracing Twitter for PDL relates to the anytime, anywhere nature of the service. Although this is often mentioned as one of the primary benefits of using Twitter for PDL, school leaders need to be realistic and sensitive to their expectations of staff. The always-on environment of Twitter can make it difficult for educators to maintain an acceptable work–life rhythm. Thus, school leaders must avoid pushing too hard and, in the process, causing school staff to develop negative perceptions of the value of Twitter for PDL.

Another limitation school leaders must consider prior to implementing a Twitter PDL plan is whether they have the authority and autonomy to grant credit or hours to school staff who participate in these activities. Nearly all state departments of education throughout the U.S. require teachers to engage in documented PDL experiences during some predefined period. Some states specify higher-education credit hour requirements (i.e., graduate-level coursework), while others have clock-hour requirements. However, many states limit how and where certified staff members can obtain these PDL credits and hours, often requiring them to come from state-approved agencies and providers. School leaders who have the authority and autonomy, which is often determined at the local level, to grant hours for teacher engagement in Twitter should fully embrace this opportunity to further develop their Twitter-for-PDL initiative.

Staff Inclusion

It is important for school leaders to determine which staff members to include in their Twitter-for-PDL initiative. Although PDL is most often associated with certified staff, depending on the needs of the school, the school leader might also include noncertified staff members. School leaders have several strategies for delivering PDL. Both a schoolwide and a targeted approach might fit into a school leader's PDL agenda. For example, Twitter may be used to deliver PDL to all school staff, both certified and noncertified, to address big-picture issues such as school climate; diversity, equity, and inclusion; communication approaches with the larger school community; social-emotional learning; or school safety and security. Using Twitter for these PDL topics would give all school staff opportunities to participate outside of the regular school day. For more targeted PDL, school leaders can use Twitter to focus on specific instructional and classroom-management issues for all certified staff, a new curriculum or program for a specific grade level or content area, or to examine the role of paraprofessionals and other support staff to help all students find success.

In brief, some of the key factors for school leaders to consider prior to implementing a Twitter PDL initiative include time, cost, staff for inclusion, and ability to give credit to staff who participate. School leaders who have embraced Twitter for PDL know these factors create the necessary conditions for Twitter to become an increasingly valuable part of their school's PDL agenda.

Twitter as the Preferred SMN Platform for PDL

The use of Twitter for PDL is a great way for teachers to stay relevant and current. A wealth of education-related information is available on Twitter, as are a growing number of educators worldwide exchanging ideas about teaching, learning, and school leadership. Learning about the experiences of leaders from high-needs schools who have successfully used Twitter for PDL can help others determine whether this approach is feasible in their schools. Although school leaders who embrace SMN for PDL utilize a variety of SMN services, the preferred service for PDL is Twitter for a variety of reasons.

Twitter is conversational, easy to use, and concise. Conversations on Twitter are easily archived for later consumption with the use of hashtags. The ability for staff to start slowly and accelerate their participation as their comfort level increases is a primary advantage of Twitter compared to other SMN services. The availability of various Twitter chats makes both schoolwide and targeted PDL possible for sustained growth and learning for all school staff. Whereas cost and time are both obstacles to more traditional PDL delivery modes, for leaders of high-needs schools, time is the greatest obstacle that can be overcome by using Twitter. School leaders can encourage staff to use the service whenever it best fits their individual schedules, thereby protecting instructional time without having to hire substitute teachers or arrange classroom coverage. Then, students will benefit from the instruction their regular classroom teacher provides to optimize daily learning opportunities for all.

Twitter for PDL has been beneficial for school leaders because it allows them to connect and interact with other school leaders. The service allows educators to engage in PDL in the comfort of their own homes, and some school leaders believe that Twitter empowers and enables teachers to participate and engage in more PDL because they can participate at their convenience (Fancera, 2020). Thus, perhaps one of the biggest benefits school leaders have observed with the use of Twitter for PDL is that it has opened conversations among staff within and among schools. Leaders in high-needs schools have reported that their Twitter PDL initiatives have influenced more teacher interaction within their schools, and they have observed increases in conversations across content areas and grade levels. These types of collaborative discussions help to improve teaching and learning throughout a school.

Successes

School leaders have shared many successes regarding the use of Twitter as a PDL tool. Many agree that Twitter enables connected educators to engage with others to share content knowledge and instructional strategies from the comfort of their home or school. Current high-needs school leaders who actively use Twitter for PDL offered the following comments, which are valuable for other school leaders to consider when evaluating the potential of Twitter as part of a school's PDL agenda:

> Twitter is flattening the walls of our building. Great people, great educators that we can learn from without having to pay lots of money to go to conferences.
>
> —*Middle school principal of a high-needs school*
> *in the Midwest region of the U.S.*

> I have some of the smartest people in my pocket.
>
> —*Elementary school principal of a high-needs school*
> *in the Northeast region of the U.S.*

Twitter has changed me as an educator. It has taken me off the island and connected me with people around the world that I would never have known if I didn't have Twitter. It's also given me more confidence, because participating in a Twitter chat, you put yourself out there.

—Elementary school principal of a high-needs school
in the Midwest region of the U.S.

While most staff use Twitter more sporadically or for knowledge consumption purposes only, some high-needs school leaders suggest the "rock star" staff members in their schools are the ones who consistently use Twitter for both knowledge consumption and creation. The rock stars are confident that what they do in their classrooms works for their students and share their strategies, engage in conversations about teaching and learning, and offer help to educators who are looking for strategies, in other parts of the U.S. as well as globally. Consistent use of Twitter is essential because this type of learning happens more readily when teachers make connections with other educators and participate in both knowledge consumption and creation.

School leaders agree that Twitter chats offer a valuable forum for targeted learning, and some have established either schoolwide or districtwide Twitter chats that occur at regularly scheduled intervals. Educators typically create school and district Twitter hashtags, which allows staff to search for and archive individual tweets. Many school leaders provide staff with certificates of completion for participating in Twitter chats, which staff then use for documentation of professional responsibilities for evaluative purposes or for documenting attainment of PDL credits or hours. This is one of the most inconsistent areas among school leaders who use Twitter for PDL, however, because some have the authority and autonomy to document teacher participation in Twitter for PDL requirements, while others are unable to do so because of local or state policies. The value of Twitter for PDL is likely to continue to grow, so discussions at state and local levels about how to appropriately reward educators for using Twitter for PDL are urgently needed. Indeed, the skills and knowledge that educators can attain by participating in Twitter chats that require both knowledge consumption and creation often surpass those attained during more traditional PDL formats, including workshops, meetings, and conferences.

Pitfalls

Leaders in high-needs schools readily share their successes with using Twitter for PDL, but most have experienced pitfalls in this pursuit, too (Fancera, 2020). One of the biggest pitfalls is the absence of social interactions. Educators, by nature, embrace social learning, so most want the same types of experiences for their own PDL. Although Twitter is social learning, it is not the same face-to-face social learning that many educators are most comfortable with. School leaders have indicated that many of their staff members have particularly mentioned this since schools reopened after the extended pandemic-related closures. Not surprisingly, many educators got tired of remote teaching and learning when it was forced upon them for extended periods of time during the COVID-19 pandemic. As a result, many continue to actively pursue more traditional and face-to-face PDL opportunities. Nevertheless, it is important to note that just as many educators have embraced the convenience offered by remote opportunities, so more research is needed to determine the preferred delivery format for PDL in the postpandemic era.

Another pitfall mentioned by school leaders is the inconsistent nature of knowledge consumption and creation when using Twitter for PDL. One can argue that traditional forms of PDL also offer inconsistent learning, however. School leaders perceive this as a greater issue when they make a push for Twitter PDL. Many educators still want PDL delivered in traditional formats, so they do not take the initiative to consistently engage with Twitter for themselves. However, things are beginning to change in this area.

One additional pitfall often mentioned by leaders in high-needs schools is using Twitter more as a tool to share happenings in the classroom or the school than for PDL. Twitter is a valuable SMN service that educators can use for school promotion and branding purposes. When staff begin to use Twitter and other SMN services more to share what is going on in their classrooms and schools than for PDL, they need to be reminded of how to use these services for meaningful PDL. This is not to suggest that school leaders should discourage educators from using Twitter for classroom and school promotion and branding but to point out that it is simply a different way of using this SMN in schools.

Future Value of Twitter PDL

Educator PDL is likely to remain a mix of formats, including workshops, conferences, meetings, expert presentations, professional learning communities, and SMN. Thus, SMN for PDL is unlikely to replace the traditional face-to-face formats. At least in the foreseeable future, school leaders are more likely to utilize SMN as an addition to the PDL menu from which staff can choose. Because much of an educator's annual PDL includes topics that are stipulated by states and local education agencies, SMN is unlikely to entirely replace any of the other traditional formats. Nevertheless, most high-needs school leaders agree that it is essential to keep SMN as a PDL tool, so it is important to make it enjoyable and ensure school staff do not perceive it as yet another thing for them to do.

Specific to the future value of Twitter for PDL, school leaders can encourage staff to participate in Twitter chats, but they should avoid making such participation obligatory. The use of Twitter chats is a great way to bring people together who gravitate toward this format. Staff attendance at conferences has tremendous value, as does bringing in experts and keynote presenters. One of the biggest challenges going forward will be to determine how to hold staff accountable for Twitter PDL. Often, the required PDL is more about seat time than actual learning, which highlights a critical issue that policy makers need to consider. The opportunity for school leaders to grant credits or hours would encourage staff to take the next step in using Twitter for PDL, but many school leaders believe this might not be a sufficient incentive to increase future use.

To increase future use of Twitter for PDL, school leaders need to encourage educators to engage with this platform on their own and take advantage of the anytime, anywhere learning that it offers. School leaders who model appropriate use of Twitter for PDL, provide training for staff, and host Twitter chats on important topics for their schools are likely to see greater use of this approach to PDL among staff members. As one school leader succinctly summarized,

> Social media is here, so use it. It's a firehose of information coming out, and you can take it in bucketfuls or spoonfuls. School leaders should decide how much flows into the overall school PDL agenda when using SMN as a PDL tool.
>
> *—Elementary school principal of a high-needs school*
> *in the Midwest region of the U.S.*

Recommendations to Begin Using Twitter for PDL

Twitter is a popular SMN service among P-12 educators, but important factors need to be considered prior to implementing Twitter for PDL. Learning about the experiences from leaders in high-needs schools who use Twitter for PDL will help others make informed decisions regarding the utility of this approach in their settings. The following recommendations can serve to guide leaders in high-needs schools who want to begin using this approach as a component of their school's overall PDL agenda. School leaders can use these recommendations in practice to develop a Twitter-for-PDL initiative in their schools (see Figure 5.2).

Model Use

Staff will benefit from the school leader's actions on Twitter. As with most initiatives in education, modeling helps individuals increase their self-efficacy beliefs. School leaders who use Twitter for their own PDL and continued professional growth set a course for others to follow. It is critical for school leaders who are considering using Twitter for staff PDL to first use it as a tool for their own PDL and then share their experiences with staff.

School leaders can model Twitter use by sharing content they find on the service with staff on a regular basis and then encourage staff to start slowly. This includes modeling how to compose a tweet, reply to tweets, retweet, and quote tweets; and

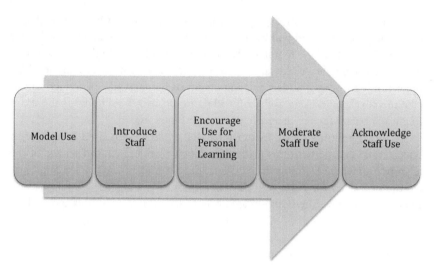

FIGURE 5.2 Strategy for Leaders in High-Needs Schools to Develop a Twitter-for-PDL Initiative

explain what a hashtag is and how staff can use hashtags to search for content or archive conversations. It is important for school leaders to participate in chats for staff to follow and then moderate chats to get staff involved and to see the value in using Twitter for PDL. Finally, school leaders need to continually encourage staff to increase their use for both knowledge consumption and creation.

Introduce Staff

Many educators are likely familiar with the different SMN services, but their experience using these services specifically for PDL will vary. This is where the school leader's experience using Twitter for their own PDL will allow them to convey concrete examples. The school leader can encourage staff to become involved in using Twitter for professional use, because most staff will likely have some experience using different SMN services for personal use. For example, many staff members may be comfortable lurking as opposed to participating in Twitter chats or conversations. So it becomes important to encourage active engagement and to explain the importance of being a connected educator. School leaders should encourage staff to follow other educators who actively use Twitter so they can begin building a personal learning network (PLN).

Encourage Use for Personal Learning

School leaders can encourage staff to engage in Twitter to make connections and interact with other educators. As school staff continue to build their PLNs, the perceived value of Twitter for PDL will increase. These early connections often allow users to determine how valuable Twitter can be when consuming and creating content to share with others. As staff members increase their comfort level by connecting with others, consuming content, and sharing resources, they will come to recognize how Twitter is a valuable tool in bringing educators together for the common purpose of improving learning for all students. When permitted, staff should be comfortable sharing pictures of students engaged in various classroom activities or other events and happenings around the school. (Be sure to comply with local school district policies prior to sharing pictures and other revealing information about students.) Staff may also be comfortable communicating lesson ideas. Although using Twitter for sharing this type of content is important for educators to tell their own stories, as well as for branding their classrooms and schools, it is critical for school leaders to encourage staff to move beyond this use of Twitter. Knowledge consumption and creation happen when users connect with others, share ideas to improve student learning, and collaborate to create meaningful learning experiences for students. This is where Twitter for PDL offers the greatest value for educators in high-needs schools.

Moderate Use

This is an important step in the process of using Twitter for PDL on a regular basis. The school leader must continually moderate staff use, not to check up on staff but to ensure that staff continue to engage in using Twitter for PDL and to further develop their PLNs. Some suggestions for moderating use include sharing specific information obtained on the service with staff, encouraging staff to participate in discussions and chats, and hosting discussions or chats on issues that are relevant and timely to improve the school. School leaders can host and moderate chats for grade-level educators, content-area experts, or all staff within the school. This is a great strategy for encouraging staff to become more involved with Twitter for PDL.

Acknowledge Use

As with all initiatives in a school, it is important for the school leader to acknowledge staff for their efforts in using Twitter for PDL. If given the authority and autonomy, granting PDL credits or hours to staff is likely to encourage continued use. Finding other ways to promote staff use is also important. Informal conversations, recognition for participation in a Twitter chat, and acknowledging the importance of sharing relevant content with colleagues can influence a staff's continued use of Twitter for PDL in positive ways. Additionally, celebrating staff members' professionalism for engaging in PDL on their own time will motivate staff to continue. All of these strategies are meaningful to leaders in high-needs schools who wish to create a culture of continued engagement in Twitter for PDL.

Key Takeaways:

1. Social media permits users to share and consume content, whereas social networking allows users to connect and interact with other users and to create content. Leaders in high-needs schools can use social media services to share school happenings with community members via blog posts and social networking services to connect and interact with other principals of high-needs schools to discuss timely issues and topics.

2. Some of the more common obstacles to traditional PDL delivery formats include time, money, and the need for teacher coverage while away from the classroom. When school leaders in high-needs schools implement a Twitter-for-PDL initiative, these obstacles can become opportunities. Twitter is free to use, educators can use it to improve their craft at their convenience, and the need for substitute teachers and classroom coverage is reduced.

3. An important reason for leaders in high-needs schools to consider using Twitter for PDL is that it enables them to protect instructional time. This instructional leadership task is paramount for the technical core of schools—teaching and learning—to function at high levels.

4. Some reasons leaders in high-needs schools prefer Twitter for PDL to other social media and networking services include its conversational nature, ease of use, brevity of individual tweets, archival feature via hashtags, and the widespread availability of Twitter education chats.

5. School leaders in high-needs schools can begin to use Twitter for PDL with both certified and noncertified staff in the following manner: model use, introduce staff to Twitter terms, encourage Twitter use for personal learning, and moderate and acknowledge staff use of Twitter for PDL.

Recommended Resources

- A Beginner's Guide to Twitter for Educators:
  www.youtube.com/watch?v=4A0Tu6tVqYs
  by Matt Miller
  This video can serve as a guide to help all educators get started on Twitter. Matt Miller reviews the basics of using Twitter, such as: the Twitter screen; components of a tweet; hashtags; and how to interact with tweets, retweet, and favorite tweets.
- How to Participate in a Twitter Chat:
  https://youtu.be/EJ0YW-JCwcQ
  by Alice Keeler

This is a resource for educators who have an interest in participating in Twitter chats to connect and interact with others on specific education-related topics. Alice Keeler discusses Twitter chat schedules, the role of hosts and moderators in Twitter chats, and the importance of using hashtags to search for and curate Twitter chats.

- TeachThought University:
  www.teachthought.com/technology/twitter-for-teachers/
  This is a beginner's guide to Twitter for teachers and other educators who have an interest in using this social networking platform from a professional orientation.
- Twitter Education Chats:
  https://sites.google.com/site/twittereducationchats/education-chat-calendar
  Teachers, school leaders, and other educators can use this resource to locate the days and times of various education-related Twitter chats for professional development and learning. This database contains the official education-related Twitter chat list, as well as a Twitter chat calendar.

References

Carpenter, J. P., & Green, T. D. (2017). Mobile instant messaging for professional learning: Educators' perspectives on and uses of Voxer. *Teaching and Teacher Education, 68*, 53–67. https://doi.org/10.1016/j.tate.2017.08.008

Carpenter, J. P., & Krutka, D. G. (2014). How and why educators use Twitter: A survey of the field. *Journal of Research on Technology in Education, 46*(4), 414–434. https://doi.org/10.1080/15391523.2014.925701

Carpenter, J. P., & Krutka, D. G. (2015). Engagement through microblogging: Educator professional development via Twitter. *Professional Development in Education, 41*(4), 707–728. https://doi.org/10.1080/19415257.2014.939294

Carpenter, J. P., Morrison, S. A., Craft, M., & Lee, M. (2020). How and why are educators using Instagram? *Teaching and Teacher Education, 96*, 103–149. https://doi.org/10.1016/j.tate.2020.103149

Carpenter, J. P., Trust, T., Kimmons, R., & Krutka, D. G. (2021). Sharing and self-promoting: An analysis of educator tweeting at the onset of the COVID-19 pandemic. *Computers and Education Open, 2*, 1–11. https://doi.org/10.1016/j.caeo.2021.100038

Chat Calendar. (n.d.). *Twitter education chats.* https://sites.google.com/site/twittereducation chats/education-chat-calendar

Fancera, S. F. (2020). School leadership for professional development: The role of social media and networks. *Professional Development in Education, 46*(4), 664–676. https://doi.org/10.1080/19415257.2019.1629615

Fancera, S. F. (2021). A scale to measure school leaders' use of Twitter for professional development and learning. *NASSP Bulletin, 105*(2), 111–129. https://doi.org/10.1177/01926365211008990

Fancera, S. F., & Bliss, J. R. (2011). Instructional leadership influence on collective teacher efficacy to improve school achievement. *Leadership and Policy in Schools, 10*(3), 349–370. https://doi.org/10.1080/15700763.2011.585537

68 Samuel F. Fancera

Hsieh, B. (2017). Making and missing connections: Exploring Twitter chats as a learning tool in a preservice teacher education course. *Contemporary Issues in Technology and Teacher Education, 17*(4), 549–568. www.learntechlib.org/primary/p/174129/

Kerr, S. L., & Schmeichel, M. J. (2018) Teacher Twitter chats: Gender differences in participants' contributions. *Journal of Research on Technology in Education, 50*(3), 241–252. https://doi.org/10.1080/15391523.2018.1458260

Michela, E., Rosenberg, J. M., Kimmons, R., Sultana, O., Burchfield, M. A., & Thomas, T. (2022). "We are trying to communicate the best we can": Understanding districts' communication on Twitter curing the COVID-19 pandemic. *AERA Open, 8*(1), 1–18. https://journals.sagepub.com/home/ero

Nochumson, T. C. (2020). Elementary schoolteachers' use of Twitter: Exploring the implications of learning through online social media. *Professional Development in Education, 46*(2), 306–323. https://doi.org/10.1080/19415257.2019.1585382

Statista. (2022a). *Number of social media users worldwide from 2017 to 2025 (in billions).* www.statista.com/statistics/278414/number-of-worldwide-social-network-users/

Statista. (2022b). *Most popular mobile social networking apps in the United States as of September 2019, by monthly users (in millions).* www.statista.com/statistics/248074/most-popular-us-social-networking-apps-ranked-by-audience/

Sturm, E., & Quaynor, L. A. (2020). Window, mirror, and wall: How educators use Twitter for professional learning. *Research in Social Sciences and Technology, 5*(1), 22–44. https://doi.org/10.46303/ressat.05.01.2

6

FEEDBACK, EVALUATION, AND GRADING

The Unique Considerations Distance Learning Poses to the Evaluation Cycle and the Task of Ensuring Equitable Practices

Kimberly Moreno

Guiding Questions:

- How do traditional grading practices create inequity among students in high-needs school districts?
- How can school districts develop equitable grading policies to combat disproportionality?
- How can teachers establish and implement equitable grading practices in their classrooms?

Introduction

Assessment has been the focus of educational reform in recent years. Nevertheless, the grading system remains the same, with punitive tactics and no resounding consensus on what constitutes "best" practice. Due to this lack of consensus, grading practices vary widely among teachers in American schools, especially at the middle and high school levels (Stiggins, 2002). School districts create policies, and teachers develop their grading systems for what students should know. Since teachers do not all share the same beliefs about grading, grading often ends up being subjective and biased, primarily if learning criteria are not clearly written and shared with students (Feldman, 2019). Further compounding the discrepancies in assessment and grading has been the rapid transition to the various digital learning models, both synchronous and asynchronous, adopted by school districts. During the early weeks and months of the COVID-19 pandemic, school districts went into survival mode, preparing for this rapid shift from in-person learning

DOI:10.4324/9781003274537-8

due to school closing. Some districts provided internet services to students in the form of wireless hotspots; others purchased Chromebooks to ensure all students had access to synchronous instruction. Due to this sudden and rapid shift, more emphasis was placed on ensuring students had access to their education than on assessment and grading. While this is understandable, it leaves the question of what other barriers there are for students during their academic careers.

One thing became crystal clear from the rapid shift to digital learning models, regardless of whether instruction was synchronous or asynchronous: access to technology can help increase equity in schools. When students have continuous access to technology, it means that they can also access instructional materials outside of school. In the case of students within high-need areas, simply having to connect to the internet as the educational platform shifted became a barrier, identifying an equity gap that schools were tasked to fill.

However, providing access to technology and the internet does not fully combat systemic disparities. School districts must ensure that students have opportunities to use technology in powerful, meaningful ways. According to U.S. Census Bureau data (U.S. Census Bureau, n.d.), disparities in internet access are correlated with socioeconomic status, among other factors. For example, from 2016, nearly 82% of U.S. households had some kind of internet subscription. Of that, 59% of households with an annual income of less than $25,000 have an internet subscription, compared to 89% of households making between $50,000 and $99,000 per year. Therefore, during the shift to online educational delivery due to the pandemic, school districts not only had to provide devices to students but also subscriptions to the internet, particularly for students in high-needs areas. That is, providing true equitable access to learning means more than distributing devices and providing internet access; it means taking a close look at all areas where disparities can occur, especially in assessment and grading practices.

With regard to assessment and grading, student performance is often communicated inaccurately when grades are connected to nonacademic factors such as behavior, bonus points, or giving zeros on a 100-point scale. The imprecise nature of these examples often ends up sending confusing feedback to students and parents around intended learning outcomes. The effect of these grading inconsistencies is further compounded by the current high-stakes testing processes that focus on measuring only student academic mastery (Brookhart et al., 2016).

Grades awarded under these conditions may not accurately reflect students' knowledge and skills. This can particularly affect students with special needs, English language learners, students from low socioeconomic backgrounds, and Black people, Indigenous people, and people of color (BIPOC). If the inequities in grading are not addressed, these inequities can perpetuate inequity with regard to future opportunities.

The first step in combating inequities in grading involves identifying and defining equitable grading practices. Equitable grading practices reflect students' mastery of knowledge and skills in measurable and observable ways (Feldman,

Feedback, Evaluation, and Grading **71**

2019). Whether in a digital, hybrid, or in-person learning environment, teachers must accurately assess what students can do, which can be challenging. Traditional grading practices whereby teachers award or subtract points for behaviors are subject to misinterpretation and implicit bias.

Grading should reflect the learning outcome. In our current educational system, students' educational background can significantly impact the overall grade they receive. Providing authentic, effective, and timely feedback modifies teaching and learning (Black & William, 1998). Moving away from points-based grading to a more qualitative assessment that is feedback oriented, such as rubrics, allows teachers to judge a student's demonstrated competency in a particular skill. This type of grading is necessary to combat existing inequities (Feldman, 2018). The current points-based system disproportionately puts lower-income students and students of color at a disadvantage due to funding inequality across school districts (Feldman, 2019).

As grading shifts to reflect learning outcomes, students have the opportunity to understand their learning and make adjustments in short, incremental stages (Brookhart, 2015; Wiliam, 2010). Specifically, the formative assessment process includes clearly articulating learning objectives, recording and gathering data, providing immediate and relevant feedback, and making adjustments to improve learning at any and all times (Wiliam, 2013; Hattie & Timperley, 2007). Incorporating this process while focusing on equitable grading practices is seen by some to improve student achievement more than any other instructional strategy (Wiliam, 2013). When the formative assessment process is combined with summative assessments, more significant gains are recorded than when only using summative assessments (Wiliam, 2010). A fundamental part of the formative assessment process, as explained by Black and Wiliam (1998), involves providing ongoing, specific feedback that students can use to adjust their learning. The feedback provided is to be nonjudgmental snapshots of students' progress to aid them in making modifications to their practices (Wiliam, 2013). Therefore, the link between feedback and assessment is strong. Assessment drives feedback. This is evidenced when a teacher formatively checks for understanding and comments on what was observed. Moreover, assessments that are used formatively can shape future instruction as teachers use these data to drive instructional decisions and planning. Ultimately, feedback drives learning as students utilize the feedback to improve performance. Thus, grades are derived from student performance on assessments used summatively.

Any assessment can be used formatively or summatively, meaning each tool created for the purpose of assessment has the potential to provide data on student performance (Black et al., 2003). For example, a digital exit ticket can consist of a series of open-ended questions, with students having to respond to one or more of them. Teachers can use student data in two ways. First, they can gather formative data by reviewing students' responses for misconceptions or comprehension. Second, they can gather summative data by reviewing students' work and analyzing whether they answered the questions completely and correctly. When creating assessments, what matters most is how the data collected are used. Unfortunately, quite often, assessments and grades are used as isolated measures of a given student's achievement at a single point in time rather than as an indication of the student's overall performance trajectory. Feedback is the connection in the assessment system. It drives learning in the moment, and when the learning is measured cumulatively, grades ultimately give additional feedback to students as a measure of their mastery.

This chapter will detail strategies for equitable grading practices that can be used in digital, in-person, or hybrid educational settings. Using these practices and guiding questions when creating grading policies will allow classrooms, regardless of landscape, to disrupt the cycle of disproportionality whereby students' success is predicted based on race, resources, and native language instead of their knowledge and skills. To tackle disproportionality and promote equity, schools should implement more diverse perspectives, encourage no-grade feedback to shift the focus to motivating the student rather than the final product, and expand the repertoire of assessments to address the different ways in which students learn.

Fundamental Challenges of Traditional Grading Practices and the Impact During the COVID-19 Pandemic Digital Shift

Traditional grading practices aim to sort and separate students, which directly violates equity and access. Grading practices typically fall into three main categories: meaning, accuracy, and alignment (Brookhart, 2015; O'Connor, 2007). Grading practices that award points for feedback or formative assessments prove problematic, as the student is still engaged in the learning. Frequently, within this traditional grading system, grades have an expiration date; that is, students only have one opportunity to demonstrate mastery because of the pacing of the curriculum. These examples challenge equity among students because learning can be an uneven, indirect process for individual students (Sadler, 1989).

Accuracy is another issue with regard to the traditional grading system (Brookhart, 2015; Iamarino, 2014; O'Connor, 2007). In the A–F grading system, each letter grade is correlated to a range of 9% to 10%, except for F, which has a 59-point range. When teachers utilize a 100-point scale and average all scores, a score below 59 creates a statistical drag on all of the student's assessments, which leads to inaccurate reporting of the student's actual performance. Zeros, which are commonly used in the traditional grading system, are problematic when misused because they create a statistical drag on averaged points for a final grade, skewing the accuracy of student performance (O'Connor, 2007).

Finally, alignment is the third category that creates challenges for equitable grading. When a single letter grade is assigned to an assessment that spans multiple learning outcomes or standards, it masks the student's performance on the specific learning indicators, creating discrepancies in student performance (Iamarino, 2014). Before equitable grading practices and the standards-based grading movement, feedback might not have been clearly connected to learning outcomes (Iamarino, 2014; O'Connor, 2007).

As the learning landscape shifts to digital and hybrid educational environments, challenges to the traditional grading system and the new learning curve intensify. Lack of resources is a critical obstacle (Bingimlar, 2009). As mentioned earlier in this chapter, at the beginning of the COVID-19 pandemic, school districts worked tirelessly to ensure students had access to their instructional materials through the purchase and distribution of Chromebooks, wireless hotspots, and web cameras, as well as instructional materials such as pencils, paper, calculators, and headphones. Unfortunately, during the rapid shift to online instruction, the inequality in available resources between schools of low versus high socioeconomic status became glaringly apparent.

Although research indicates a higher prevalence of technology use by teachers in high-needs schools, according to the U.S. Department of Education's Committee for Economic Development (U.S. Department of Education, 2013), there is a gap in the computer-to-student ratio between schools with high minority populations and schools with low minority populations. Schools with students of low socioeconomic status tend to have the fewest computers available for student use. Thus, technology integration is currently implemented inconsistently in educational environments even though it has been proven to be an effective instructional strategy for improving student engagement and learning (Walsh, 2018).

Inoperable or limited-functioning computer availability and inconsistent or unavailable internet access are economic issues the schools will have to resolve before all teachers can make strides in technology integration. In this regard, funding is a national concern (Walsh, 2018) that needs to be addressed by an inflow of financial resources. As such, high-needs schools will need to focus on grant writing or fundraising to obtain enough funding to purchase the necessary hardware when internal budget constraints offer limited or no provisions, regardless of the learning landscape.

Best Practices for Building Equitable Grading and Assessment

To develop equitable grading practices, authentic assessments must reflect students' mastery of knowledge and skills based on measurable and observable course objectives. As the learning landscape changes from in-person to digital to hybrid instruction, schools must adapt their assessments and consider unique contexts that might affect student performance. The following sections present three steps to help teachers start building equitable grading and assessments.

Set Clear Objectives

Teachers cannot design sound and fair assessments without knowing their students and what they are learning. Further, students must clearly understand how they are to demonstrate their mastery of knowledge and skills. While this might seem obvious, when the learning landscape changes suddenly, the need for assessment tools, tips, and tricks begins to overshadow the reasons behind the assessment. Therefore, assessment tools must never be selected before identifying criteria for success with students and correlating the criteria for success to a purpose that impacts their learning.

Knowing the expected learning outcomes is just as important as knowing the students who will be engaging in the assessment. The standards drive instruction and provide a framework for assessment practices. Therefore, assessments should directly align with learning expectations and criteria for success. Moreover, communicating the standards to students early in the learning helps clarify progress and move students forward toward the criteria for success (Iamarino, 2014).

The criteria for success form the basis of student assessment. Through learning the intentions and success criteria, teachers can provide clarity of the standards. Instructional experiences further assist students' progress and aid them in reaching the criteria for success.

Keeping this in mind, teaching and assessing based on the standards should occur regardless of the learning landscape. To create equitable assessments, students must be able to answer the following questions regardless of where they are in their learning (Feldman, 2019):

1. What am I learning?
2. Why am I learning it?
3. How will I know when I have learned it?

When these questions guide practice and assessments, students will clearly understand what is expected of them and how they can succeed.

Develop Observable Criteria

Students need clear measures to achieve their goals or expectations successfully. Learning intentions are to be created and written based on the standards being assessed. Alignment with the standards invites students into learning and allows them to establish goals for their learning. When purposeful observable criteria are developed, the goal is to remove bias from the learning criteria and ensure objectively that the students are moving toward mastery of the standards.

There are several valuable aspects to creating learning intentions. Most important, the learning intention guides the selection of assessment tools used to determine students' understanding and mastery. Without purposeful learning intentions, assessments can become merely a list of tasks to be completed, establishing a separation between learning intention and assessments and creating confusion among the students regarding what they are supposed to learn. When developing learning intentions, it is important to keep in mind the three questions mentioned that students should be able to answer. Learning intentions should be written using language that the students understand, written in the first person, including key concepts and what the students are learning. In short, the learning intention should be concise and clearly communicated so that students understand the expectations.

Provide Opportunities for Success

Teachers should set realistic expectations, including any necessary modifications, for all students, allowing grading practices to be equitable and inclusive. A common misconception of equitable grading practices is that they will lead to lower expectations for students. However, according to Berns (2016), studies show that teachers' expectations are correlated to student motivation and academic achievement. Teachers who understand that building and prioritizing relationships, respecting cultural values, and tailoring their instructional practices to meet the diverse needs of their students provide multiple opportunities for student success (Berns, 2016; Nieto, 2013). This may mean implementing flexible deadlines for assignments or providing opportunities for students to demonstrate their knowledge and skills through varying formats and modalities over time (Perlman, 2005).

Four Steps to Equitable Grading

There are several ways to increase equity and move toward equitable grading practices. This section identifies four ways to promote equitable grading practices and level the playing field for all students. These steps can be implemented regardless of the educational landscape; that is, in-person, digital, and hybrid settings can all incorporate the steps to tackle the inequity of current grading practices.

Eliminate the Use of Zeros in Grading

As mentioned earlier in this chapter, the use of zeros creates a negative statistical drag. Sometimes, zeros or multiple zeros do not accurately reflect students' performance and end up being incurably damaging for students. Eliminating the use of zeros allows for flexibility when the goal of assessments is learning. Being mindful of students' situations or home support is necessary to ensure equitable grading practices.

Eliminate Prerequisites for Honors and Advanced Placement (AP) Classes

Entry barriers or prerequisites hinder many students of color from taking higher-level and more challenging courses. A large body of research supports the importance of student participation in honors and advanced placement classes, pointing to a positive correlation between students' participation in these advanced-level courses and their later success in postsecondary studies (Chatterji & Quirk, 2021). Therefore, districts should create support for students to consider enrolling in advanced courses. Support for these courses might include educating families about the courses, speaking to students individually, and encouraging student participation.

Move Toward Standards-Based Grading

Moving towards standards-based grading practices promotes more accurate grading of student performance and removes the subjectivity and bias that traditional grading practices can create. Proper standards-based grading is based on an understanding that students will be at different levels of learning at different times (Wormeli, 2006). Providing a variety of assessments to measure the mastery of the standards is key to delivering an individualized educational experience. Using multiple-choice quizzes or tests to measure each standard distorts the individualism needed to ensure equitable grading practices.

Review the Curriculum

School curricula should be reviewed to ensure that all students see themselves reflected in their everyday learning experiences. When schools take an inclusive and responsive approach to equity, students are more likely to see their identity represented in instructional materials, books, and visuals. Curricula should be updated to mirror current student populations to ensure students have access to authentic learning experiences, concurrently increasing content retention and engagement (Berns, 2016; Nieto, 2013).

Recommendations

The Benefits of Equitable Grading

Much evidence shows that more equitable grading practices allow grades to be more accurate and reduce achievement disparities (Feldman, 2019). When teachers utilize equitable grading practices and school districts implement equitable grading policies, failing grades significantly decrease, with the most dramatic decrease occurring for low-income students and students of color. At the same time, equitable grading decreases grade inflation. That is, more equitable grading—a reduction in the number of D and F grades for underserved student groups and a reduction in the number of A grades for White and higher-income students—reduces achievement gaps (Feldman, 2018). Focusing on equitable grading practices provides a sharper lens whereby teachers can objectively grade student performance and mastery.

TABLE 6.1 Formative Assessment Classroom Strategies

Strategy	Description
Verbal Response	Teachers use verbal response techniques that allow for simultaneous responses from each group member rather than receiving isolated answers. The ultimate goal of these verbal responses is to solicit answers from all students to check for understanding and gauge the level of understanding among the group. In other words, this is an assessment *for* learning (Black & William, 1998). The benefits of these types of assessments are twofold. First, they provide a quick read on student understanding, and second, they prompt students to evaluate their own knowledge in the moment. This information, in turn, can create opportunities for self-reflection and dialogue in seeking the correct response, thus shifting student learning from being passive to being active. Examples of verbal response techniques in the face-to-face classroom include response cards, individual whiteboards, and hand signals. These response techniques can easily be adapted as the learning landscape shifts from in-person to digital synchronous or hybrid learning. Consider the following examples as assessments *for* learning to assess students at the moment and make instructional adjustments as needed.
Wait Time	Wait time or think time is a strategy that provides students a set amount of time before they are asked to respond to a question or carry out a task. Students benefit from processing time to formulate their responses. Somewhere between 3 and 10 seconds is recommended, with longer wait times more beneficial for English language learners. Utilizing wait time strategically and purposefully allows students to think (Gambrell, 1983). The need for wait time in the virtual setting has increased due to transmission delays. Other delays also occur. For example, if students are asked to type their response in the chat, time needs to be allotted for them to do so. If students are asked to respond verbally, they may need to unmute their microphones before speaking. That is, the need for students to process their response cognitively, the audio delay, and the actions needed for them to respond to the silence that precedes the question indicate increased wait time.
Hand Signals	Even the youngest learners can use hand signals to respond to questions. The most basic hand signals are thumbs up/thumbs down and can be used to conduct a quick check among students. With older students, hand signals such as "fist to five" can be used to answer more complex questions. This technique uses different numbers of fingers to indicate levels of agreement or disagreement with a particular statement.

(*Continued*)

TABLE 6.1 (Continued)

Strategy	Description
Response Cards	Response cards are another easily adaptable technique in the virtual setting. They can be used in various formats, including signs or individual whiteboards where students hold their responses up simultaneously. Studies have shown that using preprinted or written response cards is associated with higher achievement on tests and quizzes, increased participation, and lower disruptive behavior levels than individualized call and response (Randolph, 2007). Response cards are best suited for in-person, digital (synchronous), and hybrid educational settings. Response cards are particularly effective in monitoring what is written. Each student has a whiteboard and marker at their disposal. This can be adapted for learning at home by using clear sheet protectors or plastic plates. Students can write their responses to the questions throughout the lesson and then hold up their boards, thus providing a quick and timely opportunity to gauge student understanding and address any misconceptions immediately.
Polling	When using the response strategy of polling students, teachers have their students vote on the book that will be read aloud to the class or to select students to fill classroom responsibility roles, for example. However, polling students tends to be cumbersome and is rarely utilized. With increased technology integration, polling student responses has become easier to incorporate during instruction. Integrating open-source programs such as Kahoot or Poll Everywhere allows teachers to easily use polling as an option for assessment. These open-source programs offer flexibility for student completion and allow for adaptation to in-person, digital (synchronous or asynchronous), and hybrid educational settings seamlessly. When utilizing polling, teachers construct questions in advance in the form of multiple-choice responses. Some platforms allow for open-response questions. Teachers can integrate the poll to check for understanding during the lesson and make instructional decisions to move forward or reteach content depending on the data gathered from the poll.
Teach–Back	Students need the opportunity to explain to others during the course of their instruction. When learning is shared with others, students hear the same content in multiple ways, promoting cognitive gains (Vygotsky, 1978). The opportunity to speak and write can serve to clarify one's own thinking about the task or topic of discussion. It allows students to think aloud, demonstrate self-questioning, learn to self-verbalize, and understand various strategies to complete the same task or problem. This process of restructuring one's thinking, known as cognitive elaboration, occurs when learners explain their ideas to each other and discuss gaps in their understanding (Chi, 2000).

Teach-back is a form of assessment to gauge students' learning by gathering data on their cognitive and metacognitive thinking. Once a child has learned something, teaching it to someone else can aid in transferring that learning (Biggs, 1999). Teachers can set up opportunities for students to teach their classmates, siblings, family members, or community members (Wiseman et al., 2020).

Teach-back can occur across grade spans and subject areas. Ways to incorporate teach-backs within instruction include story or text retelling, student-created podcasts, or written summaries. Using the teach-back method, teachers can gather data on what students have learned and what they still need to learn, thus ensuring that students understand what they are learning, why they are learning it, and how they will know they have learned it (Fisher et al., 2021). Teach-back can be used during in-person, digital (synchronous or asynchronous), and hybrid educational settings. Examples include utilizing think-pair-share for in-person or hybrid learning, breakout rooms for digital synchronous learning, and video or audio clips for digital asynchronous learning.

| Rubrics | Rubrics are widely used as an assessment tool for writing. They can be used during in-person, digital (synchronous or asynchronous), and hybrid educational settings and guide a range of work quality (Ghaffar et al., 2020). There are two main types of rubric formats: holistic and analytic. Holistic rubrics are used to assess large-scale writing assessments. The advantage of using holistic rubrics is that they are broad and easily understood. However, they do not lend themselves to providing less specific feedback. |

Analytic rubrics help define specific points for writers to focus on during the writing process. They are useful in assessment for learning, as both the student and teacher can concentrate on specific areas where improvement is needed. Many rubrics are written for the evaluator and not the student. Teachers may consider co-constructing rubrics with students to encourage active participation and ensure that appropriate language is used.

80 Kimberly Moreno

The Power of Equity

Teachers are reflective practitioners and are always interested in improving their pedagogy. Teachers often enter the profession because of a belief that every student deserves an opportunity to succeed. When the connection between grading and equity is discussed and brought to light, teachers and school districts become aware of how traditional grading practices undermine equity in their classrooms and schools, thus creating a sense of urgency to learn how to develop equitable grading practices and implement them with fidelity in the classroom.

Nearly every school and district across the country is committed to ensuring equity for their students, which leads to tackling traditional grading practices, which, in turn, makes existing disparities more obvious. Explicitly identifying the inequities in traditional grading practices will allow teachers and all stakeholders alike to promote equitable grading practices. Educators can identify and dismantle inequities in schools to enable every student to succeed. We must commit to making our grading practices equitable for all students regardless of the learning landscape.

Recommended Formative Assessment Strategies

As equitable grading practices are built into the instructional design, it is helpful to have a repertoire of assessment processes that can be used to match the purpose for assessment. Table 6.1 lists a number of recommended formative assessment strategies that can be utilized regardless of the learning landscape and that are easily adaptive to any student population.

Key Takeaways:

1. Equitable grading practices can and should be implemented in all learning landscapes, in-person, digital, and hybrid, to bridge the disproportionality gap.
2. Establishing purposeful assessment criteria that are aligned with the standards and communicated to students is imperative for building equitable grading practices.
3. Utilizing varying assessment strategies provides multiple points of data to be utilized to drive instructional practice.

Recommended Resources

Books:

- Fisher, D., Frey, N., & Hattie, J. (2021). *The distance learning playbook, grades K-12: Teaching for engagement & impact in any setting.* Corwin, a SAGE Publishing Company.

- Feldman, J. (2019). *Grading for equity: What it is, why it matters, and how it can transform schools and classrooms.* Corwin, a SAGE Publishing Company.

Websites:

- AES Learning Center: www.aeseducation.com/learning-center
- Apex Learning Virtual School: www.apexlearningvs.com/
- Pear Deck: www.peardeck.com/
- Poll Everywhere: www.polleverywhere.com/
- Teacher Toolkit: www.theteachertoolkit.com/

References

Berns, R. (2016). *Child, family, school, and community: Socialization and support* (10th ed.). Cengage.

Biggs, J. (1999). *Teaching for quality learning at university.* Society for Research into Higher Education and Open University Press.

Bingimlar, K. A. (2009). Barriers to the successful integration of ICT in teaching and learning environments: A review of the literature. *Eurasia Journal of Mathematics, Science & Technology Education, 5*(3), 235–245.

Black, P. J., Harrison, C., Lee, C., Marshall, B., & William, D. (2003). *Assessment for learning: Putting it into practice.* Open University Press.

Black, P. J., & William, D. (1998). Assessment and classroom learning. *Assessment in Education, 5*(1), 7–74.

Brookhart, S. M. (2015). Graded achievement, tested achievement, and validity. *Educational Assessment, 20*(4), 268–296. https://doi.org/10.1080/10627197.2015.1093928

Brookhart, S. M., Guskey, T. R., Bowers, A. J., McMillan, J. H., Smith, J. K., Smith, L. F., Stevens, M. T., & Welsh, M. E. (2016). A century of grading research meaning and value in the most common educational measure. *Review of Educational Research.* http://rer.sagepub.com/content/early/2016/10/03/0034654316672069

Chatterji, R., & Quirk, A. (2021, June 30). Closing advanced coursework equity gaps for all students. *Center for American Progress.* www.americanprogress.org/article/closing-advanced-coursework-equity-gaps-students/

Chi, M. T. H. (2000). Self-explaining expository texts: The dual processes of generating inferences and repairing mental models. In R. Glaser (Ed.), *Advances in instructional psychology* (pp. 161–238). Lawrence Erlbaum Associates.

Feldman, J. (2018). *School grading policies are failing children: A call to action for equitable grading.* Crescendo Education Group.

Feldman, J. (2019). Beyond standards-based grading: Why equity must be part of grading reform. *Phi Delta Kappan, 10*(8), 52–55.

Fisher, D., Frey, N., & Hattie, J. (2021). *The distance learning playbook, grades K-12: Teaching for engagement & impact in any setting.* Corwin, a SAGE Company.

Gambrell, L. B. (1983). The occurrence of think-time during reading comprehension instruction. *The Journal of Educational Research, 77*(2), 77–80. https://doi.org/10.1080/00220671.1983.10885502

Ghaffar, M. A., Khairallah, M., & Salloum, S. (2020). Co-constructed rubrics and assessment for learning: The impact on middle school students' attitudes and writing skills. *Assessing Writing, 45,* 100468. https://doi.org/10.1016/j.asw.2020.100468

Hattie, J., & Timperley, H. (2007). The power of feedback. *Review of Educational Research*, 77(1), 81–112. https://doi.org/10.3102/003465430298487

Iamarino, D. L. (2014). The benefits of standards-based grading: A critical evaluation of modern grading practices. *Current Issues in Education*, 17(2).

Nieto, S. (2013). *Finding joy in teaching students of diverse backgrounds*. Heinemann.

O'Connor, K. (2007). *A repair kit for grading: 15 fixes for broken grades*. Pearson.

Perlman, B. (2005). Dealing with students missing exams and in-class graded assignments. *Observer*, 18, 6. www.psychologicalscience.org/index.php/publications/observer/2006/june-06/dealing-with-students-missing-exams-and-in-class-graded-assignments.html

Randolph, J. J. (2007). Meta-analysis of the research on response cards. *Journal of Positive Behavior Interventions*, 9(2), 113–128. https://doi.org/10.1177/10983007070090020201

Sadler, D. R. (1989). Formative assessment and the design of instructional systems. *Instructional Science*, 18(2), 119–144.

Stiggins, R. J. (2002). Assessment crisis: The absence of assessment FOR learning. *Phi Delta Kappan*, 83(10), 758–765.

U.S. Census Bureau. (n.d.). Computer and internet use in the United States: 2016. *Census. gov*. www.census.gov/content/dam/Census/library/publications/2018/acs/ACS-39.pdf

U.S. Department of Education. (2013, March). *Strategic plan for FYs 2014–2018– March 2013*. [PDF]. www.ed.gov/about/reports/strat/plan2014-18/strategic-plan.pdf

Vygotsky, L. S. (1978). *Mind in society: The development of higher psychological processes*. Harvard University Press.

Walsh, N. (2018, July). Barriers to technology integration in K-12 Classrooms. *Learnovate*. https://www.learnovatecentre.org/barriers-to-technology-integration-in-k-12-classrooms/

Wiliam, D. (2010). An integrative summary of the research literature and implications for a new theory of formative assessment. In H. L. Andrade & G. J. Cizek (Eds.), *Handbook of formative assessment* (pp. 18–40). Taylor & Francis.

Wiliam, D. (2013). Assessment: The bridge between teaching and learning. *Voices from the Middle*, 21, 15–20.

Wiseman, R., Fisher, D., Frey, N., & Hattie, J. (2020). *The distance learning playbook for parents: How to support your child's academic, social and emotional development in any setting*. Corwin.

Wormeli, R. (2006). *Fair isn't always equal*. Stenhouse.

7

STUDENTS' INFORMATIONAL NEEDS

Applying the Principles of Universal Design to Address Inequity in High-Needs Schools During Virtual Learning

Gihan Mohamad and Ellen Pozzi

Guiding Questions:

- How do librarians in high-needs schools offer information literacy education?
- Which Universal Design for Learning (UDL) principles and strategies do librarians in high-needs schools use in virtual teaching situations to meet the needs of their students?
- How does applying the principles of UDL in high-needs schools help students achieve their learning goals?
- How do librarians in high-needs schools apply UDL strategies in their instruction?
- How does the UDL framework address inequities in high-needs schools during virtual learning?

Introduction

Universal Design for Learning (UDL) stems from research in the field of neuroscience and the universal design concept in architecture (Dickinson & Gronseth, 2020). UDL is a framework designed to address the needs of all learners, going beyond equitable access to require equitable opportunities for learners to develop as experts. As such, it extends the scope of equity in education to provide support and resources for students and encompasses curriculum design that facilitates learning for all abilities without the need for differentiation. The framework connects Engagement (the Why of learning), Representation (the What of learning),

DOI:10.4324/9781003274537-9

and Action and Expression (the How of learning) to create equitable learning experiences. The UDL framework encourages educators to (a) start with the learning goals in mind, (b) identify the barriers that might interfere with their learners reaching these goals, and (c) eliminate these barriers by creating flexible learning paths (CAST, 2018). According to Venkatesh (2015) and Thomas (2020), UDL principles are closely related to the principles of equity pedagogy, as both encourage the examination of the curriculum with a focus on content, instruction, and assessment. Embedded in the framework is the need for a modified curriculum that grants access to education via flexible means (Thomas, 2020; Venkatesh, 2015).

Given their importance, these principles need to be applied beyond the traditional classroom to include the school library, as librarians provide information literacy instruction to students of all abilities (Robinson, 2017). This issue has become particularly salient in relation to virtual learning, in which school librarians play a major role. Much of the existing research on librarians and UDL is outdated and focuses on academic librarians (Pittaway & Malomo, 2021; Webb & Hoover, 2015; Yang et al., 2011). Using results from surveys and semistructured interviews of school librarians from high-needs districts in New Jersey, this chapter will fill this gap in the literature by exploring how librarians met the needs of their students in a virtual learning environment.

Background

This chapter applies the principles of UDL as a basis for examining how the educational needs of students of all abilities have been met in high-needs schools. Students vary in the ways they perceive instruction (the What of learning), process learning (the How of learning), and become engaged and motivated (the Why of learning) (Rapp, 2014). As a pedagogical theory, UDL provides guidelines on how to improve instruction to meet the needs of all students in an inclusive environment (Nave, 2020). Ron Mace, the American architect responsible for coining the term "universal design," was referring to the flexible design of physical environments that allow access to all users, including those with physical disabilities (Dickinson & Gronseth, 2020). Based on this concept, the Center for Applied Special Technology (CAST) developed a UDL framework to guide educators in designing accessible learning environments that challenge students of all abilities (Figure 7.1). To achieve this goal, the guidelines suggest providing multiple avenues for Engagement, Representation, and Action and Expression. *Engagement* addresses the affective domain of learning, and since students vary in terms of background knowledge, culture, and learning style, providing just one way of Engagement, as has traditionally often been the case, discourages many students. Multiple ways of Engagement include sparking interest by providing individual choices in achieving the learning goals, for example, by allowing for many levels of challenge, personalization, and choice of sequence (CAST, 2018).

Representation, in turn, addresses the cognitive domain of learning. Students comprehend information differently depending on their cognitive and language abilities and cultural backgrounds. The UDL framework encourages educators to present information in multiple ways, such as visual, auditory, and customizable print. Embedding clarification of vocabulary and highlighting main ideas in the instruction are examples of modes of Representation (CAST, 2018).

Finally, *Action and Expression* address the psychomotor domain of learning. There are many ways to express knowledge, and providing students with options to show their mastery is essential to driving learning achievements. For example, some students with physical impairments need other ways to communicate through writing than using pen and pencil. Providing choices of alternatives such as voice, keyboard, and joystick gives every student an equal opportunity to express their learning (CAST, 2018).

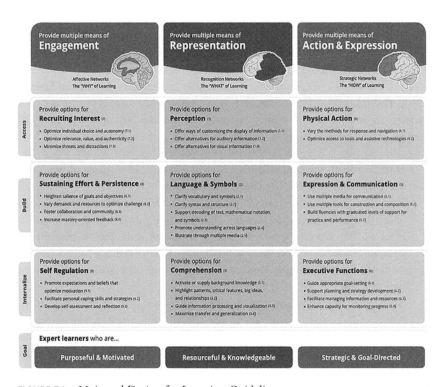

FIGURE 7.1 Universal Design for Learning Guidelines

Note: Reprinted with permission.

UDL and School Libraries

The Individuals with Disabilities Education Act (IDEA), enacted in 2004, mandates equal access to education for children and youth with disabilities (U.S. Department of Education, n.d.). For schools, this means including students with disabilities in general education classes, including school libraries (Blue & Pace, 2011). Examples of applying UDL principles to school libraries include the following. In terms of Engagement, librarians need to provide students with as many choices as possible. Library instruction should include literature in various formats, technology tools, discussions, and group activities (Sturge, 2020). Providing multiple means of Representation requires librarians to develop collections in various formats such as print, video, and audio. Also, digital resources should include read-aloud and translation features. Finally, multiple means of Action and Expression for library instruction means giving students the choice of ways to present their assignments, aided by tools such as handouts and checklists to help them monitor their progress (Sturge, 2020).

UDL and Information Literacy

According to the Association of College and Research Libraries (ACRL), information-literate individuals should be able to determine the extent of information needed, access it, evaluate it critically, and use it effectively and ethically (*Information Literacy*, 2000). Following are ACRL competencies (*Information Literacy*, 2000), along with barriers students might face with these competencies and how applying the UDL framework helps eliminate these barriers.

- **Determine the extent of information needed, including identifying the potential sources for that information.**
  Potential barriers: Some learners struggle to develop insight into the main ideas that form research topics. That is, they find it difficult to grasp some of the concepts they are reading about. Introducing assignments as an open-ended question, for example, may be problematic because some students work best with a strict routine, while others like to be more independent.
  Applying UDL guidelines: Using UDL, librarians provide multiple entry points and alternative pathways to the content, for example, exploring big ideas through artwork, literature, media, and film. Providing graduated levels of support through prompts (Hall et al., 2012) is another strategy to help learners organize information.
- **Access the needed information effectively and efficiently and design effective search strategies.**
  Potential barriers: Using one format to present information forces students to conform to its boundaries. The layout and the volume of information presented can overwhelm students and cause information overload.

Applying UDL guidelines: The UDL framework encourages educators to present instruction in more than one format (such as text, images, audio, and video), identify critical information related to the instructional goals using highlighted text and side notes, and repeat essential concepts.

- **Evaluate the information and its sources critically.**
  Potential barriers: The key to developing good comprehension skills is the ability to detect main ideas and to understand how the supporting details fit into a larger conceptual framework. This takes effort and often presents a barrier for students. *Applying UDL guidelines:* UDL guidelines suggest that educators create guides for students to self-assess. These can be a Getting-Started guide or an Assess My Work guide. Also, encouraging students to develop acronyms to decode text gives them autonomy, which drives engagement.
- **Incorporate selected information into one's knowledge base.**
  Potential barriers: Many learners struggle with connecting the ideas presented in the learning materials, finding it challenging to identify themes and patterns to make sense of them.
  Applying UDL guidelines: UDL guidelines suggest helping students design planners and templates to help them format their responses and include sentence starters.
- **Understand the economic, ethical, legal, and social issues surrounding the use of information.**
  Potential barriers: Copyright and fair-use language is packed with technical terms that often make it difficult for students to decipher.
  Applying UDL guidelines: Based on UDL guidelines, educators must prioritize value and authenticity by providing reminders and checklists to help students self-regulate and reflect on their learning more frequently.

Study Highlights

Participants

Surveys were sent to 39 high-needs schools in New Jersey, identified through public information on the New Jersey Department of Education website (www.nj.gov/education/title1/funding/allocation.shtml) as overall low performing. Schools with summative scores in the bottom 5% of Title I schools and schools with a four-year graduation rate of 67% or less in 2020 were selected. According to the New Jersey Department of Education, Title I funding "is intended to ensure that the most financially and socially disadvantaged children have a fair, equal and significant opportunity to obtain a high quality education and reach proficiency on challenging state academic standards and assessments" (State of New Jersey Department of Education, n.d.).

Although 121 schools were listed on the website as being low performing, information about the school librarians was available for only 39 schools; in these schools, the librarian was subsequently contacted. Ten individuals completed the surveys; two of the survey completers participated in online semistructured interviews. The participants worked in elementary, middle, and high schools, so all levels are represented in the survey. Survey questions referred to the strategies embedded within the UDL framework, as the participants might not be familiar with the framework itself.

Key Findings

The survey sent out to school librarians was organized around the three main principles of UDL: Multiple Means of Engagement, Multiple Means of Representation, and Action and Expression (Figure 7.1). Respondents were asked to answer questions related to each area about their experiences teaching online.

Multiple Means of Engagement

Educators strive to design instruction that engages students and sustains that engagement as long as possible. Communication and collaboration with their teacher and peers play an important role in keeping students motivated, and providing the tools that help them monitor their activities is essential for Engagement (CAST, 2018; Courey et al., 2013; Nave, 2020).

Respondents indicated they had open meetings and office hours on Zoom where students could communicate with the librarian and with each other. They also allowed students to ask for help through email and encouraged them to ask peers (one respondent urged using the "Ask 3 before me" strategy). One participant noted they told students, "The only stupid question is the one unasked." Students were provided the opportunity to communicate with their peers through chat, messaging, and discussion and almost always had a choice to work in groups, all of which allowed for fostering collaboration and community.

Students need structure, regardless of their level, to help them reach their learning goals. Based on the UDL framework, providing students with tools that help them monitor their progress, such as a checklist, note-taking, and calendars, is an effective approach (Galkiene & Monkeviciene, 2021; Nelson & Rose, 2013).

Most respondents reported that they provided tools such as calendars and to-do lists to help students with organizational skills.

For students to effectively use their time, educators need to provide them with the tools and strategies to encourage critical thinking and a goal-driven attitude. Self-reflection on the learning process is one of the approaches recommended by the UDL framework (CAST, 2018; Nave, 2021; Nelson & Rose, 2013).

Respondents were asked how frequently their assessments allowed for customization (choosing resources for book reports or topics for research) and if they provided students with rubrics and asked students to reflect on their learning (see Figure 7.2). The results were mixed. That is, around 45% of respondents provided choice "always" or "most of the time," and 55% provided choice "sometimes" or "about half the time." Three respondents never provided rubrics, and two did

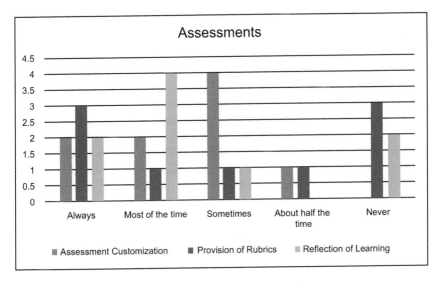

FIGURE 7.2 Frequency of Provision of Multiple Options for Assessment

so occasionally. Most librarians had students reflect on learning either "always" or "most of the time." Participants also commented that "I barely teach lessons" and "Grades are not required for the library in this school, so there wasn't much formal assessment."

Multiple Modes of Representation

The UDL framework encourages educators to provide options for how they present instruction. Students' ways of decoding information vary depending on their cultural and background knowledge and learning abilities (CAST, 2018; Robinson, 2017). According to UDL, educators must aid students' perception by providing them with more than one way to access the content. Students who have difficulty processing print text need to be given the information through various media (CAST, 2018; Hall et al., 2012).

Most respondents used a combination of text and video in their instruction, and some incorporated audio. Most offered a variety of choices for customizing text access, including read-aloud options; changing the size of images, font style and size, and background color; and a translation option. An image description was seldom used, even though this is an essential practice for students with visual impairments. Respondents also provided audio and visual playback customization, including customizing sound and audio playback and closed captions. Only one respondent provided transcripts for audio, which limits the access for students with hearing impairments or those who can read a language but do not understand it when spoken. One comment received for each question (presumably by the same respondent over several questions) was that the options depended on the software used.

To aid student comprehension, the UDL framework encourages educators to use techniques such as modeling, highlighting main ideas, using graphic organizers, and emphasizing relationships that help students connect their prior knowledge to the new information (CAST, 2018; Murawski & Scott, 2019; Nave, 2021).

Librarians in this study used graphic organizers most often, with some use of Know, Want to Know, and Learn (KWL) charts and scaffolded instruction by highlighting important text and using a bulleted list of big ideas.

According to the UDL framework, educators need to clarify the vocabulary used in instruction and preteach it in student-friendly language. For students who are not proficient in the English language, educators could use scaffolding techniques such as providing a dictionary or teaching in the students' native language (Murawski & Scott, 2019; Nave, 2021).

Respondents noted that dictionaries were made available to students for vocabulary, as was access to examples and clarification of vocabulary and translation tools like Google Translate. However, one interviewee working with a large Hispanic population did not have a Spanish/English dictionary available; another interviewee mentioned that they encouraged using Google Translate and the translation feature in databases.

Multiple Modes of Action and Expression

Students need to navigate their learning environments and express their knowledge in ways that feel natural to them. For example, some students may have language and speech barriers that impede their ability to communicate their learning orally. The UDL framework calls for providing alternative ways to express learning to reduce media-specific barriers. Providing options for action and expression allows students to share their thoughts and monitor their progress to make the most of their learning (CAST, 2018; Nave, 2021; Rapp, 2014). The key to helping students persist in the face of challenges involves balancing their tasks and providing constructive feedback that keeps them moving toward achieving their learning goals as their mastery increases (Hall et al., 2012; Nelson & Rose, 2013).

Participants were asked what choices they provided for their students to express their learning. The most common response was oral responses (7), followed by written assessment (3) and drawing a picture (3). Four respondents indicated they used all three options. Additionally, one person indicated they used Makerspace creations as a choice. Students would be encouraged to express themselves in various ways when participating in the Makerspace environment. Sharing real-life experiences is another way to allow students to express themselves, with twice as many respondents choosing to do this "always" or "most of the time."

Varying the methods by which students learn between physical actions and various modes of expression, such as using multimedia to show their learning, help them become expert learners who take ownership of their education (Galkiene & Monkeviciene, 2021; Russo, 2019).

Librarians in the survey supported students in strategizing and planning by providing checklists and breaking up tasks into mini-tasks. They also offered students a variety of tools for managing information, most often through guides, templates, bookmarking, and note-taking and less often through image capturing and audio notes. One of the participants noted that they used Google Classroom. "I would have a variety of resources available for students to choose from, trying to reach each type of learner."

Discussion

As shown by the results, the respondents to the survey are using some elements of UDL in their instruction. In general, there is a need for more awareness of the UDL principles and the importance of incorporating these principles into library instruction practices. There are also some specific challenges within the field and within high-needs schools that are elaborated in what follows along with some recommendations.

Lack of Collaboration and Job Elimination

School librarians' role as instructional collaborators is reportedly the least fulfilled task of their practice (Mohamad, 2017). A recent study of school librarian employment found a decline between 2009 and 2019 of almost 20% while at the same time, other positions such as district administrators, school administrators, and instructional coordinators increased. The only further decline was a little over 1% in teachers' positions (Kachel & Lance, 2021). According to the authors, this reflects an apparent shift in organizational priorities regarding staffing choices. Kachel and Lance (2021) surveyed all 50 states and the District of Columbia (D.C.) to investigate support for school library programs. Their data showed that only 10 states plus D.C. enforced a mandate to hire public school librarians. A lack of such mandate in many states contributes to school librarians' staffing issues.

The impact of this reality was also noted by the interviewees in the current study: "We used to do more collaboration. But when I started in the district, there were several of us; now, there are two basically." They added, "they've [students] gone without a librarian in the buildings, a consistent library in the building for almost ten years."

Time Commitment and Lack of Professional Development

Perceptions about implementing UDL principles into practice face barriers. According to Jordan Anstead (2016), these include the time commitment required and lack of adequate professional development. Again, this was also borne out in the current study, as one interviewee noted, "We haven't [had library-specific PD] in years." Another respondent said, "Up until now, we have not had a specific library-related PD. The likelihood is it'll be a representative from InfoBase. You know the database as well as World Book," indicating that the only PD provided to the librarians was from vendors.

Areas for Improvement

Based on the responses in the survey, there are several areas noted for improvement. Librarians need to do more to customize assessments and to understand the importance of providing rubrics. While some librarians indicated grades are not required in the library, learning assessment is an important element of instruction and should be practiced while students are there. Some participants noted that the limits and capabilities of the software often determined their practices, which indicates that software must be carefully chosen to provide maximum possibilities for presenting information to learners. To facilitate learning for English language learners, use of translation applications such as Google Translate should be highlighted, especially if print dictionaries are not available in the appropriate languages in the library.

Conclusions

This study has limitations, as it utilized a survey as a research instrument. Descriptive data describe current situations but lack the depth to reveal their reasons. Further studies are needed, therefore, to explore the implications of implementing the UDL framework in high-needs schools. Despite these shortcomings, the participants revealed much about their library instruction. The reported application of UDL principles reflected a lack of knowledge about the UDL framework even though respondents reported implementing many of the principles. Awareness of the framework as a unit would help educators implement the parts more effectively. The participants agreed on the importance of adopting multiple means of Representation, Engagement, and Actions and Expression in their practice but cited many obstacles, such as those listed by Jordan Anstead (2016), primarily lack of time and resources.

UDL encourages educators to give students the choice of how they learn and how to express their knowledge. To create a socially just society, educators need to focus less on classroom management and following directions and more on encouraging students to be seen and heard by embracing diversity, identity, and personalization (Novak & Chardin, 2020). Educators and school administrators must create a shared vision of how equity in education should look in the classroom.

Our study included 39 high-needs schools in which librarians could be identified. Another 36 of the high-needs schools listed on the state website responded that they do not have a librarian. Information on librarians for the rest of the schools could not be determined. The average percentage of economically disadvantaged students among the 39 schools is 63%. Only two schools had less than 30% economically disadvantaged students, while the rate was between 31% and 60% in 14 schools. Twenty-two schools had between 61% and 90% economically disadvantaged students, and one school had more than 90%. Economically disadvantaged students have less access to educational resources outside of the classroom, which often results in a lack of confidence and difficulties in attaining the skills needed to achieve academically (Li et al., 2020). Giving students choices empowers them to identify their learning barriers and attain the privileges that education grants them.

Barrett (2010) listed 19 major studies conducted around the globe showing a positive correlation between effective school library programs and student achievement. For example, qualified school librarians teach students information, reading, and technological literacies that foster achievement. Further, the characteristics of an effective school library program include the following: it is led by a state-certified full-time library media specialist, aided by paraprofessional staff, based on a flexible schedule, integrated into curriculum content, provided with professional development opportunities, and has access to resources (American Library Association, n.d.; Barrett, 2010; Todd & Kuhlthau, 2005).

While school library programs provide information literacy services to students of all physical and cognitive abilities, we argue that the decline of school library positions and the lack of librarian-targeted professional development in high-needs schools, as reflected in this and previous studies, might have a negative impact on student achievement. To help lessen this situation, we argue for the importance of implementing UDL on a larger scale. Specifically, the UDL framework addresses deficiencies in the curriculum, not the students. It promotes shared power and the provision of appropriate support. It prompts rigor and honors variability. It aims to eliminate specific learning barriers that each student might face regardless of the environment they find themselves in (Novak & Chardin, 2020; Rapp, 2014). The core of UDL practice is the belief that, with no exceptions, all students can and should achieve their learning goals.

Key Takeaways:

1. More professional development on UDL is needed for librarians to raise their awareness of its applicability to teaching information literacy skills.
2. Integration of technology that encourages implementation of UDL is needed.
3. Implementing the UDL principles in library instruction can help close the equity gap in high-needs schools by encouraging educators to focus on diversity, identity, and personalization.
4. Librarians need to be aware of their roles in providing solutions to how social positions such as class, race, and culture were historically structured to provide opportunities for some students to succeed while hindering others.

Recommended Resources

Books:

- Nelson, L. L., & Rose, D. H. (2013). *Design and deliver: Planning and teaching using Universal Design for Learning.* Paul H. Brookes Publishing Co.:
  —This book guides educators on how to implement the principles of UDL. It includes practical suggestions for educators on lesson planning.
  —*Loui Lord Nelson's UDL in 15 Minutes*: Podcast by the author of *Design and Deliver* about implementing UDL, sharing success stories and challenges. https://theudlapproach.com/media/
- Rapp, W. H. (2015). *Universal Design for Learning in action: 100 ways to teach all learners.* Paul H. Brookes Publishing Co.:
  —This book provides educators with practical ideas for how to implement the UDL principles in the areas of Engagement, Learning, and Assessment with illustrations.
  —Access a free sample pack for some of the strategies mentioned in the book using this link https://brookespublishing.com/resource-library/sample-pack-universal-design-for-learning-in-action/.
- Meyer, A., Rose, D. H., & Gordon, D. (2013). *Universal Design for Learning: Theory and practice.* CAST Incorporated.
  —This book reflects years of research at the Center for Applied Special Technology (CAST). It provides a comprehensive look at UDL based on collaborative implementations in schools and universities.
- Murawski, W., & Scott, K. L. (2019). *What really works with Universal Design for Learning.* Corwin, a SAGE Publications:
  —This book provides a practical guide to implementation of the principles of Universal Design for Learning.

Websites:

- CAST UDL Studio (http://udlstudio.cast.org/):
  CAST UDL studio allows educators to create and share educational materials and access copyright-free resources.
- The #UDLchat on Twitter:
  This Twitter conversation offers a great way to connect with other educators implementing UDL and share ideas.
- UDL Principles and Practice Video Series (www.youtube.com/playlist?list=PLDD6870F2D42327F3):
  This is the series developed by the National Center on Universal Design for Learning. The six videos in the series show examples of UDL in practice.

References

American Library Association. (n.d.). *Highly effective school libraries have a common set of characteristics.* www.ala.org/tools/research/librariesmatter/highly-effective-school-libraries-have-common-set-characteristics

Barrett, L. (2010). Effective school libraries: Evidence of impact on student achievement. *The School Librarian, 58*(3), 136–139.

Blue, E. V., & Pace, D. (2011). UD and UDL: Paving the way toward inclusion and independence in the school library. *Knowledge Quest, 39*(3), 48–55.

CAST. (2018). *The UDL guidelines.* http://udlguidelines.cast.org

Courey, S. J., Tappe, P., Siker, J., & LePage, P. (2013). Improved lesson planning with Universal Design for Learning (UDL). *Teacher Education and Special Education, 36*(1), 7–27. https://doi.org/10.1177/0888406412446178

Dickinson, K. J., & Gronseth, S. L. (2020). Application of Universal Design for Learning (UDL) principles to surgical education during the COVID-19 pandemic. *Journal of Surgical Education, 77*(5), 1008–1012. https://doi.org/10.1016/j.jsurg.2020.06.005

Galkiene, A., & Monkeviciene, O. (Eds.). (2021). *Improving inclusive education through Universal Design for Learning* (Vol. 5). Springer International Publishing. https://doi.org/10.1007/978-3-030-80658-3

Hall, T. E., Meyer, A., & Rose, D. H. (2012). *Universal Design for Learning in the classroom: Practical applications.* Guilford Press.

Information literacy competency standards for higher education. (2000). [Brochure]. Association of College & Research Libraries. https://alair.ala.org/bitstream/handle/11213/7668/ACRL%20Information%20Literacy%20Competency%20Standards%20for%20Higher%20Education.pdf?sequence=1

Jordan Anstead, M. (2016). *Teachers' perceptions of barriers to Universal Design for Learning* (Publication No. 3746213) [Doctoral dissertation, Walden College]. ProQuest Dissertations and Theses Global. p. 334.

Kachel, D. E., & Lance, K. C. (2021). The status of state support of school library programs. *Teacher Librarian, 48*(5), 8–13.

Li, H., Peng, M. Y., Yang, M., & Chen, C. C. (2020). Exploring the influence of learning motivation and socioeconomic status on college students' learning outcomes using self-determination theory. *Frontiers in Psychology, 11*, 1–13. https://doi.org/10.3389/fpsyg.2020.00849

Mohamad, G. (2017). *A librarian-teacher collaboration: Integrating information literacy and technology in the K-12 classroom* (Publication No. 10745746) [Doctoral dissertation, New Jersey City University]. ProQuest Dissertations and Theses Global.

Murawski, W., & Scott, K. L. (2019). *What really works with Universal Design for Learning.* Corwin.

Nave, L. (2020). Universal Design for Learning UDL in online environments: The WHY of learning. *Journal of Developmental Education, 44*(1), 30–31.

Nave, L. (2021). Universal Design for Learning UDL in online environments: The HOW of learning. *Journal of Developmental Education, 44*(3), 34–35.

Nelson, L. L., & Rose, D. H. (2013). *Design and deliver: Planning and teaching using Universal Design for Learning.* Paul H. Brookes Publishing Co.

Novak, K., & Chardin, M. (2020). *Equity by design: Delivering on the power and promise of UDL.* Corwin.

Pittaway, S., & Malomo, M. (2021). "So, you want me to read for my degree?": A Universal Design for Learning approach to reading. *Insights, 34*(19), 1–10. https://doi.org/10.1629/uksg.549

Rapp, W. H. (2014). *Universal Design for Learning in action: 100 ways to teach all learners.* Paul H. Brookes Publishing Co.

Robinson, D. E. (2017). Universal Design for Learning and school libraries: A logical partnership. *Knowledge Quest, 46*(1), 56–61.

Russo, L. J. (2019). *Teachers' perceptions and knowledge about the Universal Design for Learning model* (Publication No. 13877857) [Doctoral dissertation, Gwynedd Mercy University]. ProQuest Dissertations and Theses Global.

State of New Jersey Department of Education. (n.d.). *Title I—funding allocation of the Title I award.* www.nj.gov/education/title1/funding/allocation.shtml

Sturge, J. (2020. June 2). School libraries and UDL in the time of learning from home. *Knowledge Quest: Journal of the American Association of School Librarians.* https://knowledgequest.aasl.org/school-libraries-and-udl-in-the-time-of-learning-from-home/

Thomas, M. (2020). Making the case for equity pedagogy. *Current Musicology, 107,* 142–147. https://doi.org/10.52214/cm.v107i.7841

Todd, R. J., & Kuhlthau, C. C. (2005). Student learning through Ohio school libraries, part 2: Faculty perceptions of effective school libraries. *School Libraries Worldwide, 11*(1), 89–110.

U.S. Department of Education. (n.d.). *Individuals with disabilities education act (IDEA).* https://sites.ed.gov/idea/

Venkatesh, K. (2015). *Universal Design for Learning as a framework for social justice: A multi-case analysis of undergraduate pre-service teachers* (Publication No. 3689535) [Doctoral dissertation, Boston College]. ProQuest Dissertations and Theses Global.

Webb, K. K., & Hoover, J. (2015). Universal Design for Learning (UDL) in the academic library: A methodology for mapping multiple means of representation in library tutorials. *College & Research Libraries, 76*(4), 537–553. https://doi.org/10.5860/crl.76.4.537

Yang, C., Tzuo, P. W., & Komara, C. (2011). Using webquest as a Universal Design for Learning tool to enhance teaching and learning in teacher preparation programs. *Journal of College Teaching and Learning, 8*(3), 21–30. https://doi.org/10.19030/tlc.v8i3.4121

SECTION III

Pedagogical Strategies and Digital Tools Across the Curriculum

8

CONTENT-NEUTRAL TECHNOLOGIES AS A PEDAGOGICAL RESPONSE IN HIGH-NEEDS SCHOOLS AND COMMUNITIES

Design Thinking, Making, and Learning

Diallo Sessoms

Guiding Questions:

- How can the use of makerspaces support students in high-needs schools?
- What can schools do to develop and nurture a maker mindset in students?
- In what ways does leadership impact innovation and creativity in a school environment?
- How can educators develop a maker mindset?
- What are best practices to support educators and school administrators in developing classrooms as makerspaces?

Introduction

This chapter focuses on content-neutral technology for high-needs schools in a rural setting. The Eastern Shore of Maryland (MD) is a rural area consisting of nine counties. Each county includes high-needs schools focusing their resources at the elementary and middle school levels, which have a Title I designation. While there are targeted resources for specific populations, resources are designated as schoolwide so as to improve learning for all students. This is an important distinction because the discussion of makerspaces in this chapter is based on the idea of a universal approach to learning in high-needs schools using

DOI:10.4324/9781003274537-11

content-neutral technologies. Two of the schools in the area focus on technology that can be classified as student centered, which means students use technology to explore and create knowledge; this is an aspect of how makerspaces function. The schools in the other counties have a teacher-centered focus, which means teachers use technology for administrative purposes such as recording data, displaying information, or demonstrating concepts. While this might be how a teacher starts out in a makerspace, an evolution must occur to fully take advantage of a makerspace using content-neutral technology.

High-needs schools face many challenges, including underqualified teachers, poor teacher retention rates, limited resources, substandard facilities, and a lack of materials (Darling-Hammond, 2004) as well as a limited vision on the part of educators and school leaders (Suppes et al., 2013) with regard to infusion of innovative spaces. High-needs schools in rural areas might also face geographic challenges. As such, geographic challenges require a greater need for innovative, in-school learning experiences. That is, educators in high-needs schools in rural areas must know how to "expand the geography of innovation" (Watkins, 2019, p. 17) to mitigate such challenges as reliable public transportation and "quality of access and opportunities" (Watkins & Cho, 2018, p. 23) by transforming spaces such as classrooms into makerspaces.

In rural areas, reliable public transportation is not as accessible, and some students live as far as an hour from their home school. By contrast, urban areas have public transportation, which may be used to access quality learning experiences. For example, in Baltimore, Maryland, the Digital Harbor Foundation (DHF), which is dedicated to "fostering learning, creativity, productivity, and community through education" via youth and educator programs (Digital Harbor Foundation, 2022), provides access to a host of human and technological resources for any youth. The DHF serves as a unique type of makerspace because it serves students in high-needs areas, provides training for teachers who want to learn about makerspaces, and serves as a makerspace.

Issues that affect high-needs schools, in general, consist of a confluence of factors such as students' socioeconomic status and teacher salaries and working conditions (Carver & Darling-Hammond, 2017). Although salary and socioeconomic status are factors, teachers are more satisfied and plan to stay longer in schools that have a positive work context, independent of the school's student demographic characteristics (Johnson et al., 2012). A positive work context includes providing educators with professional development to support innovative practices such as the implementation of makerspaces. For example, Ertmer & Ottenbreit-Leftwich (2010) suggest teaching is not as effective without the appropriate use of technologies to facilitate student learning, while Suppes et al. (2013) found that "contrary to the overly pessimistic view of educational technology now held by many persons participating in or following the current national debate on the effectiveness of technology, statistically significant outcomes of technologically driven experiments can be obtained" (p. 177). Further, Kormos (2022) noted that teachers in high-needs schools did not perceive technology as an effective tool to help improve student learning outcomes based on prohibitive costs, lack of access to technology, lack of support, and lack of adequate professional development.

Ironically, lack of adequate professional development also hinders teachers from understanding how the aforementioned perceptions can be mitigated. Even in situations where support is provided, a teacher's mindset and beliefs can be a powerful hindrance to the use of technology beyond low-level applications; conversely, Tondeur et al. (2017) suggest teacher beliefs can also be a mechanism for greater technology integration. Because today's students expect to be engaged in meaningful learning experiences, makerspaces can be the innovation that inspires teachers to engage learners and positively impact learning in high-needs schools. This chapter discusses an approach to infusing technology into high-needs schools based on content-neutral technology through the implementation of makerspaces. "Content neutral" refers to the ability of learners to understand technology and transfer that knowledge "broadly enough to apply it productively at work and in their everyday lives" (Harris et al., 2009, p. 397). Makerspaces can be a solution that allows a high-needs school to scale mindsets centered around using technology to solve problems through creating and making.

Maker Movement for High-Needs Schools

The maker movement began as community-based organizations of people with similar interests gathering to share tools and expertise for the purpose of making various artifacts, using the benefit of shared knowledge (Brown & Antink-Meyer, 2017). These opportunities, in turn, facilitated collaboration, learning, sharing ideas, problem-solving, critical thinking, a do-it-yourself (DIY) ethos, and sharing creations. Although each makerspace is unique in terms of the tools, materials, and objectives used, a common thread is that a maker mentality fosters natural interest in learning and that learning is the foundation of making (Hatch, 2014).

The maker movement gained popularity in 2005, and educational institutions began adopting the concept into formal and informal spaces more than 10 years ago. In an attempt to provide access to makerspaces, public venues such as libraries and museums have adopted the maker philosophy as part of their offerings to the general public. For example, the Children's Museum Makerspace (2022) in Pittsburgh, Pennsylvania, started in 2017, serves students in local elementary schools as well as the public. This is a unique example of a partnership between public schools and community organizations collaborating to provide opportunities for local elementary schools. Two of the elementary schools are eligible for Title I funding. This endeavor required private funding, which might be seen as a hurdle in some areas with high-needs schools; however, it does provide an example of what high-needs schools can do to provide access to cutting-edge learning experiences.

Part of the inspiration for the maker movement was spurred by one of President Obama's initiatives, Educate to Innovate. This initiative focused on math and science, which inspired makerspaces to have a STEM focus. As educators became aware of the concept of a makerspace, the focus of makerspaces evolved to include a broader array of learning experiences. Educators began to understand that makerspaces provide an emergent and flexible learning environment that might combine the rigor of traditional instruction with the self-organization of natural systems (Roskos & Christie, 2011). As learners explore possibilities in makerspaces (see Figure 8.1), "complex behavioral forms emerge from the interaction of simpler ones" (Roskos & Christie, 2011, p. 77). Such scaffolded experiences support a student-centered approach, which allows a teacher to foster a culture in which students take ownership of their learning (International Society for Technology in Education [ISTE], 2017).

As leaders, educators create a vision for makerspaces (see Figure 8.2) and collaborate with their students to create a community of makers; however, learning is not necessarily defined by the teacher or a particular product. This is a significant departure from traditional classroom practices and includes research-based approaches such as the elements of the principles of Universal Design for Learning (UDL) and constructivist learning theory. UDL focuses on removing barriers

FIGURE 8.1 Student Tinkering in a Makerspace
Note: Sessoms (2022).

FIGURE 8.2 A Makerspace Is a Flexible Environment, and Each Has a Unique Look
Note: Sessoms (2022).

to improve and optimize teaching and learning for all people (The IRIS Center, 2010) through multiple means of representation, expression, and engagement. Technology plays a critical role in that process. Likewise, makerspaces remove barriers to improve and optimize teaching and learning through making, which supports the UDL principles. Based in constructivist learning theory, makerspaces encourage learners to learn from their own active engagement with raw materials provided by the teacher (Hughes et al., 2016). These materials do not have to be expensive or high tech. Makerspaces are noted for their ability to promote inquiry-based learning and for allowing students to explore a variety of technologies, giving them autonomy in choosing the tools they feel might be the best fit for what they plan to make to demonstrate learning.

A makerspace can support a variety of making and promote various levels of active learning, including group discussion (see Figure 8.3), practice by doing, and teaching others (Khalifa & Brahimi, 2017). Crafts, sewing, electronics, construction, and design are examples of making (Davee et al., 2015). Additionally, makerspaces can focus on STEM to facilitate language learning for students who do not speak English and enable creative expression through the use of rich language (Lee et al., 2013), promote civic engagement through invention (Barton et al., 2017), engineering, computer science, social-emotional learning, and use of technology as a means of personal expression (Bull et al., 2017). "Being a

FIGURE 8.3 Collaborating in a Makerspace

Note: Sessoms (2022).

maker in these spaces involves participating in a space with diverse tools, materials, and processes; finding problems and projects to work on; iterating through designs; becoming a member of a community; taking on leadership and teaching roles as needed; and sharing creations and skills with a wider world" (Sheridan et al., 2014, p. 529).

Some view innovative practices, including makerspaces, as limited to well-resourced schools (Singh & Kim, 2019). This mindset can be pervasive among professional educators based on the assumption that learners of certain backgrounds need more "remediation" than "innovation." Contrary to this belief, a makerspace is even more critical for high-needs schools. According to Dale Dougherty (2016), known as the godfather of the maker movement, the power of the term "maker" is based on its broad application, inclusiveness, and lack of close alignment with any specific content or interests. This means that any teaching in high-needs schools, at any level of education, can create a makerspace and is free to claim the identity for itself. As a result, the maker movement has sparked interest due to its potential role in breaking down barriers for students who would otherwise not have access to learning and attainment in a variety of areas such as but not limited to STEM (Barton et al., 2017). When learners from high-needs schools are exposed to cutting-edge practices, pedagogies, and technologies, they are not limited in how they reach their potential; rather, they are allowed to develop critical mindsets and skills necessary for a successful future.

Makerspaces can be implemented in any educational setting, formal and informal. Formal spaces such as classrooms must work within the context of curricular expectations, while informal spaces such as after-school programs or public libraries have more flexibility and fewer academic constraints. In high-needs schools, makerspaces can address some of the educational issues to improve student engagement, create student-centered learning, and inspire creativity from educators as well as learners without using expensive tools.

Makers and Their Tools

Well-resourced schools embrace the maker movement by equipping labs with expensive items such as digital fabrication tools. It may appear that high-needs schools are left behind, under the presumption that high-tech equipment is required to establish a makerspace. The problem with this presumption is that learning in high-needs schools is passive, and the teaching approach focuses on discipline and management of student behavior. Makerspaces are defined by those who create the space, and "the most important guiding principle is the interest of students. Due to the learner focus of a makerspace, it is absolutely critical to take into account the interests of the targeted population" (Kurti et al., 2014, p. 9). This implies that high-tech digital fabrication tools might not be what is needed, depending on the context of the community (see Figure 8.4).

FIGURE 8.4 Hi- and Low-Tech Makerspace Tools

Note: Sessoms (2022).

One of the unique qualities of a makerspace is that the tools that are readily available are the only important tools.

In any educational setting, including high-needs schools, it is important to understand the interests of students and what arouses their curiosity. This is why makerspaces are diverse in terms of the focus and the types of tools selected. For example, in a makerspace at a public library in Toronto, the makerspace consisted entirely of tools for textiles and fashion. On the campus of Salisbury University (see Figure 8.5), there is a maker lab that only focuses on digital fabrication with 3D printers, while a makerspace at a local public-school library focuses on robotics.

Each makerspace has different equipment, although there is some overlap. Providing access to hands-on activities is crucial to fostering a maker mindset, where students learn more through play, develop growth mindsets, understand that failing is an iteration of learning, and collaborate with peers to solve problems, thereby developing attributes that are critical to 21st-century learning (Singh & Kim, 2019). Some tools and concepts can be classified as having "low thresholds, high ceilings, and wide walls" (Resnick et al., 2005, p. 3). This means a makerspace should not be intimidating and should provide learners with successes from failures, have powerful tools that can lead to student-centered solutions, and support a wide range of explorations.

FIGURE 8.5 Salisbury University Makerlab

Note: Reprinted with Permission from Salisbury University (Pusey, 2016).

Content-Neutral Technologies as a Pedagogical Response **107**

There are several ways for high-need schools to create makerspaces even with limited funding. An example is the concept of open-source tools. Open-source tools are created by a community of individuals who freely share their creations with the world. The Lifelong Kindergarten (n.d.) develops technologies focused on enhancing learning for all. In 2007, the group launched Scratch. Built around a community of coders, "Scratch promotes computational thinking and problem-solving skills; creative teaching and learning; self-expression and collaboration; and equity in computing" (About Scratch, n.d.). The tool can be used as a web-based platform or downloaded to a computer. Another open-source tool is Audacity, which is audio editing software. This tool, which can be downloaded for free, allows learners as young as in the third grade to create audio recordings for a variety of applications, such as podcasting or self-evaluation of reading skills. In addition, a variety of other tools allow any learner to create websites (e.g., Wix), share content (e.g., YouTube), create documents (e.g., Google Docs), and create 3D models (e.g., Tinkercad). For a high-needs school, these are the types of high-level software programs that allow learners to be creative and develop skills while demonstrating knowledge. Each of the tools is content neutral and can be used in various contexts.

High-end tools are a part of some makerspaces; however, students can benefit from a makerspace if high-end tools are not readily available. A student who creates a 3D model in Tinkercad can print that model even if the school does not have 3D printers by visiting a local library, a university space, or a community organization that has 3D printers. For example, among the Title I schools in Salisbury, Maryland, schools use 3D printers within schools (e.g., some of the schools have 3D printers in a media center), connect with the local university (e.g., Salisbury University), or access the entrepreneurship center in downtown Salisbury. Salisbury is not considered an affluent area; however, it still offers opportunities for high-needs schools to access quality experiences.

Projects that represent the intersection of high-tech tools and social ideas is one approach that can be used in a high-needs setting. Figures 8.6 and 8.7 show a stamp that was designed using Tinkercad and printed using a 3D printer at the Dave and Patsy Rommel Center for Entrepreneurship in Salisbury, Maryland. This is an example of how a concept such as social entrepreneurship may be infused into a public school curriculum as students use technology and research to address issues in a given community. Even if students in a high-needs school are not able to print an object, for example, addressing a social issue and designing an object as part of a bigger plan can yield a level of satisfaction, accomplishment, and demonstration of learning.

Other tools that can be found in a makerspace include low-tech tools that a teacher might already have in the classroom such as traditional craft materials, plastic bottles, cups, cardboard, and any other available materials. Because of the expense, the only tool that might be difficult for high-needs schools to obtain is hardware, which may include 3D printers, laser cutters, robots, and computers.

FIGURE 8.6 Kindness Stamp Created by Students in an Education Program
Note: Sessoms (2022).

FIGURE 8.7 Bottom of the Stamp Stating, "Certified Kindness Spreader"
Note: Sessoms (2022).

But although hardware can be expensive, and there are limited ways to obtain open-source hardware tools, options are available that allow a high-needs school to access high-end hardware tools. For example, Birdbrain technologies has a loaner program to which teachers can apply for a classroom set of robots to use for a specified period of time. While robots are not completely content neutral, as math and science might be the first thought with respect to robots, there are creative applications of robots in other content areas such as language arts and humanities. From a language arts perspective, robots can be used to enhance reading comprehension. After reading a text, a pair of students might program the robots to interact and communicate in ways relevant to the content of the book. Robots such as Dash & Dot have an audible component, which would facilitate this type of activity.

As emphasized, the most important aspect of the makerspace is the mindset of making to learn. Even though a high-needs school may not have some of the more expensive equipment, it is possible to instill a variety of skills in students using low-cost and free tools. Companies such as SparkFun might donate hardware to schools that are starting makerspaces, especially those serving high-need populations. When high-needs schools are considering a makerspace, it is not necessary to focus on the cost, because a makerspace can be started with donated materials or materials found in the community. You will read about William Kamkwamba in a later section, which will highlight the importance of not thinking about cost; rather, the focus should be on developing the ingenuity of learners in high-needs schools through making.

Maker Philosophy and Pedagogy

A makerspace must include an intentional focus on processes such as critical thinking, problem solving, collaboration, and sharing. At the core of the makerspace concept is "developing ideas and theories and pursuing answers and solutions to real-world issues" (ISTE Standards for Students, 2021, 1.3.d). A variety of learning methodologies can be used interchangeably based on the objective of the learning experience, as it is not uncommon for educators to shift from one instructional method to another depending on the needs of the students. For example, direct instruction might be employed to teach students a new skill such as sewing or how to create a simple circuit, whereas a problem-based learning approach might be used to provide learners with an opportunity to independently find solutions to a given problem using the new skills gained from direct instruction.

As students gain new skills, learning can naturally morph from a teacher-centered to a student-centered approach, in which students drive their own learning, which requires educators to plan for students to create or make artifacts. Engagement with technology must transcend current practices in which technology is used unconsciously, without making room for students to understand how to learn with technology (Anderson et al., 2021).

Design Thinking, Making, and Learning

An educator's ingenuity, tenacity, and development of learning experiences might be the only reliable intersection with cutting-edge technology applications, both hardware and software, that students in high-needs schools encounter. As Watkins and Cho (2018) concluded, "school was the last, best chance for many of the students in their study to find their unique pathway to opportunity" (p. 16). Similarly, any high-needs school has the capacity to be innovative by creating spaces that focus on mindsets, even if there is limited access to the latest technology.

Access to technology, access to an educator willing to explore and implement technology-infused learning experiences, and school leadership that understands the possibilities of transforming student learning with technology are concrete steps to manifesting a culture of making with technology in a high-needs school (Kormos, 2022; Anderson et al., 2021; Suppes et al., 2013). Technology use in schools has the potential to improve learning outcomes for all students, creating a necessity to prepare teachers with a technical and pedagogical set of skills that allows them to integrate various technologies in the classroom (Chapman et al., 2010). While tools are not the focus of the learning, they are an integral part of the depth to which learners can pursue, discover, create, and share knowledge.

Leadership includes a comprehensive vision for technology infusion and support of educators through timely professional development, both technological and pedagogical. Educators and administrators must learn to understand technology infusion across grades and content areas to create an environment that leverages the affordances of technology (Suppes et al., 2013). This is not an easy task because of all that must be done to ensure the well-being of students and their learning; however, students can thrive in tough conditions, as highlighted in experiments such as the power of self-organized learning (Mitra, 2012). The issues that many students in a high-needs school experience can create a barrier to success; however, to some extent, this can be mitigated by an educator who is skilled at cultivating relationships and willing to apply an innovative approach to teaching.

One method to accomplish the infusion of technology and create maker mindsets is implementing a makerspace. Employing a variety of technology-based learning experiences can encourage critical thinking, creativity, problem solving, collaboration, and empathy across all content areas. This might include high-tech applications such as 3D modeling, which has already entered K–12 education at all levels. In high-needs schools, 3D design and 3D artifact production can be curriculum-based learning activities that combine arts, crafts, and STEM subjects in multidisciplinary learning projects (Leinonen et al., 2020). For example, 3D modeling and literacy might be combined to create an interesting lesson focused on developing literacy skills, design thinking, and understanding social issues.

Creating artifacts is a cross-cutting concept that fits any content area; for example, a learner can create an artifact that represents a mathematical concept or objects that represent perceived meaning in literary works. In the following example, the focus is on an elementary school application that can be easily used in a high-needs setting and expanded to any grade level. The only aspects that will change are the level of the books used and the complexity of what is created using 3D software, as older students might have greater capacity for creating.

Elementary Level

Children's literature such as *Ruth and the Green Book* (Ramsey & Strauss, 2013) can be used for a multipart lesson. Lessons using children's literature might start with a class read-aloud, followed by a discussion in which students are given opportunities to delve into the story and share their thoughts—this can also be used at the high school level because reading aloud may inspire older students to read for pleasure (Ecroyd, 1991; Trelease, 2013). With *Ruth and the Green Book*, a variety of conversations are possible, for example, about comprehension, empathy, understanding historical challenges, and so on. After robust discussion, students can be assigned either of the following tasks: select an object from the book that they want to recreate or think of their own object to create to represent a theme in the book; both require critical thinking and creativity. With either choice, the object must represent a theme or concept from the book, which also requires the use of decoding and comprehension skills. After the object is selected, students can sketch ideas of how their object should look. This will also help with how a student might approach designing the object in the next phase, which is to use 3D modeling software such as Tinkercad. At this point, some trial and error might occur as students design their objects.

Finally, the objects can be printed and shared with the class. This might require coordination with a media specialist because, typically, a 3D printer, if available, is found in the media center of a school. Meaningful collaboration with a media specialist is useful for a variety of reasons anyway, as this human resource might have specialized skills. Even if no 3D printer is available, the process of creating the object can be achieved with free software, and "an empowering learning experience could stem from holding the self-fabricated artifact in hand and giving it a name" (Leinonen et al., 2020, p. 609). Using 3D modeling in this way is also an example of how a tool seemingly dedicated to math and science can be used across disciplines with creative applications.

Beyond the Elementary Level

Creating solutions for a community or for other students is a way to differentiate learning opportunities for older students. For example, ideas and inspiration could be drawn from the book *The Boy Who Harnessed the Wind*. This coming-of-age story about William Kamkwaba from a village in Malawi is also a story about the resilience of humans and how determination can be a catalyst for learning. As a young man, William grew up in poverty and, at night, he had to prematurely end his day because his family did not have electricity. Motivated by the desire to stay awake beyond sunset and with little money to attend his local high school, William began a journey of learning and invention that would change the lives of his family and his community and his own life—he invented a windmill to solve a problem for himself, his family, and his village.

With the self-determination of learning about science, specifically about the properties of electricity, William read books and embarked on a quest to learn all he could about how things worked, such as dynamos. Fascinated by science, he began to apply what he read in old books by constructing devices that would generate electricity. His resources for constructing a windmill consisted of whatever he could find in his community such as old wire, batteries, metal, and old bicycles. In stages, William brought electricity first to his room, then to his house, and then to others in his village. Unknowingly, he employed a design thinking process (Shanks, 2010).

Using the design thinking process, students in a high-needs school might be challenged to address an issue of interest to them in their community that parallels William's experience. This would have the potential of combining multiple content areas such as mathematics (data collection and analysis), language arts (writing), digital literacies (creating and sharing), and social studies (studying and enhancing communities). It could also include subjects such as levels of government, because a good starting place for students might be to speak with local officials who are familiar with pressing issues in a community. For example, students could investigate what has been tried and already exists, which could lead to new solutions or improvements to old ones.

An application of the concept illustrated in William's experience is the Building Unique Inventions to Launch Discovery, Engagement, Reasoning, and STEM (BUILDERS)—a project-based learning program that incorporates a makerspace concept. Students who participated in the program participated in an intensive summer learning experience focused on using science and technology to improve their community. In another project, Escobar and Qazi (2020) found that it is necessary to provide underserved students with learning opportunities focused on designing, building, and inventing. The goal of this program, which was conducted in an impoverished area of Alabama called the Southern Black Belt, was to incorporate activities as part of students' real lives. Connecting science and technology experiences with students' lives helps them be more successful in learning new concepts (Escobar & Qazi, 2020), similar to the experience of William as he realized he could harness the power of electricity to improve conditions in his personal life as well as his community (Kamkwamba & Mealer, 2016).

This example is illustrative of how makerspaces and the tools are content neutral—tools are used in ways discovered by learners to solve a particular problem. Students in the program began with introductory maker activities such as using common materials to solve a problem posed to the group, which focused on "building a sound attenuating enclosure that could mask the sound of a ringing cell phone" (Escobar & Qazi, 2020, p. 37). Similarly, William's first task, which can be viewed as an introduction to maker concepts, was to use a dynamo to generate power that would produce light for his room.

The teams of students held discussion sessions to hypothesize about the varying degrees of effectiveness for their enclosures. A problem-based learning approach was used in this makerspace, which also included the design thinking process. The process involved students moving through the phases of Figure 8.1. From sketching and prototyping to building and testing, the design thinking process was a natural part of what the students were doing in the BUILD project as they selected their own problem to be solved. Similarly, William was using a problem-based learning approach to solve a problem that he defined. An additional component of the makerspace was a set of mentors. Mentors are not always a part of a makerspace but are beneficial when available. Mentors might be teachers or local community members with expertise to share. What Escobar and Qazi (2020) and Kamkwamba and Meale (2016) demonstrated is something many educators know, which is, given the opportunity and proper guidance, any student can be successful at learning and using technology to solve problems despite the socio-economic context.

Conclusion

The maker movement is an innovation that does not belong to any particular community; it belongs to all communities. Making to learn is good for students at well-resourced schools as well as students in high-needs environments. Implementing a makerspace changes mindsets and promotes resourcefulness with the use of content-neutral technology. This means that a high-needs school can adopt the mindset and use makerspaces to engage learners at a deeper level using a variety of tools. While high-tech tools in a makerspace may be the purview of well-resourced schools, these tools do not define what students can do, and most tools in a makerspace can be content neutral. When students and teachers use creativity, almost any technology or tool can be used for a different purpose than originally intended. For example, a hanger was designed to organize clothes in a small space, but it can also be used as an antenna.

In 2013, former Secretary of Education Arne Duncan (2013) stated that it is up to all stakeholders (schools, districts, parents, and technologists) to ensure access to cutting-edge technology in low-income communities. Creating a maker environment and a maker mindset in high-needs schools is possible with the proper focus and leadership. Makerspaces have many benefits and adhere to the concept of Universal Design for Learning with a "no one-size-fits-all" ethos (Brown & Antink-Meyer, 2017). This also includes the space because any space can be used with the proper vision, materials, and the learning experiences generated by teachers in collaboration with students. Access to a maker environment and a maker mindset simultaneously benefits educators and learners: Learners are able to explore interests that might become lifelong passions, while educators can use their ingenuity to create opportunities based on their students' interests.

Key Takeaways:

1. Implementing a makerspace starts with a desire to provide learners with new learning experiences. Include students in the process if possible.
2. Generally, any technology can be repurposed to be content neutral. For example, iPads were not originally designed for public school settings. They were meant to be an easy way for the average person to consume content quickly and easily. Educators and researchers determined how they would be used in content-specific contexts.
3. Creating makerspaces in high-needs schools is no different than creating a makerspace in a well-resourced school; do not wait for the perfect situation to start building your makerspace. Do not wait for the perfect set of tools or resources. Now is the time to start, and any room in your building can be a makerspace.
4. It is important to develop new skills (e.g., complete courses about new makerspaces or visit a makerspace and talk to the developers).
5. Visit makerspaces in all contexts (e.g., libraries, museums, universities, and communities).
6. Get inspired by other makers.

Recommended Resources

- Finch Loan Program, www.birdbraintechnologies.com/loan-program/
  This is a loan program for educators to apply for and borrow robots.
- Free Software Foundation (FSF): www.fsf.org/resources/
  This foundation promotes the development and use of free software.
- Fundforteachers (www.fundforteachers.org/):
  Numerous grant resources for educators are offered by professional organizations (e.g., The National Education Association), local businesses, and other organizations.
- MakerED (https://makered.org/):
  This nonprofit organization provides maker resources to transform teaching and learning.
- Makergirl (https://makergirl.org/):
  This organization was created to inspire young girls to pursue STEM fields.

- MIT Lifelong Kindergarten (www.media.mit.edu/groups/lifelong-kindergarten/projects/):
  The MIT Media Lab develops technologies, activities, and communities to engage young people from all backgrounds in creative learning experiences so they can develop their thinking, their voices, and their identities.
- OLPC: https://laptop.org/
  OLPC provides computer access to students in high-needs schools.
- Raspberry Pi Foundation (www.raspberrypi.org/courses/learn-python):
  The Raspberry Pi Foundation offers free courses as well as professional development (pi academy).
- Sparkfuneducation (www.sparkfuneducation.com/):
  SparkFun provides open-source products that promote people sharing and learning.
- SparkFun Community Partnership Program (www.sparkfun.com/community_outreach):
  This is an example of an organization that donates hardware.
- The Hour of Code (https://code.org):
  Code.org provides free courses, classroom materials, and other resources about computer science.
- Tinkercad (www.tinkercad.com/):
  This is a free 3D modeling software with tutorials.

References

About Scratch. (n.d.). *Scratch.* https://scratch.mit.edu/about

Anderson, J., Rainie, L., & Vogels, E. A. (2021). Experts say the 'new normal' in 2025 will be far more tech-driven, presenting more big challenges. *Pew Research Center.* https://www.pewresearch.org/internet/2021/02/18/experts-say-the-new-normal-in-2025-will-be-far-more-tech-driven-presenting-more-big-challenges/

Barton, A. C., Tan, E., & Greenberg, D. (2017). The Makerspace movement: Sites of possibilities for equitable opportunities to engage underrepresented youth in STEM. *Teachers College Record, 119*(6), 1–44.

Brown, R. A., & Antink-Meyer, A. (2017). Makerspaces in informal settings. *Educational Technology, 57*(2), 75–77. www.jstor.org/stable/44430529.

Bull, G., Schmidt-Crawford, D. A., McKenna, M. C., & Cohoon, J. (2017). Storymaking: Combining making and storytelling in a school makerspace. *Theory into Practice, 56*(4), 271–281.

Carver-Thomas, D., & Darling-Hammond, L. (2017). *Teacher turnover: Why it matters and what we can do about it.* Learning Policy Institute.

Chapman, L., Masters, J., & Pedulla, J. (2010). Do digital divisions still persist in schools? access to technology and technical skills of teachers in high-needs schools in the United States of America. *Journal of Education for Teaching, 36*(2), 239–239.

Children's Museum of Pittsburgh. (2022, September 19). https://pittsburghkids.org/

Darling-Hammond, L. (2004). Inequality and the right to learn: Access to qualified teachers in California's public schools. *Teachers College Record, 106*, 1936–1966.

Davee, S., Regalla, L., & Chang, S. (2015, May). *Makerspaces: Highlights of select literature.* http://makered.org/wp-content/uploads/2015/08/Makerspace-Lit-Review-5B.pdf

Digital Harbor Foundation. (2022). *Learn, create, explore, build community.* www.digitalharbor.org

Dougherty, D. (2016). *Free to make: How the maker movement is changing our schools, our jobs, and our minds.* North Atlantic Books.

Duncan, A. (2013). Why we need high-speed schools. *Scientific American, 309*(2), 69–71. https://doi-org.proxy-su.researchport.umd.edu/10.1038/scientificamerican0813-69.

Ecroyd, C. A. (1991). Motivating students through reading aloud. *The English Journal, 80*(6), 76–78.

Ertmer, P. A., & Ottenbreit-Leftwich, A. T. (2010). Teacher technology change: How knowledge, confidence, beliefs, and culture intersect. *Journal of Research on Technology in Education, 42*(3), 255–284.

Escobar, M., & Qazi, M. (2020). Builders: A project-based learning experience to foster stem interest in students from underserved high schools. *Journal of STEM Education: Innovations & Research, 21*(3), 35–43.

Harris, J. B., Mishra, P., & Koehler, M. (2009). Teachers' technological pedagogical content knowledge and learning activity types: Curriculum-based technology integration reframed. *Journal of Research on Technology in Education, 41*(3), 393–416.

Hatch, M. (2014). *The maker movement manifesto: Rules for innovation in the new world of crafters, hackers, and tinkerers.* McGraw Hill.

Hughes, J., Laffler, J., Mamolo, A., Morrison, L., & Petrarca, D. (2016). *Full STEAM ahead: Building preservice teachers' capacity in makerspace pedagogies.* Paper presented at the Higher Education in Transformation Symposium, Oshawa, Ontario, Canada.

International Society for Technology in Education. (2017). *Standards for educators.* www.iste.org/standards/iste-standards-for-teachers

ISTE. (2021). *ISTE Standards for students.* www.iste.org. https://www.iste.org/standards/iste-standards-for-students

Johnson, S. M., Kraft, M. A., & Papay, J. P. (2012). How context matters in high-need schools: The effects of teachers' working conditions on their professional satisfaction and their students' achievement. *Teachers College Record, 114*(10), 1–39.

Kamkwamba, W., & Mealer, B. (2016). *The boy who harnessed the wind.* Puffin.

Khalifa, S., & Brahimi, T. (2017, February). Makerspace: A novel approach to creative learning. In *2017 Learning and Technology Conference (L&T)—The MakerSpace: From imagining to making!* (pp. 43–48). IEEE.

Kormos, E. (2022). Technology as a facilitator in the learning process in urban high-needs schools: Challenges and opportunities. *Education & Urban Society, 54*(2).

Kurti, R. S., Kurti, D., & Fleming, L. (2014). The environment and tools of great educational makerspaces. *Teacher Librarian, 42*(1), 8–12.

Lee, O., Quinn, H., & Valdés, G. (2013). Science and language for English language learners in relation to Next Generation Science Standards and with implications for Common Core State Standards for English language arts and mathematics. *Educational Researcher, 42*, 223–233.

Leinonen, T., Virnes, M., Hietala, I., & Brinck, J. (2020). 3D printing in the wild: Adopting digital fabrication in elementary school Education. *International Journal of Art & Design Education, 39*(3), 600–615.

Lifelong Kindergarten. (n.d.). *MIT media lab.* www.media.mit.edu/groups/lifelong-kindergarten/overview

Pusey, K. (2016). *People in a makerlab at Salisbury University* [Photograph]. Salisbury University. www.salisbury.edu/libraries/news/article/su-libraries-makerlab.aspx

Ramsey, C. A., & Strauss, G. (2013). *Ruth and the green book*. Lerner Publishing Group.

Resnick, M., Myers, B., Nakakoji, K., Shneiderman, B., Pausch, R., Selker, T., & Eisenberg, M. (2005). Design principles for tools to support creative thinking. In *NSF workshop report on creativity support tools* (pp. 25–35).

Roskos, K. A., & Christie, J. F. (2011). Mindbrain and play-literacy connections. *Journal of Early Childhood Literacy, 11*(1), 73–94.

Sessoms, D. (2019, August). *Participants collaborating on a raspberry pi project* [Photograph].

Sessoms, D. (2022a, March). *Kindness stamp created by students in an education program* [Photograph].

Sessoms, D. (2022b, March). *Bottom of the stamp stating, "Certified Kindness Spreader"* [Photograph].

Sessoms, D. (2022c, April). *Student creating blackout poetry* [Photograph].

Sessoms, D. (2022d, April). *Makerspace created by Dr. Sessoms at Salisbury University* [Photograph].

Sessoms, D. (2022e, August). *Makerspace tools* [Photograph].

Shanks, M. (2010). *An introduction to design thinking.* www.web.stanford.edu/~mshanks/MichaelShanks/files/509554.pdf

Sheridan, K., Halverson, E. R., Litts, B., Brahms, L., Jacobs-Priebe, L., & Owens, T. (2014). Learning in the making: A comparative case study of three makerspaces. *Harvard Educational Review, 84*(4), 505–531.

Sing, R., & Kim, Y.J. (2019). Systematic approach to develop sustainable makerspaces in resource-constrained schools. In *Proceedings of Fablearn 2019* (pp. 164–167). https://doi.org/10.1145/3311890.3311917

Suppes, P., Holland, P. W., Hu, Y., & Vu, M. T. (2013). Effectiveness of an individualized computer-driven online math K-5 course in eight California Title I elementary schools. *Educational Assessment, 18*(3), 162–181.

The IRIS Center. (2010, 2020). *Assistive technology: An overview.* https://iris.peabody.vanderbilt.edu/module/at/

Tondeur, J., van Braak, J., Ertmer, P. A., & Ottenbreit-Leftwich, A. (2017). Understanding the relationship between teachers' pedagogical beliefs and technology use in education: A systematic review of qualitative evidence. *Educational Technology Research and Development, 65*(3), 555–575.

Trelease, J. (2013). *The read-aloud handbook*. Penguin.

Watkins, S. C. (2019). *Don't knock the hustle: Young creatives, tech ingenuity, and the making of a new innovation economy*. Beacon Press.

Watkins, S. C., & Cho, A. (2018). *The digital edge*. NYU Press.

9

STRATEGIES TO FACILITATE DIGITAL LEARNING IN URBAN HIGH-NEEDS SOCIAL STUDIES CLASSROOMS

Erik Kormos and Joe Sherman

Guiding Questions:

1. What are challenges related to digital learning in social studies class-rooms composed of urban high-needs learners?
2. How can social studies teachers in urban high-needs schools effectively incorporate technology in the teaching and learning process?

Introduction

This chapter explores the impact of the digital divide on digital learning in high-needs urban schools and suggests teaching strategies and technologies that can be incorporated into teaching practices in these settings. More specifically, the information is intended to serve as a starting point of a broader discussion on how interactive technologies can effectively be used in digital learning for all grade levels and content areas, including the importance of effective technology implementation in K–12 social studies classrooms as a means of increasing collaboration, communication, creativity, and critical thinking skills to enhance learning and prepare learners for success. As schools across the country face challenges related to online teaching, the digital divide within their school community, and engaging learners with technology, a more in-depth examination of high-needs schools is needed.

According to a statement by the United States Department of Education, "technology is at the core of virtually every aspect of our daily lives and work, and we must leverage it to provide engaging and powerful learning experiences and content" (2010, p. ix). For young learners, the U.S. Departments of Education and Health and Human Services developed the Early Learning and Educational

DOI:10.4324/9781003274537-12

Technology Policy Brief, which is intended to provide a template for educators in early learning settings. Among other things, the policies encourage collaboration between researchers and media and app developers. Within an educational setting, collaboration can be summarized as either a process or an outcome of joint activity (Nganga, 2019). When analyzing definitions across the literature, a trio of fundamental aspects differentiate collaboration: Learners (a) interact interdependently with two or more peers, (b) participate in an authentic joint activity, and (c) pool their knowledge, skills, and efforts (Budiarti et al., 2021).

The instructional design of social studies teaching and learning in urban high-needs schools should model the four Cs of P21's Framework for 21st Century Learning (critical thinking, communication, collaboration, and creativity) and develop globally competitive leaders (Partnership for 21st Century Skills, 2008). The four Cs are vital in the social studies learning process, as they incorporate executive function skills such as planning, organizing, and strategizing. When utilized effectively, these skills promote learner self-regulation along with working memory and cognitive flexibility, which encourages students to seek out new ideas as well as develop social-emotional capabilities (Budiarti et al., 2021). Utilizing elements of Universal Design for Learning (UDL), the four Cs can be used to create student-centered personalized learning opportunities; however, lessons and teaching strategies using this framework must be designed with intention (Nganga, 2019). For social studies educators, the component of creativity can maximize the UDL principles by leveraging knowledge and understanding to generate innovative ways of thinking to identify solutions to new problems and create new materials. To that end, educators should employ a variety of idea-creation techniques such as brainstorming to foster new and worthwhile ideas that also promote student ownership. Further, students should work in creative settings to promote inclusion of new and diverse perspectives (Budiarti et al., 2021).

Unfortunately, educators often face a dearth of knowledge to help identify learning technologies that best supplement traditional curriculum. It is important to recognize that education plays a vital role in training learners to be globally competitive learners. A predetermined framework is crucial for achieving implementation that fosters learning (Townsend & Cronin, 2017). The primary features of the 21st Century Learning framework include learning and innovation skills, as well as life and career readiness. As a result, social studies educators should design instruction and utilize technology to match the needs of their students.

Challenges and Obstacles in High-Needs Social Studies Classrooms

Like the communities they serve, urban high-needs schools are exceptional and unique learning environments. Urban student demographics are frequently primarily composed of African American learners, along with a significant increase in the number of Hispanic students over the last two decades (Bristol, 2018). Many variables in these schools, including financial resources and teacher professional development, merge to create a "digital divide," defined by Tustin (2014) as "the inequality in access to technology that exists between communities due to regional and demographic differences, particularly socioeconomic groups" (p. 4). Prior research revealed urban schools were significantly more likely to face substantial obstacles with regard to budgetary issues, teacher knowledge and capability, quality of teaching and supply, and behavioral issues than rural or suburban schools (Kormos, 2021; Lee et al., 2019).

Social studies teachers of high-needs learners must circumvent these and multiple other challenges to lessen the digital divide. While these districts generally feature larger student populations, the cumbersome bureaucratic framework can delay effective technology integration. In addition, high rates of teacher and administrative turnover in high-needs schools also lead to conflicting priorities. This lack of consistency often results in technologies being introduced only to be discarded soon after (Delpit, 2012; Michie, 2005). High-needs teacher self-perceptions of their ability to integrate technology are an additional threat. For example, Herold (2016) found K-12 educators were unlikely to report increased levels of self-efficacy and training in the use of educational technology. A third area of concern is teacher preparedness related to technology. Urban educators of color are twice as likely not to receive the necessary adequate professional development, skills, and knowledge to utilize technology in their teaching practices (Cosby et al., 2017). Taken together, these inequalities directly impact technology implementation in many high-needs social studies classrooms.

Compared to their colleagues in more affluent schools, teachers in high-needs settings have been found to demonstrate innovative integration at significantly lower rates and to be more likely to use technology for rote learning (Harris, 2016). High-needs educators also were more inclined to provide passive digital learning experiences centered around memorization instead of critical thinking. High-needs schools should seek educators who create learning activities that emphasize collaboration, creativity, leadership, and communication (McKnight et al., 2016). In the 21st-century classroom, social studies teachers may work asynchronously in a remote environment using communication platforms such as Zoom, Google Meet, or Microsoft Teams. However, high-needs educators are more inclined to promote introductory options for learners to demonstrate understanding of the subject matter such as presentation software or group work during class time (Buczynski & Mathews, 2016). As a large percentage of high-needs schools are low socioeconomic communities, technology integration may be hindered by financial limitations. In terms of per-capita student spending, high-needs schools trail districts in other settings (Lee et al., 2019).

Student Internet and Technology Access at Home

Even with robust financial resources dedicated to technology, there are challenges for successful implementation of digital learning in high-needs social studies classrooms. One obstacle is the high percentage of learners who lack reliable internet and technology access at home. For example, a quarter of households in Alabama lack home internet access. Further, the majority in four counties located in rural areas are devoid of the necessary infrastructure to provide connection at home. To the west in Mississippi, 30% of households are unable to connect to the internet. Even in Utah, the most wired state in the United States, approximately 10% of households are without home internet access (Archibald, 2019). However, the presence of internet access does not prevent connectivity issues. For example, 12% of families in the southeastern portion of Ohio have no internet or cable devices, and an additional 15% lack access to the minimum standard internet speed of 25 by 3 megabits per second (Doyle, 2020).

Unfortunately, urban schools encounter many of the same challenges related to reliable home technology and internet access for learners. According to the Cleveland (Ohio) Metropolitan School District, approximately 30% to 40% of their nearly 38,000 students do not have reliable home internet access. In other large urban districts, educators may struggle to contact their students using the internet. In the Los Angeles Unified School District, the second most populous in the U.S., nearly 13% of high school students never logged in during the initial COVID-related shutdown, and nearly one-third did not regularly participate in online learning (Goldstein et al., 2020). High-needs schools also may include substantial immigrant and nonimmigrant English language learner populations, two groups that are often left behind when it comes to digital learning. Yet learning technologies, such as Flipgrid and Google Suite for Education, can be particularly effective for these learners, as prior research found students became more comfortable speaking English after using the technology during the academic year (McLain, 2018).

The focus of any lesson plan involving digital learning should include directions, content, and outside resources so learners will continue hitting objectives based upon critical standards. Administrators and teachers should implement routines and structures to ensure students and families can stay connected to the learning process. Given the reality of the digital divide, schools need to ensure students have access to digital and nondigital content. Students of color are disproportionately affected: 37% of American Indian and Alaska Native children lack access to the internet at home, along with 19% of Black children and 17% of Hispanic children, compared to 12% of White and Asian children (Camera, 2020).

Suggested Technologies and Teaching Practices in High-Needs Social Studies Classrooms

Implementation Strategies

When planning to provide effective digital learning, it is essential to recognize that digital learning involves more than just moving content online to a learning management system from a seated classroom (Goldstein et al., 2020). Whether course content is delivered face-to-face or through a virtual modality, technology should serve as a pipeline through which the high-needs social studies teacher selects instructional strategies that are appropriate for their specific course, objective, or topic (Flanagan, 2019). When positive elements of technological and pedagogical knowledge are embraced, they can provide a high-level educational learning experience. Pelz (2009) identified three principles of effective digital learning pedagogy:

1. Let the students do most of the work. The more time students spend engaged with the content, the more they will learn.
2. Interactivity is the heart and soul of effective asynchronous learning.
3. Strive for presence: social, cognitive, and teacher presence. Effective online pedagogy promotes this interactivity and encourages teacher and student presence as essential to an effective online learning community.

Effective implementation of digital learning strategies will meet these criteria and provide the building blocks that can allow urban social studies teachers to develop a diverse pedagogical framework to help their learners.

While this point might seem obvious, it is important that high-needs social studies teachers continue to model principles of impactful learning. At the onset of any lesson incorporating technology, therefore, educators should introduce a clear plan of action and objectives and consistently offer students an opportunity to assess where they are within that structure. This can include classroom calendars and checklists to help students keep abreast of class deadlines and assignments to promote ownership and organization.

Urban, high-needs social studies educators should identify innovative strategies to establish an interactive digital learning community. One such option is through regularly framing questions to allow incorporation of students' personal experiences. For instance, teacher-created blogs can allow students to reply not only to the original prompt but to the replies of peers. By inviting active discussion in a digital platform that can be monitored, social studies teachers can use learner responses as an opportunity for more wide-ranging discussions. Through social learning, students can become more involved and gain understanding from each other to produce more effective content and learning experiences (Bandura & Walters, 1977). As an example, a student's response to a writing prompt about dealing with unease and anxiety around controversial topics can stimulate a discussion of the impact on mental health, cultural implications, and other topics. For social studies teachers, it would be best practice to record initial lessons centered around digital teaching and analyze them upon completion to specify strengths and weaknesses for improvement.

During the design and implementation process, high-needs social studies educators should pay special attention to ensuring equitable and high-quality educational opportunities that reflect the diversity of their learners. Interaction and differentiated learning pedagogy should be supported to help high-needs students navigate any shift to remote learning during these unsettled times (Catalano et al., 2021). Further, teachers from all content areas should investigate cross-curricular collaboration to focus on critical thinking and maximize student work time from home.

Regardless of student population or available educational technology tools, it is important for high-needs social studies educators to seek out and implement digital tools that students can access from home and that are user-friendly. An ever-increasing number of choices include built-in features such as quizzes, lectures, assessments, simulations and games, and interactions. Following are specific practices, strategies, and tips to ensure successful implementation of a digital learning plan that is research based, promotes student collaboration, and allows for demonstration of understanding pertaining to class standards and curriculum. It is important for social studies educators to examine multiple options to ensure appropriate technologies are selected. The vetting process should be centered around the collective and individual goals to create and deliver content and communicate with stakeholders.

An appropriate place to begin is allotting time to determine how to monitor, disseminate, and track student learning using a learning management system (LMS). The use of an LMS can simplify the process of managing remote learning by automating functions such as communication, learning materials assigned, submission of assignments, and grading. A final benefit of LMS usage is the capability to disseminate content on multiple electronic devices such as laptops, smartphones, and tablets (Townsend & Cronin, 2017). This is especially relevant for digital learning in high-needs schools that incorporate BYOD (bring your own device) policies so students can access course materials and content outside of school hours.

When selecting an LMS, it is important to ensure it is grounded in sound research. Features to evaluate include whether content is to be delivered synchronously or asynchronously. Many LMSs, such as Google Classroom and Canvas, can also allow high-needs social studies educators to elect their own online procedures. LMSs are great as well for creating a virtual classroom, where students can check in informally and submit assessments.

Technologies for the Urban High-Needs Social Studies Classroom

As with the incorporation of any new technology, it is imperative to conduct faculty training on LMS implementation. Training can occur in a seated environment or remotely utilizing platforms such as Zoom or Microsoft Teams.

One particular technology platform that may be of interest to urban, high-needs social studies teachers is Flipgrid. Students and educators may use this internet application on a computer, smartphone app, other devices, or as an integrated application. For the purpose of social studies education, the technology creates a learner-oriented community in which student voices can be heard and shared. Prior studies have indicated that video-recording applications are beneficial for student engagement and encouragement within a learning community (Dyment et al., 2020). Further, Flipgrid encourages learners of all ages to demonstrate higher-order thinking skills through verbal discussions, not just text-based messages of course content (Flanagan, 2019). This low-stakes platform can help students to develop their communication skills, particularly public speaking and nonverbal communication.

Learners receiving remote instruction often experience a sense of isolation due to the absence of peers to communicate with (McLain, 2018). In Flipgrid, topics can be created quickly and easily, allowing students to discuss ideas. Social studies teachers can create brief or extended-length videos on relevant topics based upon the knowledge level or conversation expected. Responses can range from 30 seconds up to 10 minutes, which enable learners to provide a snapshot into their understanding of content. The technology can also serve as a medium for communicating many teaching-related items such as expectations, parent encouragement, or assignment directions. Benefits include providing a forum for learners to view videos multiple times at their own convenience and enabling teachers to conduct formative assessments with individual students to measure understanding. When students record a video, they can either speak, right, read, or just listen to their peers and teachers. Learners can then interact with peers by recording video replies to each other's original recording.

Further, using the video prompt encourages students to build content through communication. Flipgrid allows for the utilization of spoken-word and nonverbal communication to help social studies learners develop a better understanding of class material. As students learn content, they develop the critical thinking skills necessary to navigate across information being presented. Lastly, students can produce an artifact, such as a poster or poem, to demonstrate mastery of a topic. For example, students could create a presentation using Google Slides, an infographic using Piktochart, or a piece of hand-drawn art as an assessment. Learners could then share their artifacts and get feedback from peers and their teacher to close learning gaps.

Communication between districts, schools, and educators should prioritize student connections with trusted school personnel. Platforms such as Remind, ClassDojo, and social media provide a clear, consistent, concise, and accessible communication plan that also allows for family access to information and resources. Materials and communications should be provided to ensure accessibility to students and parents with language needs. It is important that a two-way communication channel is developed to encourage and maintain interaction with clearly defined terms and ideas to avoid miscommunication. For both educators and students, expectations related to response time of emails and assignment feedback should be clearly stated and communicated to all stakeholders (Archambault et al., 2016).

Digital Learning in Urban High-Needs Social Studies Classrooms 125

When communicating with students using technology, teachers should maintain classroom customs and norms as much as possible. Educators should remind students of what is the best channel of communication to correspond with their teachers and peers, especially when students participate in a digital learning environment. Lastly, a minimum threshold for contact should be established and clearly defined for both teachers and students. When communicating with families, content-specific terms or educational jargon should be avoided as much as possible to avoid miscommunication or confusion. Teachers and administrators could utilize surveys to identify the specific needs of individual families to provide the best possible services to alleviate any deficiencies.

When possible, communication with families in the language with which they are most comfortable is recommended. Many English language learners may not have a support network at home since their parents may speak a native language other than English and, therefore, are unable to help them with class assignments (Tuttle et al., 2017). However, solutions are available such as Google Docs. The program offers translation capabilities for more than 70 languages to allow teachers to communicate with parents and caregivers who may speak another language.

School administrations may also provide recommendations for families on how to support their children to ensure academic and overall success during digital learning. Districts can also solicit caretaker feedback and provide timely information related to any updates concerning evolving policies (Smith et al., 2017). Criteria for communication among school employees should be established as well. This includes all relevant staff members and not just social studies teachers, especially paraprofessionals and related service providers, who are often left out of the communication loop. The communication channel for staff should address educational issues while also providing professional support.

When creating a digital learning plan, it is not enough to consider access to technology. Since homes often serve as a second classroom setting, it is vital to consider a broad range of family and home contexts. Faced with rapidly changing developments including health and economic disruptions, social studies teachers should ensure their method of digital learning accounts for a variety of factors. For instance, many high-needs students are at home alone after school hours while adults and parents may be at work in another location. Furthermore, many students are the caretakers of younger siblings or ill family members. In low-socioeconomic school districts, students may also need to take jobs to help financially support their families.

In addition, social studies teachers may also need support, encouragement, and compassion from administrators and peers to be successful and resilient. Many who work remotely, for example, are planning for the delivery of teaching material while also providing care for family members and helping their own children with schoolwork. It is vital that these educators are placed in a position in which they can balance their personal and professional responsibilities.

Conclusion

This chapter identified specific strategies for the urban social studies classroom in an effort to develop a digital learning framework that is inclusive of all students regardless of age, location, cultural background, socioeconomic status, and availability of technology resources at home. However, when planning to use these suggestions, it is important to take into consideration that each urban school community is unique. Together, social studies educators continue to share their time, thinking, and commitment to students in a fast-changing world. Hopefully, the strategies and tips provided in this chapter will allow them to discover a renewed commitment to their teaching practices. As most educators know, collective effort and thinking make their work all that more important.

To support administrators, educators, parents, and caregivers, the chapter provides a list of instructional resources that can be used to assist in making digital learning successful. The specific resources were selected because they are aligned with the major components of successful digital learning. They have the potential to be incorporated into digital teaching practices and include multiple options for content and grade-level instruction. All resources are either free or offered at a reduced price to educators and students and are intended as supplemental resources for social studies educators. The list is in no way exhaustive. It is recommended, therefore, that readers seek out additional support through searching the internet, speaking with peers, and building a database for personal, district, or building use.

Key Takeaways:

1. Develop interactive, technology-based lessons utilizing multiple resources to facilitate the exchange of information related to inquiry, participation, and evaluation. Technology provides an opportunity to bring history alive through oral histories, interviews, and the use of primary sources.
2. Provide learners opportunities to speak their truth related to course content and controversial social studies–related topics. Many students possess bold experiences that can serve as a platform for promoting diversity and challenge as social studies educators work on reducing prejudice or bias in content and provide student voice from multicultural perspectives.
3. Incorporate elements of computational thinking looking at historical monuments or buildings, attaining maps of historical events, creating ancient civilizations, or mapping migration patterns.

Recommended Resources

- Annenberg Learner (www.learner.org/subject/social-studies-history/): Resources for Grades 3–12 for American history, world history, economics and geography.
- Autism Speaks (www.autismspeaks.org/education-and-autism): Teaching students in Grades K-12 about the importance of understanding and acceptance of people with autism.
- Flip (https://info.flip.com/): Flip, formerly known as Flipgrid, connects millions of PreK to Ph.D. educators, learners, and families through short videos.
- National Constitution Center (https://constitutioncenter.org/learn/educational-resources): A site for Grades 3–12 with lessons and games to promote student understanding of the Constitution and how it continues to impact society.
- News in Slow (www.newsinslow.com/): Language learning for Grades 3–12 through current events. Educators can access news videos and courses with language lessons.
- Teaching Tolerance (www.tolerance.org/): Lessons and teaching strategies for Grades K-12 about social justice through a global and historical lens.
- Teaching With Primary Sources (TPS) (https://tpscollective.org/): Online hub for Grades K-12 that offers resources, professional development, and support for teachers who use primary sources.
- Smithsonian Learning Lab (https://learninglab.si.edu/): Offers Grades K-12 educators with millions of accessible, customizable, and shareable open educational resources.

References

Archambault, L., Kennedy, K., Shelton, C., Dalal, M., McAllister, L., & Huyett, S. (2016). Incremental progress: Re-examining field experiences in K-12 online learning contexts in the United States. *Journal of Online Learning Research, 2*(3), 303–326.

Archibald, R. (2019, December 27). Rural disconnect: Majority in some Alabama counties don't have internet access. *Alabama.com.* www.al.com/news/2019/12/rural-disconnect-majority-in-some-alabama-counties-dont-have-internet-access.html

Bandura, A., & Walters, R. H. (1977). *Social learning theory* (Vol. 1). Prentice Hall.

Bristol, T. J. (2018). To be alone or in a group: An exploration into how the school-based experiences differ for Black male teachers across one urban school district. *Urban Education, 53*(3), 334–354.

Buczynski, S., & Mathews, K. (2016, January). An urban school district's 21st century teaching vision: Integration and readiness to incorporate technology. In *Proceedings of the Global Science and Technology Forum* (p. 34). International Conference on Education and e-Learning (EeL), Singapore.

Budiarti, M., Macqueen, S., Reynolds, R., & Ferguson-Patrick, K. (2021). Global project based learning as an approach to teaching the 4Cs in schools. *Journal of International Social Studies, 11*(1), 33–62.

Camera, L. (2020, April 1). Disconnected and disadvantaged: Schools race to give students access. *U.S. News and World Report*. www.usnews.com/news/education-news/articles/2020-04-01/schools-rush-to-get-students-internet-access-during-coronavirus-pandemic

Catalano, A. J., Torff, B., & Anderson, K. S. (2021). Transitioning to online learning during the COVID-19 pandemic: Differences in access and participation among students in disadvantaged school districts. *The International Journal of Information and Learning Technology*, *38*(2), 258–270.

Cosby, M., Horton, A., & Berzina-Pitcher, I. (2017). Math is all around us: Exploring the teaching, learning, and professional development of three urban mathematics teachers. *Journal of Computers in Mathematics and Science Teaching*, *36*(3), 287–305.

Delpit, L. (2012). *Multiplication is for White people: Raising expectations for other people's children*. The New Press.

Doyle, C. (2020, August 25). Ohio's rural schools face unknown with in-person classes amid COVID. *The Columbus Dispatch*. www.dispatch.com/story/news/education/2020/08/25/ohiorsquos-rural-schools-face-unknown-with-in-person-classes-amid-covid/113488360/

Dyment, J., Stone, C., & Milthorpe, N. (2020). Beyond busy work: Rethinking the measurement of online student engagement. *Higher Education Research & Development*, *39*(7), 1440–1453.

Flanagan, B. (2019, April). *Creating community, enhancing engagement, and fostering verbal expression through a video discussion platform*. Presentation at the 2019 International Universal Design for Learning Implementation & Research Network Summit, Orlando, FL. https://doi.org/10.13140/RG.2.2.24667.62247

Goldstein, D., Popescu, A., & Hannah-Jones, N. (2020, April 8). As school moves online. Many students stay logged out. *The New York Times*. www.nytimes.com/2020/04/06/us/coronavirus-schools-attendance-absent.html

Harris, C. J. (2016). The effective integration of technology into schools' curriculum. *Distance Learning*, *13*(2), 27–37.

Herold, B. (2016, July 5). Teachers in high-poverty schools less confident in ed-tech skills, survey finds. *EdWeek Market Brief*. https://marketbrief.edweek.org/marketplace-k-12/teachers-in-high-poverty-schools-less-confident-in-ed-tech-skills-survey-finds/

Kormos, E. (2021). Technology as a facilitator in the learning process in urban high-needs schools: Challenges and opportunities. *Education and Urban Society*, *54*(2). https://doi.org/10.1177/00131245211004555

Lee, C. C., Akin, S., & Goodwin, A. L. (2019). Teacher candidates' intentions to teach: Implications for recruiting and retaining teachers in urban schools. *Journal of Education for Teaching*, *45*(5), 525–539.

McKnight, K., O'Malley, K., Ruzic, R., Horsley, M. K., Franey, J. J., & Bassett, K. (2016). Teaching in a digital age: How educators use technology to improve student learning. *Journal of Research on Technology in Education*, *48*(3), 194–211.

McLain, T. R. (2018). Integration of the video response app Flipgrid in the business writing classroom. *International Journal of Educational Technology and Learning*, *4*(2), 68–75. https://doi.org/10.20448/2003.42.68.75

Michie, G. (2005). *See you when we get there: Teaching for change in urban schools*. Teachers College Press.

Nganga, L. (2019). Preservice teachers perceptions of teaching for global mindedness and social justice: Using the 4Cs (collaboration, critical thinking, creativity and communication) in teacher education. *Journal of Social Studies Education Research*, *10*(4), 26–57.

Partnership for 21st Century Skills. (2008). *A report and mile guide for 21st century skills.* www.21stCenturyskills.org/downloads/P21_Report.pdf

Pelz, B. (2009). (My) three principles of effective online pedagogy. *Journal of Asynchronous Learning Networks, 14,* 103–116.

Smith, S. J., Ortiz, K., Rice, M., & Mellard, D. (2017). *Parents' perceptions of special education service delivery when their children move to fully online learning.* University of Kansas, Center on Online Learning and Students with Disabilities.

Townsend, S. D. C., & Cronin, A. L. (2017, December 27–28). The universal access framework: An architecture for uniting learning with mobile phones. In *Proceedings of the 29th International Conference on Teaching, Education & Learning (ICTEL),* Bangkok.

Tustin, N. (2014). The role of patient satisfaction in online health information seeking. *Journal of Health Communication, 15,* 3–17.

Tuttle, N., Mentzer, G. A., Strickler, L., Bloomquist, D., Hapgood, S., Molitor, S., & Czerniak, C. M. (2017). Exploring how families do science together: Adult-child interactions at community science events. *School Science and Mathematics, 117*(5), 175–182.

United States Department of Education. (2010). *Transforming American education: Learning powered by technology.* www.ed.gov/sites/default/files/netp2010.pdf

10

DESIGNING A CULTURALLY RESPONSIVE MULTILINGUAL ARTS-INTEGRATION PROGRAM

Read-Aloud and Book-Inspired Art-Making Videos

Heejung An, Triada Samaras, Maria Lanni, and Nisreen Rajab

Guiding Questions:

- How can educators embed culturally responsive teaching elements into read-aloud and art-making videos?

  o How can educators identify culturally responsive books to record?
  o How can arts integration facilitate culturally responsive learning opportunities?

Introduction

During the COVID-19 pandemic, when most U.S. public schools were closed for in-person instruction, read-aloud instructional videos gained popularity as millions of K-12 students had to take courses online from home (Ferfeli, 2022; Fuada & Marhamah, 2021; Nesset et al., 2022). A broad range of content was easily accessible on YouTube and helped fulfill urgent learning needs. For example, listening to books read by adults via video has been found to promote feelings of contentment among students, which, in turn, enhanced their capacity to learn (Marchessault & Larwin, 2013). In addition, listening to books has been documented to be more entertaining, engaging, exciting, and theatrical (Rahiem, 2021) than other modes of communication.

When attempting to leverage the aforementioned positive aspects of this instructional video format to promote inclusive education, it is important to ensure that read-aloud videos represent the current demographics of classrooms

DOI:10.4324/9781003274537-13

in the United States, where the student population is becoming increasingly diverse—ethnically, culturally, and linguistically (National Center for Education Statistics, 2022). As such, conscientious planning before recording or selecting read-aloud videos is essential to increase their benefit for diverse students, particularly in high-needs schools. Liu (2015) noted that when the cultural content of the text is familiar, students find it easier to connect with it. Further, if they have some understanding of the target culture, students are more likely to predict vocabulary usage and the meaning of the content. In addition, growing evidence indicates that dual-language learners benefit from emergent literacy instruction that promotes their bilingual and biliterate development at an early age (Anthony et al., 2011; Soto et al., 2020), leading to a deeper understanding of language and how to use it more effectively (Cummins, 2001).

Understanding the culturally relevant content of a text and its usage can also be deepened by art-making activities via arts integration. That is, through incorporation of the arts, students learn to explore content in a multitude of ways with multiple sign systems (Reif & Grant, 2010). Horowitz and Webb-Dempsey (2002) described the relationship between the arts and other content learning as "parallel, symbiotic, interactive or multi-layered" (p. 100). Specifically, the benefits of incorporating the arts include greater academic achievement (Rabkin & Redmond, 2006; Ruppert, 2006), increased cultural understanding, enhanced self-esteem, and a healthier cultural identity (Graham, 2009; Purnell et al., 2007), all qualities needed in our increasingly diverse society.

In response to these findings, the authors enhanced and expanded the impact of read-aloud videos by incorporating book-inspired, hands-on arts activities in multiple languages designed to foster the transition from the digital world to the real world and accelerate learning in both of these realms, thereby enriching the overall learning experience. Moreover, as an added benefit, we suggested using materials easily found in students' homes, which has been found to invite students' cultures directly into their work and encourage cross-cultural responses (Krauss & LaRiviere, 2022).

In this chapter, we present a culturally responsive, multilingual art-integration program called Learning Arts at Home (LAH) (www.learningartsathome.com) that contains two types of videos: read-aloud videos and book-inspired art-making videos. LAH was originally developed at the onset of school closures necessitated by the COVID-19 pandemic during the spring of 2020 to support high-needs school communities, especially schools with a high percentage of students who speak Spanish, Arabic, and Bengali. The program has since been expanded as a teaching and learning tool.

Background

Since 2017, the first author of this study has been directing an arts–integration program entitled "Inclusive Arts Integration" to support partner high-needs schools in the Paterson Public Schools District, New Jersey, funded by the Geraldine R.

Dodge Foundation. All New Jersey public school districts are assessed by District Factor Groupings (DFGs), a single measure of socioeconomic status based on the percentage of adult residents who failed to complete high school, along with their income, level of unemployment, and the percentage living below the poverty level. From the lowest SES to the highest, the categories are A, B, CD, DE, FG, GH, I, and J (New Jersey Department of Education [NJDOE], n.d.). The Paterson Public School District falls in the lowest of these eight groupings, Group A. In this district, more than 4,000 students are classified as having limited English proficiency, with Spanish, Arabic, and Bengali being the home languages most frequently spoken.

As shown in an interactive map depicting internet and computer access in New Jersey (O'Dea, 2018) prior to the COVID-19 pandemic, approximately 70% of households in the district did not have either internet or computer access. During the COVID-19 lockdowns, the gaps in opportunities, access, and a sense of belonging that many Paterson students experienced due to systemic inequities became even more evident. As such, it has become a nationally pressing issue for teachers to make purposeful efforts to foster mutual respect among students by decreasing negative stereotyping (Noll, 2003), developing empathy (Gordon, 2019), and eliciting more participation and engagement in instructional conversations with children (Christ & Sharma, 2018) by "helping them acquire a critical awareness of other cultures, beliefs, languages, and experiences" (Ambe, 2006, p. 691). Thus, LAH was created as a way to provide continuous support as a part of the grant partner schools.

Program Design: Learning Arts at Home

Conceptual Framework

LAH's design draws upon the theoretical lens of culturally responsive teaching (CRT), defined as "using the cultural characteristics, experiences, and perspectives of ethnically diverse students as conduits for teaching them more effectively" (Gay, 2002, p. 106). CRT is based on the assumption that when academic knowledge and skills are situated within students' lived experiences and frames of reference, they are more personally meaningful, have higher interest appeal, and are learned more easily and thoroughly. Further, CRT emphasizes that culture and education are not only inseparable but interconnected, which involves incorporating cultural diversity into educative processes intended for ethnically diverse students. "Culture" here refers to the "customs, languages, values, beliefs, and achievements of a group of people" (Will & Najarro, 2022, para 8). Finally, CRT includes the contributions of different ethnic groups in various areas of mainstream culture, helping students continuously build their ethnic identities and develop positive cross-cultural relationships (Gay, 2018).

Despite some similarities, culturally responsive education differs from multicultural and social justice education. Specifically, according to Hammond (2017), multicultural education focuses on celebrating diversity and centers around creating positive social interactions across differences, whereas social justice education focuses on exposing the social-political context that students experience and centers around raising students' consciousness about inequity in everyday social, environmental, economic, and political aspects of life. Culturally responsive education, on the other hand, focuses on improving the learning capacity of diverse students who have been marginalized educationally and, therefore, centers around the affective and cognitive aspects of teaching and learning, as summarized in Table 10.1. According to Hammond (2017), multicultural and social justice education plays more of a supporting role in culturally responsive teaching. Finally, Hammond (2017) emphasized that educators must understand the importance of having a social-emotional connection with their students in order to create a safe space for learning.

LAH advocates for a culturally responsive teaching approach that encourages and prepares students to ultimately become independent learners and succeed in a diverse society. As such, the CRT framework guided (a) the selection of books

TABLE 10.1 Distinctions of Equity

Multicultural Education	Social Justice Education	Culturally Responsive Education
Focuses on celebrating diversity.	Focuses on exposing the social-political context that students experience.	Focuses on improving the learning capacity of diverse students who have been marginalized educationally.
Centers around creating positive social interactions across differences. *Diversity and inclusion efforts live here.*	Centers around raising students' consciousness about inequity in everyday social, environmental, economic, and political situations. *Antiracist efforts live here.*	Centers around the affective and cognitive aspects of teaching and learning. *Efforts to accelerate learning live here.*
Concerns itself with exposing privileged students to multiple perspectives and other cultures. For students of color, the focus is on seeing themselves reflected in the curriculum.	Concerns itself with creating a lens to recognize and interrupt inequitable patterns and practices in society.	Concerns itself with building cognitive capacity and an academic mindset by pushing back on dominant narratives about people of color.
Social Harmony	**Critical Consciousness**	**Independent Learning for Agency**

Note: From Hammond, Z. (2017). *Culturally responsive teaching and the brain.* © Corwin. Reprinted with Permission.

for read-aloud videos, (b) the design of art-making activities, and (c) the means by which the narrators facilitated teaching strategies in the LAH program.

LAH Goals

Taking into account the barriers that students were facing in the partner high-needs schools, such as (a) a lack of access to computers and internet network servers, (b) language barriers, (c) insufficient art supplies and art activities, and (c) home environments that were not conducive to reading, LAH included digital read-aloud videos and interactive art-making activities inspired by books narrated in English, Spanish, Arabic, and Bengali that students could watch on their phones while using art supplies easily found at home (Note: Except for a few entries currently posted on the LAH website, videos narrated in Bengali are still being developed and, therefore, will not be presented in this chapter).

The primary goals of LAH are as follows:

1. To provide and support teachers and students with culturally responsive read-aloud videos and art-creation videos for use in both general and bilingual classes as well as at home.
2. To use arts integration as a means of teaching content areas, especially literacy and social studies.

Criteria for Selecting Books to Record

To select culturally responsive books for our LAH target students, a three-part model that blended quantitative and qualitative measures of text complexity with reader/viewer and task considerations was used to assess the complexity of the texts for the read-aloud. The cultural diversity element was considered across the three measures (see Figure 10.1). Even though these three measures were equally important when selecting text, the qualitative measures and reader and task considerations were prioritized. The quantitative measures were not dominantly used since the teachers were performing the actual act of reading the text. However, this measure was used to select the books for the read-aloud since it was important to set parameters for choosing books that met students' grade levels, which, in the case for LAH, were K-6.

Three-Part Model

The following provides a detailed description of each measure of the model and its application to the book *Soñadores* (*Dreamers*) by Yuyi Morales as an example of how this text was selected in the LAH project.

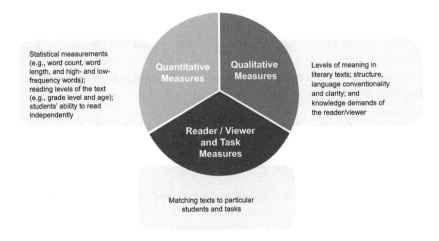

FIGURE 10.1 Criteria for Selection of Books to Record

Quantitative Measures

Quantitative measures refer to the statistical measurements of texts and consider features that can be quantified. Additionally, quantitative measures can determine the reading levels of a text (Learning A-Z, 2022). These measures include (a) word count, word length, high- and low-frequency words, sentence length, text cohesion, the complexity of the meaning, and sentence structure (Common Core State Standards Initiative, 2022); (b) grade levels and age ranges; and (c) whether students have the skills necessary to independently read a particular book or need adult support.

Along with the other two measures (qualitative measures and reader and task), the quantitative measures add another layer of coherence to book selection when it comes to the students' decoding skills and language proficiency, especially for English learners (ELs). To quantitatively measure text complexity, teachers can use tools such as Lexile, ATOS®, Degrees of Reading Power (DRP)®, Flesch-Kincaid, and the Pearson Reading Maturity Metric, among others (Common Core State Standards Initiative, 2022).

As an example, according to Lexile, the nonfiction book *Soñadores* by the Mexican author Yuyi Morales has a Spanish Lexile measure of AD260L and a Spanish Guided Reading Level of "O" (Scholastic, 2022). The same book in the English version, *Dreamers*, has a Lexile measure of AD480L and a Guided Reading of Level M. According to Lexile.com (2022), the recommended age range for the book is 4 to 8 years, or Grades K to 3, and the book is suggested to be used for read-alouds by an adult rather than having students read independently at that age level.

Qualitative Measures

Qualitative measures include text attributes that indicate the difficulty of a text. These measures are determined by a human reader and are comprised of four factors, referred to as aspects of text complexity (Common Core State Standards Initiative, 2022):

a.   **Levels of meaning or purpose.** Literary texts include single or multiple levels of meaning indicating the difficulty for the reader. Similarly, informational texts contain explicit or implicit purposes that determine the level of reading comprehension.
b.   **Structure** refers to conventional or unconventional structures, manipulation of time and sequence, common genres, conventions of a specific discipline, and even the complexity of the illustrations.
c.   **Language conventionality and clarity** indicate whether the text relies on literal or conversational language, as well as domain-specific vocabulary.
d.   **Knowledge demands** take into consideration the appropriateness of the text to the readers' experiences and cultural, literary, and discipline knowledge.

The CRT element was taken into consideration when choosing read-aloud books for the LAH, which includes various types of diversity listed in the wheel shown in Figure 10.2. Since young children, in an unconscious manner, absorb stereotypes presented to them, the books chosen for the read-aloud in LAH portray positive perspectives of all the cultural groups that are represented in the text—in their content and illustrations. Given this importance, the text and images were examined to ensure that they genuinely depicted people with distinctive rather than stereotypical features and avoid derogatory and inaccurate messages about any cultural group (Derman-Sparks, 2016). Moreover, the biographical information of the authors and illustrators of the books were taken into account to corroborate the book creators' backgrounds and qualifications to represent the cultures they portrayed in their books. Certainly, authors tend to write from their personal perspective and upbringing (Derman-Sparks, 2016). Accordingly, authors from various nationalities such as American, Cuban, Mexican, Peruvian, Guatemalan, Puerto Rican, African-American, Chinese, West African, East African, Egyptian, Spanish (Spain), Arab-American, Arab-Canadian, Palestinian, Jordanian, and so on were incorporated in the LAH read-aloud videos.

As an example, the nonfiction book *Soñadores* (*Dreamers*) by Yuyi Morales, Mexican author and illustrator, is mainly located under Race/Ethnicity in the diversity wheel shown in Figure 10.2. While the content and the structure of the book may not be appropriate for the reading levels of lower-elementary students, given the purpose of choosing texts to be read aloud by an adult, books may be read at levels higher than the students' reading levels. In addition, best practice

A Culturally Responsive Multilingual Arts-Integration Program   137

suggests choosing syntactically complex texts and engaging students in rich academic language for read-aloud activities.

Another qualitative attribute observed in this book is the presence of multiple levels of meaning in the text such as, "we bundle gifts in our backpack," which refers to the culture, value, tradition, hope, and so on, migrants bring to the new country. The book also includes figurative language, such as "The sky and the land welcomed us in words unlike those of our ancestors," referring to the new and unknown language the characters encounter when they move to the new country. Moreover, the book presents some literary and complex discipline-specific knowledge, so in order for the LAH students to have access to the story and be able to comprehend the text, they need specific relevant information. As a result, during this read-aloud video, background knowledge is encouraged from students and built for them. Furthermore, this picture book shows rich illustrations that are used to connect to the storyline to support students' comprehension. Even though some of the cultural elements in the illustrations are familiar to a large portion of students, specifically students from Mexico, students with a different Latino Spanish-speaking background might not be familiar with them. Therefore, the narrator purposely explains the meaning of the cultural Mexican

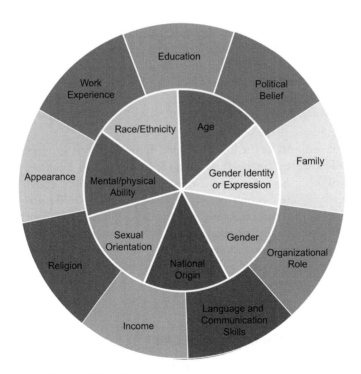

FIGURE 10.2   Diversity Wheel

Note: Johns Hopkins Office of Diversity and Inclusion. Reprinted with permission.

elements illustrated in the book, specifically the ones representing the "gifts" the character brings to the United States. Besides, the narrator connects these illustrations to the "gifts" immigrants from any country bring to their new country. Finally, the knowledge demands on the LAH audience were taken into consideration when selecting this book to meet the criterion of relating the story to students' life experiences.

Reader/Viewer and Task Measures

The reader/viewer and task measures focus on the variables that are specifically considered for a particular reader/viewer and for a particular task when determining if a text is appropriate for a given student. In order for teachers or other adults to assess and match texts to students and tasks, they must bring into play their own experiences and expert opinions about their students and the subject areas. These measures are directly connected to the appropriateness of the texts to students' knowledge or reading skills required to be able to reach the standards and learning objectives. According to Common Core State Standards Initiative (2022), the variables for reader include students' cognitive capabilities, motivation, and knowledge of the vocabulary and topic. For instance, when the text tells a story or contains information that the students are interested in, they are motivated to put in extra effort to read even harder texts and accomplish more complex tasks.

Finally, the task-related variables derived from a particular text include (a) the complexity of the task designed for the students; (b) the difficulty of the questions created for the students; (c) the reader's purpose; that is, whether students just browse the text or study the information in the text; and (d) the reader's intended outcome, such as increasing knowledge, looking for a solution to a problem, or simply engaging with the text.

Since the majority of the LAH audience in the grant partner schools are the children of immigrant families from Latino Spanish-speaking countries, the read-aloud based on the book *Soñadores* (*Dreamers*) is directly responsive to those families' experiences, interests, and motivations to read and listen to the story. Indeed, the book is about a Mexican family moving to the United States, carrying with them their culture as they encounter several cultural differences between the two places to finally achieve their dream in the new country. During this read-aloud, the narrator encourages children to develop critical analytic abilities by using open-ended questions and making inferences that are part of the standards teachers have to address.

Teaching Pedagogies Employed in LAH

The types of pedagogies employed to facilitate culturally responsive teaching in LAH fall into three areas: (a) arts-integration pedagogy, (b) literacy-development pedagogy, and (c) artistic-development pedagogy.

Arts-Integration Pedagogy

Arts integration may be described as "an interdisciplinary teaching practice through which nonarts and arts content is taught and assessed equitably in order to deepen students' understanding of both" (New Jersey Principals and Supervisors [NJPSA], 2020, p. 15). In LAH, book read-aloud videos are combined with concrete art-making lessons that bridge the virtual and "real" worlds for students. In addition, students learn the main concepts of the books across two or more disciplines, that is, involving inter- and transdisciplinary education.

In arts-integration pedagogy, the flow of ideas across disciplines and cultures and the crossing of former boundaries naturally create a lively and humanistic learning experience and inspire learners to venture into new learning territories. Arts-integration activities in LAH are inspired by the content areas in the books and by the goal to create culturally responsive art activities. LAH lessons encourage students to experience art creation and learning more holistically.

Arts-integration pedagogy in LAH supports cultural pedagogies. That is, students are able to draw on their "funds of knowledge," defined as the "assets, skills, and cultural capital they bring to the learning experience every day" (Overby et al., 2022, p. 20). Students' lived experience is implicit in the creation of the read-aloud and art-making videos, and no singular story is dominant. Further, LAH videos embed the implicit recognition of a variety of learning intelligences (Gardner, 2011).

Literacy Development Pedagogy

In the process of producing culturally responsive read-aloud videos, we used the following instructional techniques to facilitate literacy development.

Using Props

The use of props in read-aloud activities is an enriching experience for students because it not only encourages an enjoyable connection between children and books but also helps to draw their attention to the stories by deepening their understanding (Brun, 2018).

Doing a Picture Walk

Picture walks involve students closely examining the illustrations and structure of a book to look for elements that might be challenging or surprising for them. In addition, warming up before the read-aloud allows students to prepare, get in the proper mindset, and be more engaged in the reading activity. Besides generating interest and excitement, picture walks can also serve as a preview for main concepts and vocabulary, which will make the read-aloud more accessible to students

(Hudson, 2018). Thus, in some of the LAH read-aloud videos, the narrators spend time showing and explaining the cultural meaning of illustrations to connect with students' background knowledge and make them aware of aspects of cultures different from theirs.

Encouraging Students' Background Knowledge

The process of comprehending meaning requires readers to be familiar with the vocabulary and to be able to associate essential information from the reading with their prior knowledge. Besides linguistic knowledge, students should use their world knowledge and experiences to comprehend a text (Fathi & Afzali, 2020). Indeed, the ability to understand a text is based not only on the reader's linguistic knowledge but also on their general knowledge of the world. Therefore, it is important to consider the reader's cross-cultural background knowledge, given that culturally relevant information, such as prior and familiar experience, is a valuable instructional strategy for reading comprehension.

Making Connections

In order to foster students' literacy development, Küçükoğlu (2013) addressed three types of making connections, all of which the narrators in LAH employed in the read-alouds: (a) text-to-self connections—when students connect the ideas in the text to their own experiences and knowledge, (b) text-to-the-world connections—when students connect the events from the outside world to their own experience and knowledge, and (c) text-to-text connections—when the characters or story elements relate to each other between stories. These types of connections are used to help students understand the readings, since activating their prior knowledge makes reading meaningful (Küçükoğlu, 2013).

Asking Open-Ended Questions

In order to encourage students to develop higher-level thinking while reflecting, reacting, and connecting to a story, LAH incorporates open-ended questions. Furthermore, open-ended prompts help students increase their expressive language, fluency, and attention to detail. These kinds of questions are better used with picture books, especially with books that have rich and detailed illustrations (Whitehurst, 2002).

Modeling Fluent Reading

In order to interpret the characters and concepts in a book during the read-aloud, the reader/viewer has to gain an understanding of how words are phrased and expressed. Also, fluency during the read-aloud increases students' engagement and enjoyment (Children's Literacy Initiative, n.d.). It is suggested that by listening to good models of fluent reading, students can learn how a reader's voice can help written texts make sense. Thus, the read-aloud activities in LAH demonstrate expressive sounds (tone, phrasing, mood, rhythm, pitch, and pacing) to facilitate modeling of how a fluent reader sounds while reading (Texas Education Agency, 2022), thereby fostering children's ability to make sense of the story and to scaffold their comprehension.

Artistic Development Pedagogy

With the goal of creating culturally responsive art-making videos, we used the following strategies to facilitate artistic development.

Using Materials Found at Home

By asking students and their families to use simple art materials and other items found at home to create art projects, LAH emphasizes culturally responsive teaching, including an acknowledgment of students' real lives. In LAH, students are encouraged to use their natural "funds of knowledge." Students can create book-inspired artworks at home, enabling LAH to recognize the voices of those who have historically been on the margins. When students use their funds of knowledge to create art that is personally meaningful and culturally relevant, their creative process becomes more transparent and integral to their home environment, inviting family participation and shared experiences (Overby et al., 2022).

Exposing Students to a Variety of Art Media and Practices

Art-making lessons in LAH are designed with a variety of media and techniques in mind. Lessons include the creation of artworks in both 2D and 3D art media, the use of digital art-making techniques using the cellphone, the frequent use of recycled art materials, and the use of culturally informed art techniques and methods. Lessons are all designed to engage students, inform them about art creation, and elicit their responses to the books chosen for the read-alouds.

Making Connections Through a Digital Community Art Display

Students who watch the art-making videos are encouraged to submit their work to be posted on the LAH website. Displaying student art to the LAH community in a safe digital space is a form of socializing and community building that supports the goals of social and emotional learning (SEL) practice stated in the New Jersey Student Learning Standards for Visual and Performing Arts (Department of Education, State of New Jersey, 2020). LAH embraces the SEL values of "feeling seen, heard and valued" (Fennell, 2022, p. 4). In LAH, relationships as well as artistic development are prioritized, giving students a sense of belonging and agency (NJDOE, 2021). Students and families benefit from the rich opportunities for culturally relevant conversations and art analysis inherent in a welcoming and shared online environment that is easy for families to access.

Videos Narrated in English

Table 10.2 shows four sets of representative read-aloud videos and associated book-inspired art-making videos narrated in English. All of the videos narrated in English can be found at *www.learningartsathome.com/lessons-in-english*. Please note that this list is continuously growing. As shown in Figure 10.3, the descriptions were written in English, and the video was narrated in English.

TABLE 10.2 Four Sets of Representative Videos Narrated in English

Read-Aloud Videos (Number in LAH)	Book-Inspired Art-Making Videos (Number in LAH)	Themes
Gustavo the Shy Ghost by Flavina Z. Drago **E25.**	Art-making video inspired by *Gustavo the Shy Ghost* **E25.**	This story is about Gustavo, a shy ghost who loves playing the violin and finds it difficult to make friends. This art-making video demonstrates how to create art inspired by the Mexican Day of the Dead celebration.
Talking to Faith Ringgold by Faith Ringgold, Linda Freeman, and Nancy Roucher **E8.**	Art-making video inspired by *Talking to Faith Ringgold* **E13.**	This is a story about the life of an artist, Faith Ringgold, who narrates the story of her life and challenges as an African-American and female artist born in Harlem, New York City, in 1930. This art-making video demonstrates how to create colored paper at home for use in a collage.
Cuckoo by Lois Ehlert **E27.**	Art-making video inspired by *Cuckoo* **E28.**	This is a Mexican folktale about a bird who boasts of her beauty too much and the consequences that arise from her behavior. This art-making video demonstrates creating a cuckoo bird using a computer screen and recycled materials found at home.
Too Many Tamales by Gary Soto **E32.**	Art-making video inspired by *Too Many Tamales* **E33.**	This is a story about celebrating Latinx family culture by cooking tamales for a family holiday. This art-making video demonstrates creating artwork in the kitchen about the cooking process.

E33. Making Art inspired by *Too Many Tamales* by Gary Soto

TYPE

Art making

DESCRIPTION

This video demonstrates cooking *arepas** and creating art simultaneously. It features two women from Colombia: Laura and Tatiana. Laura comes from the *Paisa Region*** where arepas are especially important to the local peoples. Spanish and English are spoken in this video.

MATERIALS

Art: markers, plain white paper, Play-Doh or homemade play dough

FIGURE 10.3 Example of the Art Making Video "Too Many Tamales" Narrated in English

As an example, we describe one set of videos, *Too Many Tamales*, narrated in English, that were designed within the CRT framework while highlighting the pedagogical strategies described in the Literacy Development Pedagogy and Artistic Development Pedagogy sections. The book was selected for its ability to solicit background knowledge and cultural connections.

The read-aloud video appeals to students who are familiar with making tamales at the holidays in another culture, its traditions, and associated vocabulary. For students unfamiliar with this cultural tradition, the video provides a window (Bishop, 1990) into another way of life using a familiar Mesoamerican food, tamales, a traditional dish made of masa that is steamed in a corn husk or banana leaf popular in numerous Spanish-speaking countries, including Mexico and other Latin American countries. Emphasis is placed on inviting students to connect the story to their lived experiences. For example, open-ended questions invite the students to think about the outcomes in the book, and a picture walk of the story reminds students what shape, color, texture, and form make up the tamale.

The art-making video asks students to create a deeper relationship with *Too Many Tamales* by using simultaneous art-making and cooking activities at home with family members. The shared art-creating and cooking experiences demonstrated in the video create an opportunity for students to discuss the story with family members and to respond creatively to the read-aloud experience. Students are encouraged to create art in 2D by drawing with a marker on paper and to create art in 3D using play dough, giving them an art experience in more than one medium. The art-making video suggests that the kitchen can be conducive to both creativity and learning. Finally, students are encouraged to send in images of their work for digital display, linking the worlds of home and school in an organic and emotionally empowering way.

Videos Narrated in Spanish

Table 10.3 shows four sets of representative read-aloud videos and associated art-making videos narrated in Spanish. All of the videos narrated in Spanish can be

TABLE 10.3 Four Sets of Representative Videos Narrated in Spanish

Read-Aloud Videos (Number in LAH)	Book-Inspired Art-Making Videos (Number in LAH)	Themes
Soñadores (Dreamers) by Yuyi Morales S20.	Art-making video inspired by Soñadores (Dreamers) S21.	This is a story of an immigrant mother and her young son moving to the United States from Mexico and their experience of navigating an unfamiliar country. The book also emphasizes the gifts immigrants bring. This art-making video demonstrates how children can make books with materials easily found at home in which they can describe their history based on their own experiences and their own imagination.
Aunt Isa Wants a Car by Meg Medina S23.	Art-making video inspired by Aunt Isa Wants a Car S24.	This is a real-life and inspirational story of a young Cuban immigrant lady and her niece, who want to save money for a car that will take the whole family to the beach. This art-making video demonstrates how children can build a piggy bank using materials easily found at home. Children can come up with different sizes and designs of piggy banks, depending on the size of material they gather.
Gracias el pavo del dia de accion de gracias (Gracias, the Thanksgiving Turkey) by Jonah Winter S27.	Art-making video inspired by Gracias el pavo del dia de accion de gracias (Gracias, the Thanksgiving Turkey) S28.	This is a story of a Puerto Rican boy, Miguel, who lives with his family in a New York City neighborhood. Miguel develops an attachment to a turkey given to him by his father to be eaten on Thanksgiving. This art-making video demonstrates how to build a turkey using materials that are easily found at home.
¿Qué puedes hacer con una paleta? (What Can You Do With a Popsicle?) by Carmen Tafolla S29.	Art-making video inspired by ¿Qué puedes hacer con una paleta? (What Can You Do With a Popsicle?) S31.	This book is about a paleta—the traditional Mexican popsicle treat sold from a wagon with the sound of a tinkly bell. Throughout the book, various cultural elements are presented, such as the serape (which is a long, brightly colored shawl worn by people from certain regions in Mexico), tacos, accordion, and so on. This art-making video demonstrates how to make popsicles using materials found at home or in a neighborhood store.

found at www.learningartsathome.com/lessons-in-spanish. Please note that this list is continuously growing. As shown in Figure 10.4, the descriptions were written in two languages, Spanish and English, and the videos were narrated in Spanish.

Using it as another example, *Soñadores (Dreamers)*, narrated in Spanish, was designed within the CRT framework while highlighting the aforementioned teaching pedagogies. In the read-aloud video, the narrator shows a small collection of books to the students to symbolize the "public library" that is included in the storyline of the book *Dreamers*. During this read-aloud, the library shown in the illustrations is purposefully connected with the one used as a prop in the video.

The narrator "picture walks" the illustrations of the book to boost students' engagement and interest while also directing students' attention to the illustrations so they can make connections with the description of concepts and vocabulary provided in the read-aloud. In that way, children can make more accurate associations between their previous knowledge and the storyline of the read-aloud. For instance, the narrator shows students some familiar illustrations of Mexican culture such as customs, language, cultural elements, and so on.

S21. Arte inspirado en Soñadores por Yuyi Morales

Making Art Inspired by *Dreamers* by Yuyi Morales

TIPO
Obra artística

TYPE
Art making

DESCRIPCIÓN
Este video demuestra arte creativo inspirado por el libro *Soñadores* por Yuyi Morales

DESCRIPTION
This video demonstrates creating artwork inspired by the book *Dreamers* by Yuyi Morales

MATERIALES
Cartones, papeles blancos y de colores, engrapador, lápiz, pegamento, tijeras, variedad de material que se puede encontrar en la casa.

MATERIALS
Cardboard, colored paper, stapler, pencil, glue, scissors, and assorted materials found at home.

FIGURE 10.4 Example of the Art-Making Video Inspired by *Soñadores* (*Dreamers*) Narrated in Spanish

During this read-aloud, the narrator's own experiences as an immigrant are shared, and students are encouraged to connect their own stories and their family stories to the topic of the book *Dreamers*. In order for students to better comprehend the text, the narrator must take into consideration students' background knowledge, thus continuously extending it. Therefore, in this read-aloud video, the narrator encourages students to make text-to-self and text-to-the-world connections, specifically associating their immigrant experiences with the new life they encountered in the United States. *Dreamers* includes several examples of common immigrant experiences; for example, when the character unknowingly goes into a water fountain to cool off without realizing that it was merely a town decoration; when she gets confused looking at the train route map; and when she is answering the phone and does not understand the English language the person on the line is speaking, among others.

Students are encouraged to make their own connections to the story by writing their own immigrant experience, similar to those described in the book. Likewise, in this read-aloud, students are encouraged to get a library card, as shown in the setting of the storyline. In addition, the detailed illustrations in the book facilitate the use of open-ended questioning techniques. However, simple questions are also used to scaffold the students in responding to higher-order thinking questions, such as "What place do you think this is?" (Library), "What do you see in the library?" "What do you think is going to happen next?" "What do you think they are doing in the illustrations?" "Why are the mother and her baby reaching out their arms?" "What is your story?" and "What is the story of your family?" Lastly, after ensuring that the students have the linguistic and world knowledge needed to understand this read-aloud, the narrator uses the relevant fluent reading strategies to strengthen comprehension and the appropriate intonation and expressive sounds to make the story coherent for students. For instance, in the part of the story when the mother made mistakes or when reading about the "gifts" immigrants bring to the new country, the narrator uses different intonations.

The art-making video inspired by *Dreamers* connects important events from the read-aloud video to art creation. The 3D art video creation involves constructing a book with assorted materials easily found at home, which helps students to realize the valuable resources they possess in their home environment. The narrator guides students to use and transform those assets through their own construction by following the systematic demonstration of an art creation. In the art-creation video, students are encouraged to write their own story based on their experiences as well as their imagination. This art-making video additionally provides students more options of art creation such as drawing, coloring, designing, decorating, and utilizing recycled art material at home. Furthermore, it incorporates and integrates concepts of various subjects, including mathematical calculation, problem solving, describing parts of the book, using vocabulary, encouraging family participation, and more. The art-making video also requests students to submit pictures of their art creation to share their voices with the community.

Videos Narrated in Arabic

Table 10.4 shows four sets of representative read-aloud videos and associated art-making videos narrated in Arabic (Please note that the list is continuously

TABLE 10.4 Four Representative Sets of Videos in Arabic and English

Read-Aloud Videos (Number in LAH)	Book-Inspired Art-Making Videos (Number in LAH)	Themes
The Donkey Is Right (الحمار علي حق) by Rahma Ayyad **A17.**	Art-making video inspired by *The Donkey Is Right* **A18.**	This Arabic folklore story talks about a hard-working farmer and a donkey that helped him on his land. The events in the story show the value of loyalty and friendship among different creatures. This art-making video demonstrates how to make a simple friendship card using materials that you can find at home.
The Chicken and The Golden Egg (الدجاجة والبيضة الذهبية) by Rahma Ayyad **A19.**	Art-making video inspired by *The Chicken and The Golden Egg* **A20.**	This Arabic folklore story talks about a fair Muslim prince, a greedy guard that worked at the prince's palace, and a magical hen that lays golden eggs. When greed manifests as the intense and selfish desire for gold and money, a downfall is inevitable—greed leads to the loss of fortune. This art-making video demonstrates a simple craft of constructing the most famous Arabic/Muslim architecture features—a dome and a minaret—with construction paper and materials easily found at home.
Tell Me More About Ramadan (أخبرني المزيد عن رم) by Bachar Karroum **A25.**	Art-making video inspired by *Tell Me More About Ramadan* **A26.**	This is the story of Laila, a curious little Muslim girl who wants to learn about Ramadan—the holy month of fasting for Muslims. Ramadan has significant importance because of the important message it teaches to humanity. This art-making video demonstrates how to make a decorative line of colorful paper Ramadan lanterns.
I'm a Princess Too (!انا ايضا أميرة) by Nina Kharoufeh **A27.**	Art-making video inspired by *I'm a Princess Too* **A28.**	This is the story of Ameena, an Arab/Muslim girl who wears hijab (head covering). Even though life can be tough for a Hijabi girl, Ameena is trying to live a normal life. Hard work and dedication are what is needed to rise to the top. This art-making video demonstrates how to make girls' room décor; a handmade princess ballerina wall-art.

growing). As shown in Figure 10.5, the descriptions were written in two languages, Arabic and English, and the videos were narrated in Arabic.

As an example, we describe a set of videos, *Tell Me More About Ramadan*, narrated in Arabic, that were designed within the CRT framework while highlighting the aforementioned teaching pedagogies described in the Literacy Development Pedagogy and Artistic Development Pedagogy sections. The book, by Bashar Karroum, was selected for its ability to solicit background knowledge and cultural connections. The read-aloud video appeals to students who are familiar with this family holiday setting, its traditions, and associated vocabulary. For students with little or no knowledge of this holiday, the book provides a window into another culture (Bishop, 1990). Before the read-aloud, to help the students get into the mindset, be better prepared, and more engaged, the narrator used a picture-walk strategy of a day in the month of Ramadan. The pictures show the main things that are carried out; for example, the dawn meal (*Sohoor*), sunrise,

A26. Making Art Inspired by *Tell Me More About Ramadan* by Bachar Karroum; Illustrated by Tanja Varcelija

TYPE

Art making

Make paper lanterns' line decoration at home.

FIGURE 10.5 Example of the Art-Making Video Inspired by "Tell Me More About Ramadan" Narrated in Arabic

fasting, sunset, sunset meal (breaking the fast; *Iftar*), night prayers (*Taraweeh*), and the traditional Ramadan lanterns. During and after the read-aloud, emphasis is placed on inviting students to connect the story to their lived experiences. Students are asked open-ended questions to infer the moral lessons that the month of Ramadan teaches to people who observe it. To create a fully expressive and enjoyable listening experience, the reader's voice models fluent Arabic reading that interprets the characters and the concepts in the story.

The art-making video asks students to create a deeper understanding of the symbolism of the lanterns (*Fanous*) in the month of Ramadan. They illuminate streets in a sea of color, creating a beautiful and magical atmosphere. Throughout Arabic/Islamic history, lanterns were originally used at night in the month of Ramadan to light up the dark streets for people who go to night prayers and night social gatherings. The lanterns have become a worldwide symbol to represent the holy month of Ramadan. The art-making video inspired by *Tell Me More About Ramadan* demonstrates how to make a decorative line of colorful paper lanterns. The shared art creation demonstrated in the video provides an opportunity for students to discuss the story with their family members and to respond creatively to the read-aloud experience. The video suggests the use of materials found at home such as construction paper, crayons, scissors, a thick clothesline, and laundry baskets. The line of lanterns can be displayed on a wall or in windows. Finally, students are encouraged to send in images of their work for digital display, linking the worlds of home and school.

Recommendations for Teachers and Publishers

Children's books are some of the earliest forms of media that can be used to teach young students about diversity in the world. Children learn about the world around them and other cultures through the social messages found in stories, which helps them understand how society perceives their culture and the cultures of others, thereby influencing their social and identity development. Further, social messages that they glean from picture books will likely stay with them for the rest of their lives (Henderson, 1991; Roethler, 1998). As such, learning materials that accurately portray diverse cultures in multiple languages can positively influence young students' self-image and help them build bridges of cultural understanding (Larrick, 1965). Thus, providing authentic resources that bring about the beauty of their cultures allows young students to meet people like themselves and develop an appreciation for their culture's uniqueness. To this end, as technology becomes a core outlet for Generation Z, those born between the mid-1990s and ending around 2012 (Seemiller & Grace, 2016; Twenge, 2017), who tend to learn from online video materials (Chicca & Shellenbarger, 2018), it is important to develop accessible digital story collections that reflect cultural diversity. In the process of developing read-aloud videos, we found it challenging to find educational PreK-6 books that include references to diverse cultures, particularly stories portraying Arabic and Bengali cultures. Instead, books for young students found at public or school libraries typically represent the middle-class White population's culture (Lafferty, 2014). It was even more challenging to find books in bilingual form. In addition, some library books that were available in Arabic, in particular, were not translated in a semantically proper way.

The absence of a student's culture from print and digital media stories can be problematic. When young students never see their culture represented in their school library and in the print or digital learning materials they are to work with, they receive a resounding message that their culture is not important enough to be featured. This is referred to as "the null curriculum" (also known as "excluded curriculum"); that is, students do not have an opportunity to learn about their culture but, instead, learn content without certain experiences, interactions, and discourses in the classroom (Eisner, 1994). Such invisibility can be harmful to a student's self-image and self-esteem, which are primarily influenced by how the student and the overall society view the cultural group to which the student belongs (Vygotsky, 1986). Moreover, materials that provide inaccurate and ste-reotyped depictions of diverse languages and cultures can negatively influence young children (Myers, 2014). Sadly, this phenomenon is applicable to digital learning materials available on the internet.

Given these realities, we suggest that instructional designers, instructors, and publishers focus on recruiting authors and illustrators from diverse cultural and linguistic backgrounds to create more inclusive digital books for PreK-12 stu-dents. More efforts, including funding, to produce proper translations of digital books in the various languages represented by the school population are also needed. Translators should be mindful of the content of the translated stories to and from other languages so they don't produce materials that misrepresent or reinforce negative images of certain cultures.

Suggestions for Teachers

Based on our observations while using the LAH videos with students and teach-ers, we submit the following recommendations for general education and bilin-gual education classrooms.

- Plan activities around English language arts and social studies standards in an interdisciplinary way with arts integration activities.
- Use the read-aloud videos as homework with bilingual students to be com-pleted by the students alone or with their families.
- Use the read-aloud and/or art-making videos during class time with bilin-gual and students with special needs, encouraging them to rewind the videos as many times as they need to in order to promote greater understanding of and confidence using the content and materials presented.

- Use the read-aloud and/or art-making videos with all students as homework to be completed by the students alone or with their families.
- Use the art-making videos during class time with visual and kinesthetic learners and students who need to learn at their own pace.
- Use the read-aloud and/or art-making videos during class time with students who would benefit from having a perceived one-on-one relationship with the teacher via the videos, making learning less emotionally intimidating.
- Display various kinds of artwork made after watching art-making videos (e.g., art-making books generated by the *Dreamers* video, paintings, and art and crafts) in a virtual gallery such as Dojo and Google Classrooms, or on a bulletin board at school, and encourage oral and/or written responses to the artworks.
- Create your own videos for your students and encourage them to create their own read-aloud and art-creation videos. Children engage more with the story when they see their teacher performing the digital read-aloud and art-making activities.

Conclusion

ELs and bilingual students are a growing student population in the United States, comprising 10% of students nationwide, coming from a wide variety of cultural and linguistic backgrounds (National Center for Education Statistics, 2022; Santos et al., 2018). In diverse classroom settings, it is critical for teachers to reach students through multiple pathways and varied instructional techniques (Gay, 2018). Further, Gardner (2011) reminds us that students vary in their learning preferences.

These considerations led us to recognize that digital read-aloud videos need to support students to learn not only the arts but also the subject matter. As a result, we designed an arts-integration program using the CRT framework in multiple languages to support the target school community students' primary languages and cultures. The pilot study with four teachers (An et al., 2020) showed that the videos (a) enabled students to interact with the teachers as their work was shared; (b) gave students and parents a sense of being in a learning community and belonging; (c) increased the transparency of the instruction in that parents were able to view the videos and follow the directions step by step with their children and listen to the stories together; and (d) allowed users to replay the videos as many times as wanted or needed.

These findings are promising with regard to the use LAH as a teaching tool. Yet, further systematic research studies are needed in order to examine the effectiveness of LAH in regular and bilingual classrooms that are aligned with the goals of this program and to determine the impacts on learning outcomes.

> **Key Takeaways:**
>
> 1. Book reading and book-inspired art making are some of the ways in which arts integration can be used to enrich student learning.
> 2. When developing read-aloud videos, the selection of books is critical for fostering culturally responsive pedagogy. The selection process should be analyzed from several angles, including quantitative and qualitative measures. In addition, the characteristics of the reader/viewer and the associated tasks that go into reading should be taken into account.
> 3. Culturally responsive art education fosters an appreciation of local culture in a global context.

Recommended Resources

Books:

- Brouillette, L. (2019). *Arts integration in diverse K-5 classrooms: Cultivation literacy skills and conceptual understanding.* Teachers College Press.
- Campbell-Whatley, G. C., Rodriguez, D., & Agrawal, J. (2021). *STEAM meets story: Using adolescent fiction and film to spark deeper learning.* Teachers College Press.
- Cornett, C. E. (2015). *Creating meaning through literature and the arts: Arts integration for classroom teachers* (5th ed.). Pearson.
- Raines, S. C., & Canady, R. J. (1989). *Story stretchers: Activities to expand children's favorite books.* Gryphon House.

Websites:

- Best YouTube Art Channels for Teachers and Students: www.educatorstechnology. com/2022/03/best-youtube-art-channels-for-teachers.html
- Five (Easy-to-Implement) Ways Video Can Have a Powerful Impact on Teaching and Learning: www.edsurge.com/news/2018-04-23-five-easy-to-implement-ways-video-can-have-a-powerful-impact-on-teaching-and-learning
- How to Use Video in the ESL Classroom | Videos for ESL Students: www. eslactivity.org/use-video-in-the-esl-classroom/
- Inclusive Arts Integration Program (https://inclusiveartsintegration.weebly.com/): This is the website of the arts integration grant program at College of Education, William Paterson University, funded by the Geraldine R. Dodge Foundation.
- STEAMEmpowerment (http://steamempowerment.blogspot.com/): This blog includes exemplary arts integration activities conducted at the partner schools of the Inclusive Arts Integration Grant Program at William Paterson University.

- The Institute for Arts Integration and STEAM (https://artsintegration.com): This is the world's largest online professional development provider for teachers and leaders using arts-integrated approaches, founded by Susan Riley in 2013.

References

Ambe, E. B. (2006). Fostering multicultural appreciation in pre-service teachers through multicultural curricular transformation. *Teaching and Teacher Education, 22*(6), 690–699. https://doi.org/10.1016/j.tate.2006.03.005

An, H., & Seplocha, H. (2010). Video-sharing websites: Tools for developing pattern languages in children. *Young Children, 65*(5), 20–25.

An, H., Yoon, S. Y., & Samaras, T. (2020, October 21). Overcoming the digital divide: The development of a culturally responsive video-based arts integration tool for high-needs New Jersey urban schools. In *Proceedings of the Fall 2020 Semiannual Conference of Korean Society for Educational Technology* (pp. 136–145). South Korea.

Anthony, J. L., Williams, J. M., Durán, L. K., Gillam, S. L., Liang, L., Aghara, R., Swank, P. R., Assel, M. A., & Landry, S. H. (2011). Spanish phonological awareness: Dimensionality and sequence of development during the preschool and kindergarten years. *Journal of Educational Psychology, 103*(4), 857–876. https://doi.org/10.1037/a0025024

Bishop, R. S. (1990). Mirrors, windows, and sliding glass doors. *Perspectives: Choosing and Using Books for Classroom, 6*(3), ix–xi.

Brun, H. (2018). *#ToddlerTales—Use of props in story starter sessions.* www.beanstalkcharity.org.uk/blog/toddlertales-use-of-props-in-story-starter-sessions

Chicca, J., & Shellenbarger, T. (2018). Connecting with generation Z: Approaches in nursing education. *Teaching and Learning in Nursing, 13*(3), 180–184. https://doi.org/10.1016/j.teln.2018.03.008

Children's Literacy Initiative. (n.d.). *Fluency.* https://learn.cli.org/building-blocks/fluency.md

Christ, T., & Sharma, S. A. (2018). Searching for mirrors: Preservice teachers' journey toward more culturally relevant pedagogy. *Reading Horizons: A Journal of Literacy and Language Arts, 57*(1), 55–73. https://scholarworks.wmich.edu/reading_horizons/vol57/iss1/5/

Common Core State Standards Initiative. (2022). *English language arts & literacy in history/social studies, science, and technical subjects.* www.corestandards.org/assets/Appendix_A.pdf

Cummins, J. (2001). Bilingual children's mother tongue: Why is it important for education? *Sprogforum, 7*(19), 15–20. www.joycerain.com/uploads/2/3/2/0/23207256/bilingual_childrens_mother_tongue_1.pdf

Department of Education, State of New Jersey. (2020). *New Jersey student learning standards for visual and performing arts.* www.nj.gov/education/standards/vpa/Index.shtml

Derman-Sparks, L. (2016). Guide for selecting anti-bias children's books. A teaching for change project. *Teaching for Change.* https://socialjusticebooks.org/guide-for-selecting-anti-bias-childrens-books/

Eisner, E. W. (1994). *The educational imagination: On the design and evaluation of school programs.* Macmillan College Publishing Company.

Fathi, J., & Afzali, M. (2020). The effect of second language reading strategy instruction on young Iranian EFL learners' reading comprehension. *International Journal of Instruction, 13*(1), 475–488. https://doi.org/10.29333/iji.2020.13131a

Fennell, A. (2022). Arts teacher as reflective practitioner for personal SEL growth. The Heart of the Arts Article Series. The Center for Arts Education and Social and Emotional Learning. *ArtsEdSEL, 2*(4), 1–4. https://artsedsel.org/wp-content/uploads/HotA_Volume-2_Issue-4_final-for-web.pdf

Ferfeli, P. (2022). Book or music video? How own voices picture books revolutionized verbal and visual media. *Interactive Film & Media Journal, 2*(1), 187–200. https://doi.org/10.32920/ifmj.v2i1.1510

Fuada, S., & Marhamah, M. (2021). Read aloud video Sebagai Media Pembelajaran Daring pada Masa Pandemi Covid-19 di TK Aisyiyah Sidoharjo-Wonogiri. *International Journal of Community Service Learning, 5*(2), 151–161.

Gardner, H. E. (2011). *Frames of mind: The theory of multiple intelligences* (3rd ed.). Basic Books.

Gay, G. (2002). Preparing for culturally responsive teaching. *Journal of Teacher Education, 53*(106), 106–116.

Gay, G. (2018). *Culturally responsive teaching: Theory, research, and practice* (3rd ed.). Teachers College Press.

Gordon, L. K. (2019). *Developing empathetic responses in third-grade students through multicultural literature* [Unpublished doctoral dissertation]. Florida Atlantic University.

Graham, M. (2009). The power of art in multicultural education: The international stories project. *Multicultural Perspectives, 11*(3), 155–161.

Hammond, Z. (2017). *Distinctions of equity chart.* https://crtandthebrain.com/wp-content/uploads/Hammond_Full-Distinctions-of-Equity-Chart.pdf

Henderson, V. M. (1991). The development of self-esteem in children of color. In M. V. Lindgren (Ed.), *The multicolored mirror: Cultural substance in literature for children and young adults* (pp. 15–30). Highsmith.

Horowitz, R., & Webb-Dempsey, J. (2002). Promising signs of positive effects: Lessons from the multi-arts studies. In R. Deasey (Ed.), *Critical links: Learning in the arts and student academic and social development* (pp. 98–101). Arts Education Partnership.

Hudson, J. (2018, April 27). Get your students warmed up with a picture walk. *Children's Literacy Initiative.* https://cli.org/2016/01/21/warming-up-with-a-picture-walk/

Krauss, S., & LaRiviere, M. (2022). Unexpected gifts: Art teaching in the COVID-19 pandemic and authenticity in the classroom. *Art Education: The Journal of the National Art Education Association, 75*(2), 56–58.

Küçükoğlu, H. (2013). Improving reading skills through effective reading strategies. *Procedia—Social and Behavioral Sciences, 70,* 709–714. https://doi.org/10.1016/j.sbspro.2013.01.113

Lafferty, K. E. (2014). What are you reading: How school libraries can promote racial diversity in multicultural literature. *Multicultural Perspectives, 16*(4), 203–209.

Larrick, N. (1965). The all-White world of children's books. *Saturday Review, 11,* 63–65.

Learning A-Z (2022). *Learning A-Z text leveling system.* www.raz-kids.com/main/viewpage/name/text-leveling-system/

Lexile. (2022). *About Lexile codes.* https://lexile.com/parents-students/find-books-at-the-right-level/about-lexile-text-codes/#AD

Liu, Y. C. (2015). The perception of cultural familiarity and background knowledge on reading comprehension for intermediate EFL students. *International Journal of Language and Literature, 3*(1), 71–75.

Marchessault, J. K., & Larwin, K. H. (2013). Structured read-aloud in middle school: The potential impact on reading achievement. *Contemporary Issues in Education Research, 6,* 241–246.

Myers, C. (2014, March 15). The apartheid of children's literature. *The New York Times.* www.nytimes.com/2014/03/16/opinion/sunday/the-apartheid-of-childrens-literature.html

National Center for Education Statistics. (2022). *English learners in public schools.* Institute of Education Sciences. https://nces.ed.gov/programs/coe/indicator/cgf

Nesset, V., Davis, E. C., Stewart-Robertson, O., & Bible, J. B. (2022). Bonded design in the virtual environment: The transition of a participatory design methodology. *Journal of Documentation, 78*(3), 513–528.

New Jersey Department of Education (NJDOE). (2021). *Social and emotional learning (SEL).* www.nj.gov/education/roadforward/summer/sel/

New Jersey Department of Education (NJDOE). (n.d.). *District factor groups (DFG) for school districts.* www.state.nj.us/education/finance/rda/dfg.shtml

New Jersey Principals and Supervisors Association (NJPSA). (2020). *New Jersey's arts integration think and do workbook: A practical guide to think about and implement arts integration.* http://njpsa.org/images/artsintegrationWorkbook2020.pdf

Noll, E. (2003). Accuracy and authenticity in American Indian children's literature: The social responsibility of authors and illustrators. In D. L. Fox & K. G. Short (Eds.), *Stories matter: The complexity of cultural authenticity in children's literature* (pp. 182–197). National Council of Teachers of English.

O'Dea, C. (2018). *Interactive map: Internet and computer access across NJ reflects a digital divide.* www.njspotlight.com/2018/12/18-12-10-interactive-map-internet-and-computer-access-across-nj-reflects-a-digital-divide/amp/?fbclid=IwAR3bc7HPydku0XzZymCpG8fqpbVS_J2kjQ65Ng9VkgWQ4VU6i5RDIXo7P50

Overby, A., Constance, J., & Quenzer, B. (2022). Reimagining art education: Moving toward culturally sustaining pedagogies in the arts with funds of knowledge and lived experiences. *Art Education: The Journal of the National Art Education Association, 75*(1), 20–25.

Purnell, P., Ali, P., Begun, N., & Carter, M. (2007). Windows, bridges, and mirrors: Building culturally responsive early childhood classrooms through the integration of literacy and the arts. *Early Childhood Education Journal, 34*(6), 419–424.

Rabkin, N., & Redmond, R. (2006). The arts make a difference. *Educational Leadership, 63*(5), 60–64.

Rahiem, M. D. (2021). Storytelling in early childhood education: Time to go digital. *International Journal of Child Care and Education Policy, 15*(1). https://doi.org/10.1186/s40723-021-00081-x

Reif, N., & Grant, L. (2010). Culturally responsive classrooms through art integration. *Journal of Praxis in Multicultural Education Spring, 5*(1), 100–115.

Roethler, J. (1998). Reading in color: Children's book illustrations and identity formation for Black children in the United States. *African American Review, 32*(1), 95–105.

Ruppert, S. S. (2006). Critical evidence: How the arts benefit student achievement. *National Assembly of State Arts Agencies.* www.nasaa-arts.org/publications/critical.pdf

Santos, M., Palacios, M. C., Cheuk, T., Greene, R., Mercado-Garcia, D., Zerkel, L., Hakuta, K., & Skarin, R. (2018). *Preparing English learners for college and career: Lessons from successful high schools.* Teachers College Press.

Scholastic. (2022). *The teacher store for educators only.* https://shop.scholastic.com/teachers-ecommerce/teacher/books/sonadores-9781338605136.html

Seemiller, C., & Grace, M. (2016). *Generation Z goes to college.* Jossey-Bass.

Soto, X. T., Crucet-Choi, A., & Goldstein, H. (2020). Effects of a supplemental Spanish phonological awareness intervention on Latinx preschoolers' dual language emergent literacy skills. *American Journal of Speech-Language Pathology, 29*(3), 1283–1300. https://doi.org/10.1044/2020_AJSLP-20-00029

Texas Education Agency. (2022). Fluency: Instructional guidelines and student activities. *Reading Rockets.* www.readingrockets.org/article/fluency-instructional-guidelines-and-student-activities#:~:text=fun%2C%20and%20rewarding.-,Model%20fluent%20reading,fluent%20reader%20sounds%20during%20reading

Twenge, J. M. (2017). *iGen: Why today's super-connected kids are growing up less rebellious, more tolerant, less happy—and completely unprepared for adulthood and what that means for the rest of us.* Atria Books.

Vygotsky, L. (1986). *Thought and language.* MIT Press.

Whitehurst, G. J. (2002). Dialogic reading: An effective way to read aloud with young children. *Reading Rockets.* www.readingrockets.org/article/dialogic-reading-effective-way-read-aloud-young-children

Will, M., & Najarro, I. (2022, April 6). What is culturally responsive teaching? *Education Week.* www.edweek.org/teaching-learning/culturally-responsive-teaching-culturally-responsive-pedagogy/2022/04?utm_source=summari

11

THE IMPACT OF AN ONLINE MATHEMATICS ACTIVITY ON ELEMENTARY SCHOOL STUDENTS' ENGAGEMENT AND LEARNING IN A HIGH-NEEDS CONTEXT

August Howerton and Drew Polly

Guiding Questions:

- What does a technology-rich elementary mathematics activity look like when framed within the concept of equity-based teaching?
- How can technology support mathematics learning in schools that have been determined to be high-needs contexts?
- How can this example of a technology-rich mathematics activity support my work with integrating technology in my own context(s)?

Introduction

Technology can be a powerful tool in education. That is, students can use technology tools to explore, leading to innovation and creativity. In fact, The National Education Technology Plan (NETP) has set "a national vision and plan for learning enabled by technology through building on the work of leading education researchers; district, school, and higher education leaders; classroom teachers; developers; entrepreneurs; and nonprofit organizations" (U.S. Department of Education, 2017, p. 3). Elementary schools, therefore, are experiencing a big push to enhance student learning using technology and prepare students to thrive and succeed in the 21st century.

Researchers have found that technology has the potential to increase student engagement in all contexts, especially in schools that have been classified as "high-needs" (Polly, 2011; Polly & Hannafin, 2011; Reinhold et al., 2020; Schuetz et al., 2018). Further, teachers are increasingly embedding more technology into

DOI:10.4324/9781003274537-14

their curriculum and in their classrooms (Dondlinger et al., 2016; Flowers & Rose, 2014; Martin et al., 2021). This chapter specifically examines fourth-grade students' experiences with an online mathematics activity, Thinking Blocks Multiplication (Math Playground; www.mathplayground.com/tb_multiplication/index.html), and its influence on student engagement and achievement as measured on pre- and postassessments.

Framework and Related Literature

Equity-Based Mathematics Teaching

The study was framed around the construct of equity-based mathematics teaching. According to Gutiérrez (2009), equity-based mathematics teaching consists of four domains: Achievement, Access, Power, and Identity (see Table 11.1).

While all four domains are important, Gutiérrez (2009) viewed Access and Achievement as the dominant aspects, emphasizing that all learners need (a) opportunities to engage in rigorous mathematics tasks and activities (Access) and (b) engaging experiences that help lead to learning on various measures (Achievement).

In this chapter, we posit that the Thinking Blocks Multiplication activity (Math Playground) provides learners with access to rigorous mathematics word problems while using technology as a way to provide a visual and scaffold learning. This type of tool might be more engaging than the traditional digital programs in which learners simply recall and type in answers to math questions that are focused on lower-level, basic skills. Specifically, our goal was to provide

TABLE 11.1 Dimensions of Equity-Based Mathematics

Dimension	Description
Access	Access to rigorous and current curriculum and resources
	Access to high-quality mathematics teachers
	Access to mathematics tools (e.g., manipulatives, technology)
Achievement	Engagement in mathematics
	Scores on assessments
	Preparation for STEM-based fields
Identity	Incorporation of students' personal and cultural backgrounds in mathematics
	Opportunity for students to select and use their own strategies
	Opportunity for students to use their own language
Power	Opportunity for students to discuss and share their thinking and strategies
	Student ownership of their own understanding and opportunities to make sense
	Acknowledgement of systems of power that have influenced and marginalized specific group of people

Source: Adapted from Gutiérrez (2009)

Impact of Online Mathematics Activity on Elementary Students   **159**

students with opportunities to use an internet-based mathematics word-problem activity to provide them with access to high-quality mathematics activities in order to strengthen the development of their mathematical identity. The project was carried out with a group of fourth-grade students who attended a school identified as "high-needs" based on the high percentage of students who qualified for free and/or reduced lunch as well as the high percentage of students whose data indicated that they need more experiences with foundational concepts taught in earlier grades.

Activity Design

Overview of Math Playground Activity

Students who participated in the activity spent time solving mathematics word problems using the Math Playground program (www.mathplayground.com/tb_multiplication/index.html) focused on multiplication and division word problems. This internet-based activity was selected because multiplication and division word problems are a major concept in fourth grade. Additionally, students in schools that are identified as high-needs traditionally have limited opportunities for growth related to their skills and understanding of how to solve word problems.

Figures 11.1 through 11.4 provide screenshots of the activity at its different stages. First, students are presented with a word problem that involves either multiplication or division. Students are expected to drag the blue labels to either of the boxes and then drag the blocks to the appropriate long rectangles. In this case, the rectangle near Jesse's label should have 1 rectangle since it is the smallest number, and the rectangle next to Sarah's label should have 9 rectangles since her number is 9 times the amount of Jesse's number (see Figure 11.1).

Next, students are presented with numbers. In the word problem, we know Jesse's number, but we do not know Sarah's number (see Figure 11.2). Students are expected to drag the label 9 to the spot above Jesse's label and the question mark to the rectangle below Sarah's picture.

After correctly dragging the labels to the yellow spots, the tool provides students with the numbers in each box (see Figure 11.3), helping them to determine the correct answer. Teachers like this tool since it provides a scaffold—prior to this point, students had to represent the word problem with the labels, the purple blocks, and the yellow labels for the various quantities. If students are not able to correctly label and represent the problem, they are unable to move past that part of the problem-solving process.

When students have entered the correct answer, the program provides automatic feedback (see Figure 11.4). If students enter an incorrect answer, they are encouraged to check their work and enter a different answer. This feature of the program prevents students from just typing in a number and moving on to a different word problem.

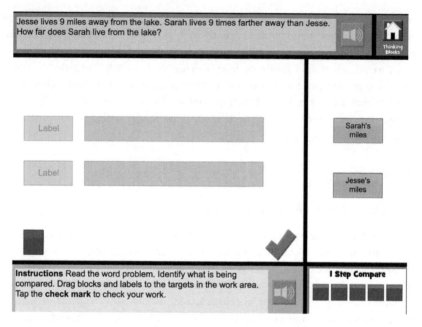

FIGURE 11.1 Thinking Blocks Before Starting

Note: Math Playground. Reprinted with permission.

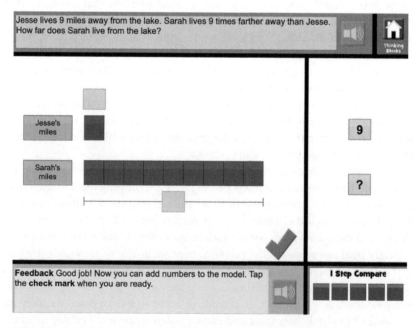

FIGURE 11.2 Thinking Blocks After Adding Representation and Labels

Note: Math Playground. Reprinted with permission.

Impact of Online Mathematics Activity on Elementary Students **161**

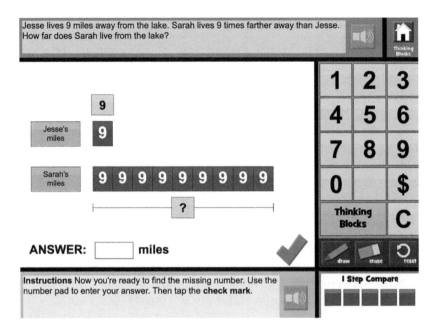

FIGURE 11.3 Thinking Blocks After Adding Numbers

Note: Math Playground. Reprinted with permission.

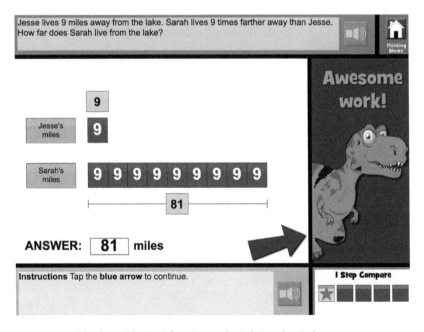

FIGURE 11.4 Thinking Blocks After Correctly Solving the Task

Note: Math Playground. Reprinted with permission.

Process of Using the Activity

The four students in the current study spent 25 to 30 minutes on the activity weekly for 3 consecutive weeks on the Math Playground website. However, the duration and frequency of use can fluctuate based on student data and teachers' choices. For example, teachers may have students work on the activity for shorter periods (10 to 15 minutes) two or three times a week.

In our context, students typically used their own Chromebooks for activities. However, we valued student-to-student conversation, so we had students pair up and work with partners on the program. This format provided more opportunities for collaboration and peer support and gave students opportunities to collaborate with other students.

In addition to the Chromebook, students also used paper and pencil. On the paper, students were expected to write the multiplication equation (e.g., $9 \times 9 = 81$). The first author provided questions to help check for students' understanding. Examples of questions included, "How did you use the blocks to represent the word problem?" "Why does this rectangle have more blocks than this rectangle?" and "How do you know that you are correct?"

Findings

In order to examine the effectiveness of the Thinking Blocks Multiplication program for a group of fourth-grade students attending a high-needs school, we examined (a) learner engagement using a survey and (b) the influence of the mathematics activity on student achievement using a pre- and posttest focused on mathematics problem solving.

Learner Engagement

The learner engagement survey was given before the intervention began. The survey asked the four fourth-grade students 33 questions about how they felt not only about their motivation but also about their engagement in mathematics. Their responses were scored using Ersoy and Oksuz's (2015) scoring chart. All four students (a) rated themselves as having a middle-level range of engagement in mathematics before the intervention; (b) agreed with the statement that mathematics was an easy subject for them; and (c) agreed that they listened carefully during mathematics. However, students disagreed with the statement, "I am afraid of solving mathematical problems that I can't do" and slightly agreed with the statement that they can explain things that they have learned in their own words in the mathematics subject.

While all students' ratings of engagement improved, Students 1 and 2 stayed in the middle range for both engagement and motivation, while Students 3 and 4 moved into the high engagement and motivation range. The changes in students' answers from the pre- to the postsurvey varied. For example, in the postsurvey, all students agreed that topics in mathematics are interesting to them, but in the survey, only two students agreed with this statement, while one student somewhat agreed and the other disagreed. All the students also agreed that they feel more confident when they succeed in mathematics. Also, all the students somewhat agreed with the statement that they can explain reasons for the use of procedures while solving mathematical problems.

In addition to the surveys, throughout the four sessions, the first author observed and took notes about each student while they were working on the activity. Major observations include the following. All students asked for help each day. Students asked for help on different multiplication equations. On the first day, students made several comments about how they were confused about how to use the website. As the days progressed, however, students became more comfortable with the website. One student even made the comment, "This app is more fun than DreamBox," the digital program they had to use multiple times a week.

While students worked on their own individual devices, they made comments to each other for motivation. For example, on the first and second days of the intervention, Student 4 constantly said that he was giving up and that he did not want to work on the problems. On the second day of intervention, Student 1 looked at Student 4 and said, "If you guess and check, you can get the answers right." After that, Student 4 began to explore the application and started to understand the concept of multiplication with missing parts, based on observation notes.

Student Achievement

Table 11.2 shows the change in student achievement scores on the mathematics pre- and postassessments.

On the pretest, none of the students actually drew a picture to show their conceptual understanding of the problems, even though they were asked to do so. Also, students did not consistently use the correct operation. In fact, on the last problem of the assessment, they added the two numbers instead of multiplying them.

TABLE 11.2 Pre- and Posttest Data

Pretest			Posttest		
Student	Points (out of 50)	Percentage	Points (out of 50)	Percentage	Change
Student 1	19	38%	25	50%	+12%
Student 2	27	54%	43	86%	+32%
Student 3	33	66%	40	80%	+14%
Student 4	24	48%	40	80%	+32%

164   August Howerton and Drew Polly

After students participated in the intervention, they were given a posttest to test their multiplication skills. The rubric used for the pretest was also used for the posttest.

As illustrated in Table 11.2, all of the students' scores improved from pre- to posttest. On the posttest, students were encouraged to transfer their work from the computer to paper by drawing a picture of the blocks. Three out of the four students demonstrated mastery, which was set as 80% or above. Student 1 still had multiple misconceptions. Even if the student wrote out equations and attempted to draw pictures, he was not yet able to solve the problem.

Recommendations and Future Considerations

Based on our findings, we offer the following recommendations regarding the use of technology-rich math activities in schools labeled high-needs: (a) ensure access to high-quality activities and (b) capitalize on the power of technology to scaffold and support learning.

Access to High-Quality Activities

Gutiérrez's equity-based framework for mathematics (2009) centers on the idea that all students should have access to high-quality mathematics activities. The program discussed in this chapter was aligned with grade-level content and provided students with opportunities to solve rigorous word problems during the activity. Researchers have noted that in schools that are called "high-needs," teachers often overscaffold the content to the point that many activities are not rigorous enough to be aligned with grade-level expectations (Berry, 2008; Polly, 2021; Rose, 2020). While students may need foundational experiences from previous grade levels to be successful with grade-level content, it is important to provide access to grade-level content as well as access to foundational experiences through differentiated experiences (McNeill & Polly, 2023; Martin & Polly, 2020; Rose, 2020).

Capitalize on the Power of Technology to Scaffold and Support Learning

In this example, the Thinking Blocks Multiplication activity used technology to scaffold and support students while they learned how to solve word problems. Figures 11.1 to 11.4 document the way that the activity required students to demonstrate an understanding of the labels and what the numbers meant in the word problem before they were allowed to use the technology to actually find the answer. This scaffolding and process of supporting students with visuals helps all students, but especially those who may be in schools called "high-needs," since it provides assistance while still allowing students to have ownership of creating the representations and pictures using the technology.

Technology-rich activities such as Thinking Blocks (www.mathplayground.com) or others such as those proposed by the National Council of Teachers of Mathematics (http://illuminations.nctm.org) provide students with opportunities to engage in meaningful mathematical activities while still providing them with scaffolds and supports to learn the mathematics concepts. McCullough and colleagues (2021) call these types of technologies "math action technologies" since learners use the technology to complete mathematical actions such as creating mathematical representations or solving mathematics problems. These types of technologies provide access and advance equity-based mathematics pedagogies in all settings. As teachers and mathematics education leaders continue to support students' mathematics learning, it is important to provide rich opportunities for students to carry out the actions of mathematics with appropriate scaffolds and supports.

Key Takeaways

1. Equity-based teaching in mathematics includes opportunities for students to use technology to create mathematical representations and be empowered to choose various strategies to use.
2. Students in high-needs contexts benefited from access to technology that involved higher-level thinking where they solved mathematics word problems.
3. Students showed gains in engagement as well as learning after multiple experiences with the digital mathematics program.

Recommended Resources

- NCTM Illuminations: https://illuminations.nctm.org/
  Various games and activities related to mathematics concepts. Appropriate from kindergarten through Grade 12.
- PhET Simulations and Activities: https://Phet.colorado.edu
  Simulations and math activities. Appropriate for Grades 3 to 12.
- Shodor: www.shodor.org/interactivate
  Online math activities and simulations. Appropriate for Grades 3 to 12
- Toy Theater: https://toytheater.com
  Various mathematics manipulatives and tools to support students' mathematics learning.

References

Berry, R. Q. (2008). Access to upper-level mathematics: The stories of successful African American middle school boys. *Journal for Research in Mathematics Education, 39*(5), 464–488.

Dondlinger, M. J., McLeod, J., & Vasinda, S. (2016). Essential conditions for technology-supported, student-centered learning: An analysis of student experiences with Math Out Loud using the ISTE standards for students. *Journal of Research on Technology in Education, 48*(4), 258–273. https://doi.org/10.1080/15391523.2016.1212633

Ersoy, E., & Oksuz, C. (2015). Primary school mathematics motivation scale. *European Scientific Journal, 11*(1), 37–50.

Flowers, J., & Rose, M. A. (2014). Mathematics in technology & engineering education: Judgments of grade-level appropriateness. *Journal of Technology Education, 25*(2), 18–34.

Gutiérrez, R. (2009). Framing equity: Helping students "play the game" and "change the game." *Teaching for Excellence and Equity in Mathematics, 1*(1), 4–8.

Martin, C. S., Harbour, K., & Polly, D. (2021). Transitioning the elementary mathematics classroom to virtual learning: Exploring the perspectives and experiences of teachers. In A. Slapac, P. Balcerzak, & K. O'Brien (Eds.), *Handbook of research on the global empowerment of educators and student learning through action research* (pp. 343–365). IGI Global. https://doi.org/10.4018/978-1-7998-6922-1.ch015

Martin, C. S., & Polly, D. (2020). Embedding formative assessment in the mathematics classroom through writing discourse and the use of digital tools: Embedding formative assessment in the mathematics classroom. In C. S. Martin, D. Polly, & R. G. Lambert (Eds.), *Handbook of research on formative assessment in pre-K through elementary classrooms* (pp. 194–205). IGI Global. https://doi.org/10.4018/978-1-7998-0323-2.ch010

McCullough, A. W., Lovett, J. N., Dick, L. K., & Cayton, C. (2021). Positioning students to explore math with technology. *Mathematics Teacher: Learning and Teaching PK-12. 114*(10), 738–749. https://doi.org/10.5951/MTLT.2021.0059

McNeill, H., & Polly, D. (2023). Exploring primary grades teachers' perceptions of their students' mathematics self-efficacy and how they differentiate instruction. *Early Childhood Education Journal, 51*, 79–88. https://doi.org/10.1007/s10643-021-01281-3

Polly, D. (2021). Advancing equity-based mathematics teaching in the primary grades: The case of two clinical practice experiences. *International Journal of Teacher Education and Professional Development, 4*(1), 68–88.

Polly, D., & Hannafin, M. J. (2011). Examining how learner-centered professional development influences teachers' espoused and enacted practices. *Journal of Educational Research, 104*, 120–130.

Reinhold, F., Hoch, S., Werner, B., Richter-Gebert, J., & Reiss, K. (2020). Learning fractions with and without educational technology: What matters for high-achieving and low-achieving students? *Learning and Instruction, 65*, 101264. https://doi.org/10.1016/j.learninstruc.2019.101264

Rose, J. (2020). The grade-level expectations trap: How lockstep math lessons leave students behind. *Education Next, 20*(3), 30–37.

Schuetz, R. L., Biancarosa, G., & Goode, J. (2018). Is technology the answer? Investigating students' engagement in math. *Journal of Research on Technology in Education, 50*(4), 318–332. https://doi.org/10.1080/15391523.2018.1490937

U.S. Department of Education. (2017). *Reimagining the role of technology in education: 2017 National education technology plan update, office of educational technology.* Author.

12

DIGITAL LEARNING FOR STUDENTS WITH DISABILITIES

Pei-Lin Weng

Guiding Questions:

- How does digital learning assist in teaching academic and functional curricula?
- Why is it crucial to incorporate the principles of Universal Design for Learning when creating digital learning materials?
- What do you look for when evaluating commercially available digital learning materials?
- What are the benefits of choosing learning devices with built-in accessibility features?
- What are the two primary resources for obtaining assistive technology devices?

Introduction

According to the most recent data from the National Center for Education Statistics (2022), 7.2 million students, equivalent to 15% of public student populations in the United States, are served under the Individuals with Disabilities Education Act (IDEA). Among these students, 33% are identified with specific learning disabilities; 19% have a speech or language impairment; 15% have other health impairments; 12% have autism spectrum disorders; 7% have developmental delays; 6% have intellectual disabilities; 5% are experiencing emotional disturbances; 2% have multiple disabilities; 1% have hearing impairments; and 0.5% are categorized as having an orthopedic impairment, visual impairment, traumatic brain injury, or deafness and blindness combined.

DOI:10.4324/9781003274537-15

Students with disabilities are considered one of the most vulnerable school populations because of the barriers created by inaccessible learning materials. For example, students who are deaf or hard of hearing have difficulties processing verbal/sound information given by teachers or verbal/sound information shown in videos if no other modalities (e.g., subtitles, audio transcriptions) are provided. In terms of assisting students with disabilities to access information, an area that warrants further examination is digital learning. Digital learning refers to "any instructional practice that effectively uses technology to strengthen a student's learning experience and encompasses a wide spectrum of tools and practices" (Every Student Succeeds Act, 2015, p. 1969).

History of Digital Learning for Students With Disabilities

Students with disabilities have used forms of digital learning since 1970 (Benjamin, 1988). With the development of technology, different terms have been used over the years, such as "computer-assisted instruction" (Hall et al., 2000; Mautone et al., 2005), "computer-based instruction" (Ayres et al., 2006; Mechling et al., 2003), "technology-based instruction" (Maccini et al., 2002), "e-learning" (Petretto et al., 2021), and "online learning" (Smith & Basham, 2014). These terms—which all fall under the big umbrella of "digital learning"—share similar qualities but are not necessarily interchangeable.

The development and emergence of different technologies have influenced digital learning and its terminology, thus necessitating a review of the history of digital learning for students with disabilities. In the late 1970s, microcomputers (e.g., desktop computers) were becoming accessible in school settings (Aslan & Reigeluth, 2011). Up until the 1980s, microcomputers were mainly confined to traditional school settings such as classrooms and were used as a supplement, such as a drill and practice (Kulik & Kulik, 1991; Woodward & Rieth, 1997). Around the early 2000s—the internet period—computers had become more prevalent in the educational system and were used with the internet to teach academic and functional curricula for students with disabilities (Aslan & Reigeluth, 2011).

With the advancement of technology (including hardware, software, and the internet), by the 2010s, digital learning had entered an era when mobile devices (e.g., laptops, tablets) were widely used in education (Hudson, 2019; Shah, 2011). Finally, in recent years, digital learning has entered a new era using cloud-based digital environments such as Blackboard, Google Classroom, and Chromebooks to increase availability and mobility. With the flexibility and availability afforded by mobile computers and cloud platforms, digital learning can be delivered not only in various K–12 school settings but also in students' homes in the community. Digital learning can also facilitate various delivery modes, such as in-person, hybrid (i.e., blended), or distance learning (Li et al., 2021). In addition, digital learning materials and digital textbooks—with or without assistive technology—are widely used in special education.

Digital Learning for Academic and Functional Curricula

Decades of meta-analyses and systematic reviews have revealed the effectiveness of digital learning for students with disabilities in learning academic curricula such as reading, mathematics, science, or social science (Benavides-Varela et al., 2020; Galuschka et al., 2014). In this section, we share an example of how digital learning materials and platforms can help level the playing field for students with disabilities in learning academic curricula at high-needs schools. On a national level, there is a critical lack of qualified teachers (García & Weiss, 2019), and the situation is especially dire in high-needs schools, in particular, among science, technology, engineering, and mathematics (STEM) teachers, including STEM teachers who specialize in teaching students with disabilities (e.g., Teachers for the Visually Impaired; DiFlavio, 2022).

Unable to find a local teacher, a school for blind and low-vision students hired a math teacher of students with visual impairments (TVI) who lives out of state to teach their students virtually. A *teacher for visual impairment* is a specific term referring to a teacher who is qualified to teach students who are blind or who have low vision. This teacher (whom the students refer to as the "teacher in the box") used video and software programs (such as JAWS, or Perky Duck) to teach her students synchronously from another state (Bouck & Weng, 2014). The class of five students who were blind or had low vision enjoyed the setup and thought the teacher was accessible to them.

An example of using digital learning materials to teach subjects in academic curricula is mathematics. Mathematics is a visual language that cannot be accurately represented via a simple text-to-speech function. Math Speak, a digital math textbook, can easily be deciphered by students with visual impairments or print disabilities because it uses supported e-texts to present math materials verbally (using Nemeth math code for math equations) and verbal descriptions of graphs and figures. For example, for an algebraic equation, the computer verbalizes the equation (the level of speech information can be adjusted based on students' familiarity with Nemeth code).

Besides academic curricula, digital learning has also been found to be effective in teaching functional curricula. Figure 12.1 illustrates the relationship between academic curricula and functional curricula (see Figure 12.1).

Functional curricula are specifically designed for students in special education to promote independence and community access throughout school and prepare students for adulthood (Bouck, 2009). The advancement of technology not only decreases barriers for students in classroom settings but also creates more opportunities for students to practice their skills in community settings with technology. For example, two decades ago, video-based instructions (such as video prompting and video modeling) were presented to students on a desktop computer. For example, students watched the video-based instruction teaching community skills, such as grocery shopping, in the classroom and then practiced the skill in a real store (Ayres & Langone, 2008). Not surprisingly, teachers had to be involved in teaching and correcting students in the store because the students

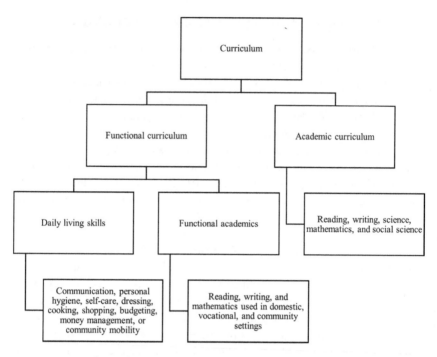

FIGURE 12.1 Relationship Between Academic and Functional Curricula

might not remember all the steps from the video they had viewed earlier. Due to advancement in technology in recent years, video-based instructions presented on mobile devices can now be used in both classroom and community settings (Weng & Bouck, 2014). As a result, with a mobile device as a learning medium, students can watch video-based instruction in a community setting and become less dependent on adult instruction or cues.

While these technologies facilitate learning, awareness of the benefits of digital learning materials is not enough. Knowing how to create or choose high-quality digital learning materials that can be used by a variety of students with different disabilities can save time and money in high-needs schools. We will discuss this in terms of content and devices. Specifically, we will look at what devices to use or purchase that can benefit all students. For content, we will concentrate on the principles (e.g., Universal Design for Learning) to incorporate when creating or purchasing digital learning materials; for devices, we suggest accessibility features and/or assistive technology to look for.

Universal Design for Learning (UDL)

All teachers, both general and special educators, have a responsibility to create digital materials that meet their students' diverse needs. The task of preparing/creating digital learning materials that can meet the different needs of all students (including those with various disabilities and those who speak different languages or come from different cultural backgrounds) can seem overwhelming. Some teachers might even ask if it would be easier if modifications were added to the learning materials after they find out which students they will be serving. But the answer is no—it would be like retrofitting a building after it has been completed by adding an accessibility ramp for wheelchairs. Retrofitting, whether either adding on to a building or adjusting learning materials (a) might be more costly in terms of time and money; (b) might only solve one problem at a time; or (c) might unintentionally single out target students. That's why it's critical for all teachers to plan and create digital materials that are accessible for all *from the very beginning.*

To help teachers create inclusive learning materials, the Center for Applied Special Technology (CAST), a federal grant-funded, nonprofit education research and development organization, developed the Universal Design for Learning (UDL) framework and guidelines for teachers on how to build learning materials for all students with and without disabilities (Center for Applied Special Technology, 2022). UDL consists of three principles: (a) provide multiple means of representation, (b) provide multiple means of action and expression, and (c) provide multiple means of engagement. By following the comprehensive UDL framework using its principles, guidelines, and checkpoints, teachers are able to create digital learning materials with the following qualities: (a) reduce barriers—but not academic challenges; (b) optimize levels of challenge and support; (c) meet the needs of all learners from the start; (d) provide equal access to learning; and (e) provide autonomy for students to control the method of accessing and expressing information.

UDL—although not limited to—is often presented in a digital form, which allows content to be presented via different affordances and multiple modalities (e.g., visual, auditory). CAST provides free digital resources, including interactive websites and UDL online e-books. If you are interested in learning more about UDL's principles, guidelines, and checkpoints, you will find more information on CAST's interactive websites:

https://udlguidelines.cast.org/?utm_medium=web&utm_campaign=none&utm_source=cast-about-udl

App and Software Evaluation

In addition to creating UDL materials, teachers can use commercially available digital options, such as software programs or applications. However, not all digital products are developed using evidence-based practice resources or undergo robust evaluation for their efficacy (Papadakis et al., 2020; Weng & Doughty, 2015). Therefore, before selecting software or applications for student use, teachers should conduct an app or software evaluation. Four examples of evidence-based practice evaluation rubrics are included in the following.

- Walker, H. (2011). Evaluating the effectiveness of apps for mobile devices. *Journal of Special Education Technology, 26*(4), 59–63.
- Boone, R., & Higgins, K. (2012). The software√-list: Evaluating educational software for use by students with disabilities. *Journal of Special Education Technology, 27*(1), 50–63.
- Weng, P.-L., & Taber-Doughty, T. (2015). Developing an app evaluation rubric for practitioners in special education. *Journal of Special Education Technology, 30*(1), 43–58.
- Papadakis, S., Kalogiannakis, M., & Zaranis, N. (2017). Designing and creating an educational app rubric for preschool teachers. *Education and Information Technologies, 22*(6), 3147–3165.

After careful evaluation of potential devices and materials, teachers should be able to select a well-designed software program or application with the following qualities:

- A simplified operating system for both teachers and students
- Affordability
- Modifiable design features (e.g., visual, auditory inputs, animation)
- Modification options to meet students' needs and preferences (e.g., font color/size, speech speed)
- Modifications to meet teachers' needs (e.g., adjustable levels, allowing for individualization, modifiable content)
- Setting options such as allowing alternative input devices (e.g., keyboard, switches, eye-tracking devices)
- Age-appropriate for users based on their age, not their abilities (Storey & Miner, 2011)

Further, it is critical that all software and applications meet the intended educational or functioning purposes (e.g., communication, learning math). It might seem time-consuming to conduct such evaluations. However, if teachers collaborate with other educators or school practitioners by sharing evaluation results, it will save time, money, and resources in the long run. The evaluation process provides teachers with a clear idea of the strengths and weaknesses of the app, but there are many other advantages, such as providing feedback to other professionals, gathering feedback from other professionals, and recommending appropriate apps for students or parents to use at home or in their communities.

Accessibility

Besides creating UDL materials, teachers also need to select devices (such as desktop computers, laptops, and tablets) appropriate for presenting digital materials. In the past, accessibility was an afterthought in the development of technology devices, which meant that teachers had to purchase additional accessibility software programs. Moreover, it typically took a long time before the students could truly benefit from add-on software programs for logistic reasons, such as a long wait on device purchase proposals, the actual purchase of the device, or installation by the school information technology department.

Fortunately, the task of selecting a device with accessibility features has become easier for teachers as more tech companies, such as Apple, began putting accessibility at the front and center of their product designs in the late 2010s because of laws and advocacy related to disabilities and accessibility. Indeed, using devices with built-in accessibility features is beneficial for teachers and students with and without disabilities. These features help teachers create/show digital learning materials and enable students to express their thoughts through multimodalities (e.g., text-to-speech, speech-to-text, audio description) without extra cost. Additionally, there are other advantages:

- Decreased stigma—It's much easier for students with disabilities to accept commercially available devices because they are using devices that others regularly use.
- Decreased financial burden—Unlike traditional add-on accessibility software programs or devices, built-in accessibility features are universal for all devices. Hence, the development cost is averaged out among all the devices.

Currently, the Apple products—iOS and macOS—systems operated on iPads and MacBooks, respectively—offer the most extensive built-in accessibility features for individuals and students with different disabilities. Many other operating systems, such as Android (for mobile devices), Chrome (for web-based computers), and Windows, also offer accessibility functions. The iOS system divides the accessibility features into three main categories—Vision, Hearing, and Physical and Motor—based on human physical senses; the Android system has five categories—Screen Reader, Display, Interaction Controls, Captions, and Audio.

It's critical to check for accessibility features before making a purchase. Take the "switch" feature in iOS and Android as an example. Both operating systems offer the "camera switch" feature (e.g., their built-in camera serves as a switch function). In iOS, the camera can distinguish between head movements (e.g., right or left head movement), which serves as switch functions; in Android, the camera can recognize facial expressions (smiles, looking right or left), which serve as switch functions.

Assistive Technology

Ideally, UDL materials—coupled with computer devices with accessibility features—should make all information accessible for students with disabilities so that they do not have to be dependent on specialized devices. However, for individuals with certain types of disabilities, specialized devices are necessary to access UDL materials and navigate computers. For example, students with limited verbal skills require augmentative and alternative communication (AAC) means, such as speech-generating devices, to express their thoughts. Alternatively, students with limited physical abilities might require switches to operate computers. Students who are blind might benefit from braille notetakers—devices with a refreshable braille display—to receive and express information via tactile means. Some might ask: Why can't students who are blind use the text-to-speech accessibility features on computers? They can. However, in some cases where too various sources of verbal information are competing with each other (e.g., text-to-speech sounds or the teacher is talking), braille notetakers—which do not make sounds—are helpful for students in processing information via additional tactile means.

The devices mentioned, such as speech-generating devices, switches, or braille notetakers, are referred to as assistive technology (AT) devices. By definition, an assistive technology device is "any item, piece of equipment or product system, whether acquired commercially, modified or customized, that is used to increase, maintain, or improve the functional capabilities of individuals with disabilities" (Assistive Technology Act [ATA], 1998).

Who is responsible for providing such critical devices, and how and where can they be obtained? According to IDEA, schools—*not* the parents of the students with disabilities—are required to provide assistive technology devices and services to students whose individualized education plans, or IEPs, specify those needs (Knighton, n.d.). Given the limited financial resources of many high-needs schools, special education service practitioners must often seek additional resources to support students who require assistive technology devices. There are two main sources for obtaining assistive technology devices for students—funding and lending resources, each serving different purposes and having its own advantages and disadvantages.

Funding resources are derived from two means: public resources (e.g., Medicaid, public special education systems, state vocational rehabilitation agencies, state grants) and private resources (e.g., private health insurance companies, private grants through organizations or companies). Medicaid is a state program for families and individuals with low incomes or limited resources. Applying funding opportunities for AT through state Medicaid and health insurance programs is a complicated process and has certain restrictions, such as AT having to be a medical necessity (Assistive Technology Industry Association, 2022; Sheldon & O'Connell, 2016). Therefore, it's important to make sure an assistive technology device prescribed by doctors is more than just a "medical necessity" and also meets other purposes, such as employment or education. The state of Minnesota provides a 10-step guide for finding funding for assistive technology (https://mn.gov/admin/at/funding-assistive-techx/).

Lending resources—including public and private resources—represent another great avenue for educators and practitioners. Public lending resources are typically offered through state agencies. Each state has its own lending libraries. Information on these libraries can be found on the Assistive Technology Act Training and Technical Assistance Center website (https://at3center.net/state-at-programs/). While lending libraries usually only provide short-term loans (e.g., 30 days) for AT devices, the process itself is much quicker, and lending applicants are not limited to professionals or practitioners who provide instruction to students with disabilities. Parents of children with disabilities can request lending services as well. For example, INDATA, one of the 58 federally funded lending libraries, is jointly run by Easterseals Crossroads (an organization founded in 1939 that provides services to children and adults with disabilities in Indiana) and the State of Indiana Division of Disability and Rehabilitative Services.

Lending opportunities are also available through private resources, such as assistive technology companies' device try-out programs. For example, teachers, practitioners, and parents can request device loan services, such as PRC-Saltillo's Evaluation Loan Program (https://saltillo.com/funding). As illustrated in Figure 12.2, obtaining assistive technology is a complex and multi-phased process, including device evaluation, tryout, application, waiting, and device maintenance phases. Both public and private loan programs provide students with a short-term solution to fill the gap before they receive their permanent assistive technology devices.

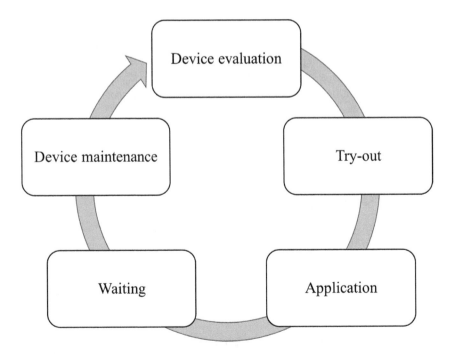

FIGURE 12.2 Five Phases of Obtaining Assistive Technology Devices

> **Key Takeaways:**
>
> 1. Retrofitting involves more time and money; that's why all teachers must plan and create digital materials accessible *for all* from the beginning.
> 2. Built-in accessibility features on commonly used devices decrease stigma and the financial burden of retrofitting.
> 3. Not all assistive technology devices can be replaced by mere accessibility features; therefore, it is critical to conduct a careful evaluation and obtain appropriate assistive technology devices.

Recommended Resources

Universal Design for Learning (UDL):

- Center for Applied Special Technology (CAST) interactive website: https://udlguidelines.cast.org/?utm_medium=web&utm_campaign=none&utm_source=cast-about-udl

App and Software Evaluation:

- Boone, R., & Higgins, K. (2012). The software√-list: Evaluating educational software for use by students with disabilities. *Journal of Special Education Technology, 27*(1), 50–63.
- Papadakis, S., Kalogiannakis, M., & Zaranis, N. (2017). Designing and creating an educational app rubric for preschool teachers. *Education and Information Technologies, 22*(6), 3147–3165.
- Walker, H. (2011). Evaluating the effectiveness of apps for mobile devices. *Journal of Special Education Technology, 26*(4), 59–63.
- Weng, P.-L., & Taber-Doughty, T. (2015). Developing an app evaluation rubric for practitioners in special education. *Journal of Special Education Technology, 30*(1), 43–58.

Assistive Technology:

- Funding: The state of Minnesota provides a 10-step guide for finding funding for assistive technology (https://mn.gov/admin/at/funding-assistive-techx/).
- Lending libraries: Assistive Technology Act Training and Technical Assistance Center website (https://at3center.net/state-at-programs/)

References

Aslan, S., & Reigeluth, C. M. (2011). A trip to the past and future of educational computing: Understanding its evolution. *Contemporary Educational Technology, 2*(1), 1–17.

Assistive Technology Act. (1998). Public law 105-193. Enacted by the 105th Congress, November 13, 1998. https://www.congress.gov/105/plaws/publ394/PLAW-105publ394.pdf

Assistive Technology Industry Association. (2022). *What is AT.* www.atia.org/home/at-resources/what-is-at/

Ayres, K. M., & Langone, J. (2008). Video supports for teaching students with developmental disabilities and autism: Twenty-five years of research and development. *Journal of Special Education Technology, 23*(3), 1–8.

Ayres, K. M., Langone, J., Boon, R. T., & Norman, A. (2006). Computer-based instruction for purchasing skills. *Education and Training in Developmental Disabilities,* 253–263.

Benavides-Varela, S., Callegher, C. Z., Fagiolini, B., Leo, I., Altoe, G., & Lucangeli, D. (2020). Effectiveness of digital-based interventions for children with mathematical learning difficulties: A meta-analysis. *Computers & Education, 157,* 103953.

Benjamin, L. T. (1988). A history of teaching machines. *American Psychologist, 43,* 703–712.

Bouck, E. C. (2009). No child left behind, the individuals with Disabilities Education Act and functional curricula: A conflict of interest? *Education and Training in Developmental Disabilities,* 3–13.

Bouck, E. C., & Weng, P. L. (2014). Hearing math: Algebra supported eText for students with visual impairments. *Assistive Technology, 26*(3), 131–139.

Center for Applied Special Technology. (2022). *Timeline of innovation.* www.cast.org/impact/timeline-innovation

DiFlavio. (2022). *A fast track to teachers for visually impaired students.* https://jsf.bz/news/a-fast-track-to-teachers-for-visually-impaired-students/

Every Student Succeeds Act. (2015). *Section 4102 (3), student support and academic enrichment grants.* www.congress.gov/bill/114th-congress/senate-bill/1177/text

Galuschka, K., Ise, E., Krick, K., & Schulte-Körne, G. (2014). Effectiveness of treatment approaches for children and adolescents with reading disabilities: A meta-analysis of randomized controlled trials. *PLoS One, 9*(2), e89900.

García, E., & Weiss, E. (2019). *The teacher shortage is real, large and growing, and worse than we thought. The first report in "The perfect storm in the teacher labor Market" series.* Economic Policy Institute.

Hall, T. E., Hughes, C. A., & Filbert, M. (2000). Computer-assisted instruction in reading for students with learning disabilities: A research synthesis. *Education and Treatment of Children,* 173–193.

Hudson, M. E. (2019). Using iPad-delivered instruction and self-monitoring to improve the early literacy skills of middle school nonreaders with developmental disabilities. *International Journal of Special Education, 34*(1), 182–196.

Knighton, K. (n.d.). *Assistive technology funding in the schools.* https://wvde.state.wv.us/osp/ASSISTIVETECHFUNDINGSCHOOLSQ&A.pdf

Kulik, C. L. C., & Kulik, J. A. (1991). Effectiveness of computer-based instruction: An updated analysis. *Computers in Human Behavior, 7*(1–2), 75–94.

Li, L., Xu, L. D., He, Y., He, W., Pribesh, S., Watson, S. M., & Major, D. A. (2021). Facilitating online learning via zoom breakout room technology: A case of pair programming involving students with learning disabilities. *Communications of the Association for Information Systems, 48*(1), 12.

Maccini, P., Gagnon, J. C., & Hughes, C. A. (2002). Technology-based practices for secondary students with learning disabilities. *Learning Disability Quarterly, 25*(4), 247–261.

Mautone, J. A., DuPaul, G. J., & Jitendra, A. K. (2005). The effects of computer-assisted instruction on the mathematics performance and classroom behavior of children with ADHD. *Journal of Attention Disorders, 9*(1), 301–312.

Mechling, L. C., Gast, D. L., & Barthold, S. (2003). Multimedia computer-based instruction to teach students with moderate intellectual disabilities to use a debit card to make purchases. *Exceptionality, 11*(4), 239–254.

National Center for Education Statistics. (2022). *Students with disabilities. Condition of education.* U.S. Department of Education, Institute of Education Sciences. https://nces.ed.gov/programs/coe/indicator/cgg

Papadakis, S., Kalogiannakis, M., & Zaranis, N. (2017). Designing and creating an educational app rubric for preschool teachers. *Education and Information Technologies, 22*(6), 3147–3165.

Papadakis, S., Vaiopoulou, J., Kalogiannakis, M., & Stamovlasis, D. (2020). Developing and exploring an evaluation tool for educational apps (ETEA) targeting kindergarten children. *Sustainability, 12*(10), 4201.

Petretto, D. R., Carta, S. M., Cataudella, S., Masala, I., Mascia, M. L., Penna, M. P., . . . Masala, C. (2021). The use of distance learning and E-learning in students with learning disabilities: A review on the effects and some hint of analysis on the use during COVID-19 outbreak. *Clinical Practice and Epidemiology in Mental Health: CP & EMH, 17*, 92.

Shah, N. (2011). Special education pupils find learning tool in iPad applications. *Education Week, 30*, 1–16.

Sheldon, J. R. Jr., & O'Connell, M. (2016). *Funding assistive technology through state Medicaid programs.* https://nls.org/wp-content/uploads/2019/02/Funding-Assistive-Technology-Through-State-Medicaid-Program-May-2016-1.pdf

Smith, S. J., & Basham, J. D. (2014). Designing online learning opportunities for students with disabilities. *Teaching Exceptional Children, 46*(5), 127–137.

Storey, K., & Miner, C. (2011). *Systematic instruction of functional skills for students and adults with disabilities.* Charles C. Thomas.

Weng, P. L., & Bouck, E. C. (2014). Using video prompting via iPads to teach price comparison to adolescents with autism. *Research in Autism Spectrum Disorders, 8*(10), 1405–1415.

Weng, P. L., & Taber-Doughty, T. (2015). Developing an app evaluation rubric for practitioners in special education. *Journal of Special Education Technology, 30*(1), 43–58.

Woodward, J., & Rieth, H. (1997). A historical review of technology research in special education. *Review of Educational Research, 67*(4), 503–536.

13

USING BITMOJI® AND GOOGLE CLASSROOM® TO SUPPORT REMOTE LITERACY INSTRUCTION IN HIGH-NEEDS SCHOOLS

Neil Grimes and Alicia Burchell

Guiding Questions:

- What parallels exist between physical and virtual classroom spaces?
- How can teachers leverage Google Classroom spaces using Bitmoji based on the parallels that exist between physical and virtual classrooms and their prior knowledge of teaching in physical classrooms in high-needs schools?
- How can teachers translate their knowledge of physical classrooms into digital classrooms within a literacy learning ecology in high-needs schools?

Introduction

The shift from teaching in the physical classroom space to the online learning space during COVID-19 brought to the surface preexisting digital divide issues, especially for students in high-needs schools in urban and rural areas, and particularly in communities of color (Ong, 2020; U.S. Department of Education, 2021). These issues included student accessibility to Wi-Fi, overall bandwidth use, and other infrastructure needs that were essential to delivering remote and online learning opportunities (Fishbane & Tomer, 2020). Nevertheless, schools were forced to come up with ways to deliver instruction regardless of the digital capabilities and accessibility that students had in their homes, leading to an increased desire to deliver instruction asynchronously and/or through hi-flex modes of instruction, which allows students to choose face-to-face or online mediums.

DOI:10.4324/9781003274537-16

Given the aforementioned challenges, Google Classroom®, a free learning management system for K-12 schools, offered an avenue for teachers to recreate the physical learning environment in a digital environment. Moreover, the use of Google Classroom to support students' learning simultaneously addressed the increasing digital divide. That is, not only did the platform offer an alternative to live video streaming, which requires tremendous bandwidth, it also allowed the transition to be more seamless as teachers began to think about ways to recreate the look of the physical classroom setting. Thus, the potential to reflect the traditional classroom space by creating a virtual space that reflected the physical classroom setting became a promising way to deliver remote instruction while utilizing the routines and dynamic pedagogical decisions guiding the physical classroom.

While many schools and districts continue to use other learning management systems, such as Blackboard, Canvas, Moodle, and Schoology, Google Classroom use has increased widely in recent years as a learning management system by K-12 schools and teachers. Launched in August 2014 and advertising itself as a one-stop shop for teachers, Google Classroom has grown to be used by a majority of K-12 schools and teachers across the United States (Education Week, 2017). Further, Google Chromebooks are currently the No. 1 selling device in the United States, Canada, Sweden, New Zealand, and the Netherlands for the K-12 community (Mainelli & Marden, 2015). Google-powered Chromebooks enabled with Google Classroom have streamlined the way that Google and its many applications are used in the K-12 environment. For example, in August 2016, a guardian summary feature was added, which allows parents to receive updates on students' work, missing assignments, or classroom announcements. Further, in 2021, Google rolled out more than 50 updates for Classroom, Meet, and other online education tools (Perez, 2021). In future years, improvements are expected to continue to be made in Google Classroom as its usage continues to grow in the K-12 community across the U.S. and the world (Perez, 2021).

As a result of the COVID-19 pandemic, and the proliferation of Google products in U.S. K-12 schools, many K-12 teachers have turned to Google Classroom as a means of recreating traditional classroom settings in a digital learning environment (Bryant et al., 2022). At the onset of the pandemic, teachers had to deliver instruction virtually as a result of school closings and learning shifting to online. Indeed, the vast majority of the K-12 schools and districts asked teachers to turn to Google Classroom in support of their teaching and learning.

The use of Google Classroom in person in the traditional classroom setting and also in the home environment impacts students' learning experiences and continues to shape American education well into the 21st century (Herold, 2020b). Unfortunately, disadvantaged or low-income families in high-needs schools cannot afford the broadband access needed for students' online learning experiences in the home environment, which has created a digital divide that affects communities of color at a disproportionate rate (Auxier & Anderson, 2020).

The digital divide can be addressed by students' families becoming more familiar with digital resources that are more accessible and familiar to students and teachers (Reich, 2019). As K-12 teachers become more accustomed to delivering instruction in virtual spaces, there is an emphasis on using the physical classroom space as a model for the virtual space (Fuentes & Grimes, 2020). The notion that if students are more familiar with the digital learning environment, it becomes more accessible to them has gained increased interest in recent years.

To help transition K-12 students to the virtual learning classroom environment, K-12 teachers have created virtual classrooms using Google Slides and Bitmoji (Fuentes & Grimes, 2020; Niess & Gillow-Wiles, 2021; Van Pate, 2022). Bitmoji® is an accessory application for social media platforms that individuals can use to create cartoon versions of themselves to be used in the digital environment as well as across various social media accounts (Lacoma, 2021). Specifically, Bitmoji are personalized cartoon avatars that can represent actual K-12 teachers in the virtual learning environment created using Google Slides. This virtual learning experience offers K-12 students the opportunity to explore and engage in a remote learning environment, and it has the potential to reinforce the learning that took place in the traditional classroom environment.

The extension of the traditional learning experience into virtual classroom spaces has the potential to offer K-12 students a more personalized and engaging learning experience. This chapter will discuss the creation of virtual classroom spaces that reflect traditional classroom spaces, with an emphasis on the importance of creating a sense of belonging. It will also share the benefits of virtual classrooms for teachers while giving an overview of literacy instruction in high-needs schools and lessons learned during the pandemic.

Background

Creating Virtual Classroom Spaces That Reflect Traditional Classroom Spaces

Teachers are well versed in designing a classroom space, and students benefit from the classroom routines developed over time. As teachers transfer their knowledge of teaching in the physical classroom space to the virtual classroom space, therefore, it is helpful for them to think about how learning new technologies and implementing them influences pedagogy in the space (physical or virtual) in which they teach. To create an interactive and engaging virtual classroom space, teachers can benefit from specific technology such as the use of Google Slides and Bitmoji. Teachers who create that virtual classroom space within a learning management system (LMS) such as Google Classroom will open up new learning experiences for their K-12 students.

The desire to create virtual spaces that reflect the physical classroom can be beneficial for students and teachers in a variety of ways. A comparison between the physical classroom and virtual classroom offers further insights

TABLE 13.1 Traditional Classroom vs. Virtual Classroom Spaces

Traditional Classroom Spaces	*Virtual Classroom Spaces*
• Fixed.	• Flexible.
• Synchronous learning.	• Synchronous and asynchronous learning.
• Heterogeneous and homogeneous student groups are used.	• Learner-centered and can be self-paced.
• Often teacher centered, and all students are expected to work at the same pace.	• Heterogeneous and homogeneous student groups are used.
• Classes are grouped by age/grade, and small groups are formed by skill level.	• Students can be grouped by subject content specific to age/grade or by subject content across ages/grades.
• Traditional teacher tools used: blackboard, notebooks, pencils, etc.	• Modern teacher tools used: multimedia, animation, and interactive.
• Learning environment can be boring, with fun kept to a minimum to prevent disciplinary issues.	• Learning environment can be stimulating and fun. Moderation tools allow the teacher to easily control the class, with the primary use of a moderation tool being to regulate and moderate the user-generated content in the virtual classroom space.
• Teacher and students collaborate in the physical classroom.	
• Evaluation involves taking tests and handing in manually graded assignments. Time-consuming and results are slow.	• Teachers and students collaborate online via audio, video, and text chat.
• High costs to provide in-person learning experience in traditional classrooms.	• More opportunities for shy or reserved students to share their voices.
• Resources are limited to school budgets.	• Automated evaluation provided through online practice or tests. Results are quick, accurate, and completely transparent.
	• Classes conducted in virtual classrooms are much cheaper.
	• Unlimited access to knowledge and free resources.

(see Table 13.1) into the two different learning spaces. Familiarity with digital learning environments places students in closer proximity to what they already know and are familiar with—the physical classroom space. Teachers have used Bitmoji of themselves on Google Slides to recreate the traditional classroom in the online environment, providing students with a sense of comfort in that they already know and have a bond with their teacher. Thinking about the dynamic power of affect and relationships in a classroom enables us to see the Bitmoji avatar as a means of maintaining the strong bonds between teacher and student that contribute to learning. Similarly, when students make a Bitmoji, they might feel a sense of belonging that otherwise might not be present when students are not together.

Thinking about the pedagogical decisions teachers make regarding the classroom environment and the ways in which those decisions can be reflected in Google Classroom (i.e., classroom libraries, word walls, sound walls, learning centers, etc.) offers an opportunity to bridge the gap between what students are familiar with in terms of learning in school and what they are not familiar with in terms of learning at home. Using Google Slides and Bitmoji allows for reinforcement and skill building in the virtual classroom space in an area such as literacy, which drives all other areas of learning. Literacy instruction in the online learning environment must be skills based (developmental) as well as creative and student centered (engaging) in order for students to benefit the most from their online learning experiences. For example, when teachers use Google Slides and Bitmoji to have their students practice their decoding or encoding using virtual manipulatives and sound walls or engage in vocabulary building by connecting to an eBook from a virtual classroom library, literacy activities become both skills-based and student-centered.

Benefits of Using Virtual Classrooms for Teachers and Students

Overall, a sense of belonging allows teachers and students to feel valued and included, and creating a sense of belonging is essential for student success in any classroom setting. The nature and makeup of K-12 classrooms presented unique challenges in that regard for distance learning and remote learning during the COVID-19 pandemic. A sense of belonging is particularly important in the Google Classroom when teacher and student Bitmoji are present on Google Slides, so that students can feel more connected to their learning experiences taking place in the virtual classroom environment. To foster that sense of belonging, both teachers and students can create virtual rooms that tell a story about who they are (see Figure 13.1).

FIGURE 13.1 Alicia's Virtual Classroom

Garrison et al. (1999) introduced the Community of Inquiry (CoI) construct as a way of understanding students' sense of belonging. This construct consists of three interrelated concepts: social presence, cognitive presence, and teaching presence, along with the interplay between them, to characterize the online educational learning experience. For students to be successful in this type of environment, they must be highly self-regulated and motivated (Garrison & Cleveland-Innes, 2005; Garrison et al., 1999). However, many younger students do not yet have the skills to navigate the distance learning environment without support (Gillow-Wiles & Niess, 2021). Further, Astin (1984) believed that conceptualizing a sense of belonging as an essential component of academic success grew from ideas around student involvement, characterized as the amount of "physical and psychological energy a student devotes to the academic experience" (p. 297). He further argued that an academic sense of belonging was essential to students' academic success.

Just as the CoI construct is important, a sense of belonging at school is an important component to online learning success. Peacock et al. (2020) identified three themes that contribute to greater student achievement in the online learning environment: interaction/engagement, a culture of learning, and support for learning. When a structured space is provided in the online environment, students and teachers are able to work collaboratively toward a pathway to deeper understanding. The following are best practices for developing a sense of belonging in an online environment that can lead to academic success: (a) teachers learn to decode and give importance to students' emotional well-being, (b) teachers make certain that each student has a role on a team and feels accepted, and (c) teachers give students opportunities to find and develop common interests with their team/group members in the classroom (St-Amand et al., 2017). Teachers that follow these best practices will engage their K-12 students more in their online learning experiences.

The greatest challenge to creating and implementing virtual classrooms is the time needed to plan in advance of delivering instruction to students. For example, the preparation of online learning environments using Google Slides requires structured preparation time to create content-specific skills development activities and structured learning opportunities. The Technological Pedagogical Content Knowledge (TPACK; Mishra & Koehler, 2006) framework describes the kinds of knowledge teachers need to successfully integrate technology in their instruction. Within regard to literacy, skills-development activities such as the use of classroom libraries to support reading practice as well as the use of sound walls, binders/notebooks, wall displays, and manipulatives are needed to close the gap between the T (technological) and the P (pedagogical) in the TPACK framework using Google Slides and Bitmoji online classroom environment. Examples of these are shown later in the chapter. Like the work of Shulman (1986), who demonstrated the reciprocal nature of content knowledge and pedagogical knowledge, the T in the Technological knowledge can begin to be seamlessly woven into the C in

Content knowledge and the P in Pedagogical knowledge by promoting teachers' use of the concept of the traditional classroom space as they know it while designing the online learning environment.

Literacy Instruction in High-Needs Schools

Providing literacy instruction in a remote learning environment during the COVID-19 pandemic was unprecedented and extremely challenging. Students in predominantly low-income schools and in urban locations lost more learning during the pandemic than their peers in high-income rural and suburban schools (Dorn et al., 2021). As a whole, low-income families were less likely to have access to the technology required to participate in online learning (Polikoff et al., 2020; Stelitano et al., 2020), and their parents were more likely to be essential workers (Berube & Bateman, 2020) with less time to devote to their children's online learning experiences. Black and Hispanic students might also have been disproportionately affected due to existing racial inequalities in school spending (Sosina & Weathers, 2019) and unequal access to high-quality teachers (Clotfelter et al., 2005; Goldhaber et al., 2015). Currently, only 35% of fourth-grade students are reading at the proficient or higher level (National Assessment for Educational Progress, 2019). As the pandemic enters its third year, a cluster of new studies shows that about a third of children in the youngest grades (K- 2) are missing reading benchmarks (Goldstein, 2022). "While children in every demographic group have been affected, Black and Hispanic children, as well as those from low-income families, those with disabilities, and those who are not fluent in English, have fallen the furthest behind" (Goldstein, 2022, para. 5).

Specifically, during the 2020–21 school year, there was a 15% reading achievement test gap score between students in low-poverty and high-poverty elementary schools (Kuhfeld et al., 2022). Students of color and low-income students suffered most. Students in majority-Black schools ended the school year six months behind in reading compared to students in majority-White schools, who ended up just three months behind (Dorn et al., 2021). As of this writing, national reading proficiency rates in high-needs schools in urban educational settings are not yet available from the COVID-19 era, in which students learned in a fully online environment for more than a year before returning to the traditional classroom learning environment in the 2021–22 school year. The national reading proficiency scores, when they finally come out from the remote learning years of the COVID-19 pandemic, will be markedly lower than in previous years based on what we currently know from available published sources (Dorn et al., 2021; Goldstein, 2022; Kuhfeld et al., 2022).

These figures are alarming, as literacy is central to all learning and can lead to either positive or negative outcomes for individual students. For example, as a whole, poor readers are more likely to drop out of high school, earn less money as adults, and become involved in the criminal justice system (Goldstein, 2022).

The available technology tools for early-literacy and literacy instruction for the K–12 environment vary widely in terms of quality. Many of the older technologies, including public television shows such as *Sesame Street*, are backed by research proving their impact, whereas many of the newer apps and software programs currently being marketed to teachers, parents, and caregivers are not (Herold, 2020a). According to Heather Schugar, a literacy professor at West Chester University, "Part of learning to read is going through struggle, but a lot of the technology we have does the thinking for kids" (Herold, 2020a, para. 14). In order to learn how to read, students need to experience the struggle of the reading experience and continually practice the skill of reading. Looking at the bigger picture of literacy education, even the best digital tools are intended to only complement classroom instruction. There's a huge difference between letting students use an app to reinforce literacy skills and teaching those same skills in a way that will motivate the individual child based on their interests, background knowledge, and strengths.

The pedagogical strategies employed by urban literacy teachers of youth at risk of failure tend to emphasize whole-group instruction and teacher control (Waxman et al., 1995). Less time is devoted to higher-order thinking skills, as teachers believe that these skills cannot be taught and supported due to low student vocabulary and reading skills (Losey, 1995; Williams, 2000). Haberman (1991, 2010) labeled these teacher-directed instructional approaches as a "pedagogy of poverty," arguing that they lead to low student engagement, passive resentment, and compliance, in addition to contributing to teacher burnout due to the high degree of accountability teachers feel for forcing students to learn. Gill et al. (2016) reimagines accountability for K–12 teachers by placing more value on teacher autonomy over federal- or state-mandated accountability that comes in the form of high-stakes testing. Students instructed with pedagogical strategies employed by urban literacy teachers that emphasize whole-group instruction and teacher control are unlikely to develop critical-thinking and problem-solving skills in literacy and typically act as passive nonparticipants in the classroom. Long-range negative effects can include lack of critical thinking skills, inexperience with formal essay and project-based research and writing, which are academic benchmarks for scholarship in higher education, and being ill prepared for the academic rigor required in higher education. Literacy instruction in the online learning environment needs to be skills based (developmental) as well as creative and student centered (engaging) for students to benefit the most from their online literacy and learning experiences. Teachers today need to have more autonomy, as emphasized by Gill et al. (2016), in order to create an online learning environment that is both developmental and engaging as well as hands-on so that students can benefit the most in their literacy and overall interactive learning experiences.

While some elements of effective in-person instruction carry over into virtual instruction such as establishing relationships, clarity of instruction, student engagement, and assessment practices (Fisher et al., 2021), the ways in which these elements are implemented can differ greatly. Teachers need to be supported in how to organize virtual learning through high-quality instructional planning. Although teachers' access to digital tools and resources for purchasing them varies widely, there are a number of free and low-cost digital tools that could be used for a variety of instruction purposes. But the number of options for interesting new digital tools to use can be overwhelming (Schwartz, 2020).

It is important to develop teachers' knowledge for teaching, TPACK, in both face-to-face and virtual contexts as well as to establish a sense of belonging so that students are more engaged in virtual learning experiences (Niess & Gillow-Wiles, 2021). Further, context is an essential component of educator knowledge development and practice (Swallow & Morrison, 2021). A major conclusion from studies done by Verloop et al. (2001) is that an understanding of teacher knowledge for teaching or context can be useful to improve teacher education and to make educational innovations more successful. Reflection also influences context, as reflection requires contextual anchors to make learning episodes meaningful for K-12 students (Loughran, 2002).

Lessons Learned: Remote Teaching During the COVID-19 Pandemic

Through an analysis of instructional practices and methods offered in remote learning settings during the COVID-19 pandemic, several areas or characteristics of effective literacy instruction emerged that will assist educators in understanding promising practices for the future. Building students' efficacy and autonomy in learning environments can be scaffolded to support positive affect and engagement in remote settings similarly to the manner in which this is accomplished in a physical classroom learning ecology and system (Cardullo et al., 2021; Miller, 2021; Thanasoulas, 2000). In this section, the importance of the classroom library, the use of binders/notebooks, the use of wall displays, the implementation of classroom management, and the use of manipulatives in a virtual classroom environment will be discussed.

Classroom Library—Finding Joy in Literacy

Teachers work hard to create a love of literacy for their students. For some, this is shown through creating a warm, organized, and enticing classroom library. Searching for classroom libraries on Pinterest will lead to cozy spaces filled with rugs, flexible seating, lamp lighting, and organized bins of books.

Teachers have been creating these same engaging spaces for students to find joy in literacy in the virtual classroom environment. Virtual classroom libraries might be organized by topic, such as authors, subjects or concepts, genres, reading levels, or phonics skills. Imagine how engaging it would be for a 6-year-old to have a virtual library filled with stuffed animals. When a student clicks on one of their favorite characters, they are taken to a live video, where they can watch a book come to life as it is being read to them. Many schools in low-socioeconomic communities lack the funding to buy books or materials to fill the classrooms. With the help of YouTube, Storyline Online, Epic, Reading A-Z, and other sites, students can gain access to countless texts and audiobooks in their virtual classrooms. Teachers can then link sites and or books to images in their virtual classroom libraries.

Binders/Notebooks

The days when students misplaced their classwork are long gone. In many traditional classroom settings, students were used to having binders or notebooks to organize notes and document their learning. Teachers are now creating and using digital notebooks to help students stay organized in their virtual classroom settings. Digital notebooks can be organized with tabs just like a real notebook and can be used in all subjects. During literacy instruction, students can use digital notebooks to complete sound, word, or sentence dictations, reading responses, or writing pieces. Students could add syllable types or cutting patterns to their notebook as they are learned. Spelling generalizations or definitions for common affixes or roots could be stored in a student's digital phonics notebook. Teachers have even used digital notebooks to organize how-to videos and anchor charts.

Wall Displays

Anchor charts are an artifact of learning and are often seen displayed in the physical classroom. Students use anchor charts as a resource. Wall space is limited in the physical classroom, but having these tools organized in a digital notebook allows students to have access to all of the anchor charts for the year, not just the past few weeks. In addition to anchor charts, teachers typically display a variety of other tools in their physical classrooms. Word walls and sound walls often take up a large amount of physical wall space. Word walls are used to organize new vocabulary and content words in any given subject, whereas sound walls help readers and writers connect a speech sound to a written symbol or letter/s. Both of these tools have been improved when brought to the virtual classroom environment. With a click, students can now hear the sound a group of letters makes or have a word pronounced to them.

Classroom Management

Classroom management is an important part of teaching. Classroom management is the process by which teachers maintain appropriate student behavior and create a sense of belonging through engaging learning activities for the class. A large part of classroom management consists of building solid relationships with students, encouraging students to do their best, and making the best choices to create the most conducive environment for learning.

Giving students a glimpse into their teachers' and classmates' lives outside of school is one way that relationships and a sense of community can be built. Teachers can use Google Slides as a place to introduce themselves to the class. By decorating a virtual room with items that represent their favorite hobbies and family members, students get to learn about the individuals that they share a classroom with whether it's virtual or brick and mortar.

Positive behavior interventions and supports (PBIS) is a program used in tens of thousands of schools in the U.S., Australia, Iceland, New Zealand, and Canada (Ryan & Baker, 2020). PBIS aims to alter school environments by creating improved systems and procedures that promote positive change in student behavior by targeting staff behaviors at the elementary (Bradshaw et al., 2008a, 2008b) and high school levels (Bradshaw et al., 2015). The Educators' Toolkit provides resources for implementation and classroom management (Ayers Institute for Learning & Innovation, 2022). Many PBIS programs include a token economy system. In the physical classroom, you might see stickers, play money, or tickets earned by students for following the schoolwide rules. Teachers have found that this same economic system can be brought into the virtual classroom setting. Students can earn virtual stickers, certificates, and other tokens created on Canva for positive behavior and turn them in to purchase rewards like admittance to virtual game rooms, homework passes, pajama day, virtual lunch with the teacher, and many others.

The Zones of Regulation is a framework and curriculum that supports the development of self-regulation of behaviors, emotions, and sensory needs and, therefore, can be an important component of classroom management (Ochocki et al., 2020). The use of Bitmoji has made it possible for teachers to provide students with visual images of specific emotions. During the pandemic, mental health became a struggle for many students. Teachers found creative ways to check in on their students virtually. Some teachers created daily check-ins using Nearpod on Google Slides to monitor their students' mental health, and Bitmoji helped students express how they were feeling without needing to find the words. They became a fun way for teachers to personalize their instructional materials for their students and develop their relationships via a virtual world.

Manipulatives

In the physical classroom, the term "manipulative" has been used to describe objects that allow a learner to explore a concept using a concrete, hands-on approach.

Some manipulatives you might see in a classroom include base-ten blocks, letter tiles, counters, and fraction bars. These same manipulatives and many others can also be used in the virtual classroom (Bouck et al., 2010; Moyer et al., 2001, 2002). Today, when someone thinks of concrete or hands-on literacy instruction, they think of the Orton-Gillingham approach. Created in the 1930s for students with dyslexia by neuropsychiatrists and pathologist Dr. Samuel T. Orton and educator-psychologist Anna Gillingham, the Orton-Gillingham approach is considered the gold standard for reading instruction. It is backed by the science of reading and works for all learners, unlike whole language or balanced literacy, which works for less than half of the population (Garnett, 2013). The Orton-Gillingham approach combines direct, multisensory teaching strategies with systematic, sequential lessons focused on phonics. Research has shown us that manipulatives don't have to be physically touched. Instead, manipulatives need to have an element of movement (Fyfe et al., 2014). In the virtual classroom setting, manipulatives can be moved on a screen, allowing for the same effect. Virtual manipulatives have allowed all students access to materials. In the physical classroom, students often have to share manipulatives due to a lack of resources. However, in the virtual classroom, teachers are able to give manipulatives to all learners who have access to the internet.

During literacy instruction, a teacher might use virtual manipulatives during a phonological or phonemic awareness task to segment syllables or phonemes in a word. Teachers can use boxes and digital letter tiles to support sound-spelling mapping (encoding) or decoding.

Classroom Discussions

Classroom discussions make up a large part of a student's learning experience. In a virtual setting, Zoom, Google Meet, Skype, and Teams allow for live discussions similar to those going on in a physical classroom. However, quiet or reserved students might not contribute in the physical setting due to anxiety or other factors. In a virtual classroom with high expectations for participation, teachers found means to promote classroom discussions and to make everyone feel comfortable and safe. Websites like Padlet, NowComment, and Flip allowed students the opportunity to practice what they would say or type their responses to engage with peers. In addition, Google Classroom has a built-in question feature, and Google Slides with the Nearpod or PearDeck add-on have a variety of tools that can be used to stimulate discussion on a given topic. These new forums for class discussions allow even the quietest students' voices to be heard.

Conclusion

The use of Google Slides and Bitmoji to create a virtual classroom environment helps to connect K-12 students to their classroom experience and fosters a sense of belonging. The virtual classroom space represents a continuation of students' traditional classroom learning experience and allows students to interact with educational technology tools and other resources while in the home environment. For the virtual classroom space to reinforce learning and to ensure equity for all students, state and federal governments must make internet and broadband affordable and accessible to all American families. If this happens, educational technology can have a greater impact on student learning, overall achievement, high school graduation rates, and preparing students for a technologically driven future, where more than 65% of today's young people will work in jobs that don't currently exist (World Economic Forum, 2016). Bitmoji Classrooms built using Google Slides have the potential to support literacy instruction in high-needs schools where students need the most learning support to prepare them for the jobs of the future that will require both high rates of literacy and technology skills.

Virtual classrooms created using Google Slides and Bitmoji offer teachers a platform that allows them to use the layout of their traditional classroom space as a model for setting up their virtual classroom space. Teachers in the K-12 environment are in various stages of online fluency. While there is still a learning curve to begin using Google Slides and designing Bitmoji, the COVID-19 pandemic presented an opportunity for many of America's K-12 teachers to replicate their physical classrooms in a remote or online learning environment. This could become a high-impact pedagogical practice that engages K-12 students in the online environment outside of the traditional in-person school day.

The learning activities set up by a teacher in the virtual classroom space can be both skill driven and student led as students become more engaged and empowered in their learning experiences. K-12 teachers who explore and implement strategies such as the use of Google Slides, Bitmoji, classroom libraries, digital notebooks, wall displays, a PBIS program that incorporates the Zones of Regulation framework, manipulatives, and classroom discussion–based tools will give their students the best opportunities to achieve success in their literacy and overall learning experiences. Virtual classroom spaces present the opportunity for learning to be more student driven rather than teacher led. Students in high-needs schools have the potential to benefit the most from the opportunity to learn in both traditional classroom spaces and virtual classroom spaces. These students need to continually practice and develop their literacy skills, including reading comprehension, phonemic awareness, phonics, morphology, vocabulary, high-frequency words, spelling, and handwriting as they engage in various student-driven activities in virtual classroom spaces. Teachers and parents who support students' learning experiences in both physical and virtual classroom spaces give students the best chance at academic success and learning growth during their K-12 experiences.

> **Key Takeaways:**
>
> 1. The digital divide can be addressed by utilizing digital resources that are more accessible and familiar to students and teachers, such as Google Classroom.
> 2. Online classrooms created using Google Slides and Bitmoji offer teachers a platform that allows them to use the layout of their traditional classroom space as a model for setting up their digital classroom space.
> 3. The use of Google Slides and Bitmoji to create a virtual classroom environment helps to connect K-12 students to their classroom experience and fosters a sense of belonging.
> 4. Building students' efficacy and autonomy in literacy learning environments can be scaffolded to support positive affect and engagement in remote settings in similar ways to the manner in which it is accomplished in a physical classroom.

Recommended Resources

Books:

Clark, H., & Avrith, T. (2021). *The Google infused classroom: A guidebook to making thinking visible and amplifying student voice*. EdTechTeam Press.

Collins, R. (2021). *Google classroom + Zoom for teachers*. Wed Books Publications.

Fisher, D., Frey, N., & Hattie, J. (2021). *The distance learning playbook, grades K-12: Teaching for engagement & impact in any setting*. Corwin.

Websites:

- Canva for Education: www.canva.com/education/: This website provides educators with templates for everything from engaging Google Slides to graphic organizers, storyboards, videos, and more.
- Creating a Classroom Library Using Bitmoji and Google Slides: www.youtube.com/watch?v=AAyQZlMcl8k
  This website provides an overview on how to create a classroom library in a K-12 educational setting using Bitmoji and Google Slides.
- Cutting patterns/dividing multisyllable words "Rooms" to match reading programs on Google Slides.

  o FUNdations
  o 95% CORE
  o Orton Gillingham
  o Handwriting Without Tears

Supporting Remote Literacy Instruction in High-Needs Schools **193**

- o Zaner-Bloser, Inc.
- o SPIRE
- o Wilson
- o Barton
- o Kilpatrick One-Minute Drills
- o Amplify
- o Really Great Reading
- o Reading Horizons
- o Heggerty

- Digital Letter Tiles: www.reallygreatreading.com/lettertiles/: This website provides educators with digital letter tiles for phonics instruction.
- Flip: https://info.flip.com/: This website is a video bulletin board. Teachers and students can record and react to videos around a central theme.
- Free and Royalty-free Images: www.freepik.com/: This website is a database that contains images that educators can use when creating their own Bitmoji classrooms.
- Googles Slides Templates: https://slidesmania.com: This website provides free Google Slides templates. Under the education tab, educators are presented with templates for digital notebooks, teacher planners, interactive games, flashcards, manipulatives, certificates, and more.
- How to Make a Digital Notebook on Google Slides: www.youtube.com/watch?v=TkXERNjcEVA
  This website provides a how-to guide in creating a digital notebook using Google Slides.
- Incorporating Pear Deck with Google Slides: www.peardeck.com/googleslides: This website presents educators the opportunity to learn how to incorporate the Pear Deck add-on in Google Slides. Pear Deck brings Google Slides to life with interactive questions, formative assessments, live whiteboards, and more.
- Nearpod: https://nearpod.com/: This website presents educators with the opportunity to learn how to incorporate the Nearpod add-on in Google Slides. Nearpod deepens student understanding and engagement on Google Slides through gamification and interactive slides for formative assessment, interactive videos, and more.
- NowComment: https://nowcomment.com/: This website turns texts, images, and videos into conversations through group annotation and comments.
- Padlet: https://padlet.com/: This website presents educators with a digital bulletin board. Teachers and students can post notes on a common page that may contain links, videos, images, and document files.
- PBIS Rewards for Online Learning: www.pbisrewards.com/resources/distance-learning/: This website presents educators with resources for implementing PBIS through distance learning.

- Specific Literacy Instruction Focus (Live or Self-Paced) Activities to Use on Google Slides provided by The Virtual Classroom, Virtual Education Consulting, Instructional Coaching, & Tutoring Service.

  o Word decoding with blending boards
  o Sound spelling mapping (encoding)
  o Vocabulary introduction or reinforcement
  o Word, sound, or picture sorts
  o Grapheme/phoneme drills, introduction, or reinforcement
  o Morphology work
  o Phonological awareness/phonemic awareness skills
  o Comprehension strategy introduction or skill reinforcement activities
  o Fluency work
  o Handwriting/letter formation
  o Genres reading/writing
  o Grammar
  o Heart words (irregular words)
  o Spelling Generalizations
  o Syllable types

- Transparent PNG images: https://favpng.com/: This website is a database that contains over 16 million free transparent PNG files that teachers can use when creating their own Bitmoji classrooms.
- Virtual Education Consulting, Instructional Coaching, & Tutoring Service www.thevirtualclassroom.org/: This website outlines research-proven teaching methods and practices in literacy and mathematics. Homeschool parents and school districts can find access to education consulting, instructional coaching, and student support services, all in a virtual classroom setting.
- Using Google Slides: www.google.com/slides/about/: This website provides an overview of Google Slides' features, templates, and plans.
- Using Hyperdocs on Google Slides: https://hyperdocs.co/: This website provides digital lesson plans and lesson plan templates that are designed by teachers and given to students. A hyperdoc is a single document that holds hyperlinks to all the resources a student would need to complete a learning cycle.
- Visual Sound Drills and Digital Blending Board: https://ogdrill.marooneyfoundation.org/#/DeckConfiguration
  This website provides educators with tools for virtual phonics instruction. Graphemes and syllable cards can be used for visual sound drills and word-blending drills.
- Virtual Whiteboard: www.whiteboard.chat/: This website provides educators with an interactive online whiteboard. Teachers can see their students' responses in real time.

References

Astin, A. W. (1984). Student involvement: A developmental theory for higher education. *Journal of College Student Personnel, 25*(4), 297–308.

Auxier, B., & Anderson, M. (2020, July 27). As schools close due to the coronavirus, some U.S. students face a digital "homework gap." *Pew Research Center.* www.pewresearch.org/fact-tank/2020/03/16/as-schools-close-due-to-the-coronavirus-some-u-s-students-face-a-digital-homework-gap/

Ayers Institute for Learning & Innovation. (2022). PBIS—Positive behavior supports and interventions. *eduTOOLBOX.* www.edutoolbox.org/rasp/2163?route=toolkit%2&list%2F6105%2F910

Berube, A., & Bateman, N. (2020, April 3). Who are the workers already impacted by the COVID-19 recession? *Brookings.* www.brookings.edu/research/who-are-the-workers-already-impacted-by-the-covid-19-recession/

Bouck, E. C., & Flanagan, S. M. (2010). Virtual manipulatives: What they are and how teachers can use them. *Intervention in School and Clinic, 45*(3), 186–191.

Bradshaw, C. P., Koth, C. W., Bevans, K. B., Ialongo, N., & Leaf, P. J. (2008a). The impact of school-wide positive behavioral interventions and supports (PBIS) on the organizational health of elementary schools. *School Psychology Quarterly, 23*(4), 462.

Bradshaw, C. P., Pas, E. T., Debnam, K. J., & Lindstrom Johnson, S. (2015). A focus on implementation of positive behavioral interventions and supports (PBIS) in high schools: Associations with bullying and other indicators of school disorder. *School Psychology Review, 44*(4), 480–498.

Bradshaw, C. P., Reinke, W. M., Brown, L. D., Bevans, K. B., & Leaf, P. J. (2008b). Implementation of school-wide positive behavioral interventions and supports (PBIS) in elementary schools: Observations from a randomized trial. *Education and Treatment of Children, 31*, 1–26.

Bryant, J., Dorn, E., Hall, S., & Panier, F. (2022, August 1). Reimagining a more equitable and resilient K-12 education system. *McKinsey & Company.* www.mckinsey.com/industries/education/our-insights/reimagining-a-more-equitable-and-resilient-k-12-education-system

Cardullo, V., Wang, C. H., Burton, M., & Dong, J. (2021). K-12 teachers' remote teaching self-efficacy during the pandemic. *Journal of Research in Innovative Teaching & Learning, 14*(1), 32–45. https://doi.org/10.1108/JRIT-10-2020-0055

Clotfelter, C. T., Ladd, H. F., & Vigdor, J. (2005). Who teaches whom? Race and the distribution of novice teachers. *Economics of Education Review, 24*(4), 377–392. https://doi.org/10.1016/j.econedurev.2004.06.008

Dorn, E., Hancock, B., Sarakatsannis, J., & Viruleg, E. (2021, November 11). Covid-19 and education: The lingering effects of unfinished learning. *McKinsey & Company.* www.mckinsey.com/industries/education/our-insights/covid-19-and-education-the-lingering-effects-of-unfinished-learning

Education Week. (2017, April). *EdWeek market brief: K-12 intel for business leaders.* Market Brief: Amazon, Apple, Google, and Microsoft: How 4 Tech Titans Are Reshaping the Ed-Tech Landscape. https://marketbrief.edweek.org/

Fishbane, L., & Tomer, A. (2020, March 20). As classes move online during COVID-19, what are disconnected students to do? *Brookings.* www.brookings.edu/blog/the-avenue/2020/03/20/as-classes-move-online-during-covid-19-what-are-disconnected-students-to-do

Fisher, D., Frey, N., & Hattie, J. (2021). *The distance learning playbook: Grades K-12*. Corwin.

Fuentes, D., & Grimes, N. (2020, October). Creating Google classrooms using Bitmoji and Google slides: An early pandemic pedagogical response. In *SITE interactive conference proceedings* (pp. 114–119). Association for the Advancement of Computing in Education (AACE).

Fyfe, E. R., McNeil, N. M., Son, J. Y., & Goldstone, R. L. (2014). Concreteness fading in mathematics and science instruction: A systematic review. *Educational Psychology Review, 26*(1), 9–25.

Garnett, K. (2013). Orton Gillingham method. In C. R. Reynolds, K. J. Vannest, & E. Fletcher-Janzen (Eds.), *Encyclopedia of special education: A reference for the education of children, adolescents, and adults with disabilities and other exceptional individuals* (4th ed.). Wiley.

Garrison, D. R., Anderson, T., & Archer, W. (1999). Critical inquiry in a text-based environment: Computer conferencing in higher education. *The Internet and Higher Education, 2*(2–3), 87–105.

Garrison, D. R., & Cleveland-Innes, M. (2005). Facilitating cognitive presence in online learning: Interaction is not enough. *The American Journal of Distance Education, 19*(3), 133–148.

Gill, B. P., Lerner, J. S., & Meosky, P. (2016). Reimagining accountability in K-12 education. *Behavioral Science & Policy, 2*(1), 57–70.

Gillow-Wiles, H., & Niess, M. L. (2021). Is there recess on mars? Developing a sense of belonging in online learning. In H. Gillow-Wiles & M. Niess (Eds.), *Handbook of research on transforming teachers' online pedagogical reasoning for engaging K-12 students in virtual learning* (pp. 1–18). IGI Global.

Goldhaber, D., Lavery, L., & Theobald, R. (2015). Uneven playing field? Assessing the teacher quality gap between advantaged and disadvantaged students. *Educational Researcher, 44*(5), 293–307. https://doi.org/10.3102/0013189X15592622

Goldstein, D. (2022, March 9). It's "alarming": Children are severely behind in reading. *The New York Times—International Edition*. https://advance.lexis.com/api/document?collection= news&id=urn:contentItem:64Y9-84P1-DYR7-C2PG-00000-00&context=1516831

Haberman, M. (1991). The pedagogy of poverty versus good teaching. *Phi Delta Kappan, 73*(4), 290–294.

Haberman, M. (2010). The pedagogy of poverty versus good teaching. *Phi Delta Kappan, 92*(2), 81–87. https://doi.org/10.1177/003172171009200223

Herold, B. (2020a, December 3). Schools already struggled to teach reading right. Now they have to do it online. *Education Week*. www.edweek.org/teaching-learning/schools-already-struggled-to-teach-reading-right-now-they-have-to-do-it-online/2020/09

Herold, B. (2020b, December 17). How Google classroom is changing teaching: Q&A with researcher Carlo Perrotta. *Education Week*. https://www.edweek.org/technology/how-google-classroom-is-changing-teaching-q-a-with-researcher-carlo-perotta/2020/12

Kuhfeld, M., Soland, J., Lewis, K., & Morton, E. (2022, March 3). The pandemic has had devastating impacts on learning. what will it take to help students catch up? *Brookings*. www.brookings.edu/blog/brown-center-chalkboard/2022/03/03/the-pandemic-has-had-devastating-impacts-on-learning-what-will-it-take-to-help-students-catch-up/

Lacoma, T. (2021, September 22). What is Bitmoji and how do you use it in 2022? *Digital Trends*. www.digitaltrends.com/mobile/what-is-bitmoji/

Losey, K. M. (1995). Mexican American students and classroom interaction: An overview and critique. *Review of Educational Research, 65*(3), 283–318.

Loughran, J. J. (2002). Effective reflective practice: In search of meaning in learning about teaching. *Journal of Teacher Education, 53*(1), 33–43.

Mainelli, T., & Marden, M. (2015). *The economic value of Chromebooks for educational institutions*. IDC White Paper. https://webobjects.cdw.com/webobjects/media/pdf/google/CB-EconomicValue-Whitepaper.pdf

Miller, K. E. (2021). A light in students' lives: K-12 teachers' experiences (re) building caring relationships during remote learning. *Online Learning, 25*(1), 115–134.

Mishra, P., & Koehler, M. J. (2006). Technological pedagogical content knowledge: A framework for teacher knowledge. *Teachers College Record, 108*(6), 1017–1054.

Moyer, P. S., Bolyard, J. J., & Spikell, M. A. (2001). Virtual manipulatives in the K-12 classroom. In *Proceedings of the International Conference on New Ideas in Mathematics Education*, Palm Cove.

Moyer, P. S., Bolyard, J. J., & Spikell, M. A. (2002). What are virtual manipulatives? *Teaching Children Mathematics, 8*(6), 372–377.

National Assessment of Educational Progress. (2019). NAEP report cards—home. *The Nation's Report Card*. Retrieved October 17, 2022, from www.nationsreportcard.gov/

Niess, M. L., & Gillow-Wiles, H. (2021). Developing teachers' knowledge for teaching in virtual contexts: Lessons from the pandemic of 2020–2021. In M. Niess & H. Gillow-Wiles (Eds.), *Handbook of research on transforming teachers' online pedagogical reasoning for engaging K-12 students in virtual learning* (pp. 643–664). IGI Global.

Ochocki, S., Frey, A., Patterson, D., Herron, F., Beck, N., & Dupper, D. (2020). Evaluating the Zones of Regulation® intervention to improve the self-control of elementary students. *International Journal of School Social Work, 5*(2), 2.

Ong, P. M. (2020). *COVID-19 and the digital divide in virtual learning*. https://knowledge.luskin.ucla.edu/wp-content/uploads/2020/12/Digital-Divide-Phase2_brief_release_v01.pdf

Peacock, S., Cowan, J., Irvine, L., & Williams, J. (2020). An exploration into the importance of a sense of belonging for online learners. *International Review of Research in Open and Distributed Learning, 21*(2), 18–35.

Perez, S. (2021, February 17). Google to roll out slate of over 50 updates for classroom, meet and other online education tools. *TechCrunch*. https://techcrunch.com/2021/02/17/google-to-roll-out-slate-of-over-50-updates-for-classroom-meet-and-other-online-education-tools/

Polikoff, M., Saavedra, A. R., & Korn, S. (2020, May 8). Not all kids have computers—And they're being left behind with schools closed by the coronavirus. *Conversation*. https://theconversation.com/not-all-kids-have-computers-and-theyre-being-left-behind-with-schools-closed-by-the-coronavirus-137359

Reich, J. (2019, February 1). Teaching our way to digital equity. *ASCD*. www.ascd.org/el/articles/teaching-our-way-to-digital-equity

Ryan, C., & Baker, B. (2020). *The PBIS team handbook: Setting expectations and building positive behavior*. Free Spirit Publishing.

Schwartz, S. (2020, March 25). Flood of online learning resources overwhelms teachers. *Education Week*. www.edweek.org/teaching-learning/flood-of-online-learning-resources-overwhelms-teachers/2020/03

Shulman, L. S. (1986). Those who understand: Knowledge growth in teaching. *Educational Researcher, 15*(2), 4–14.

Sosina, V. E., & Weathers, E. S. (2019). Pathways to inequality: Between-district segregation and racial disparities in school district expenditures. *AERA Open, 5*(3). https://doi.org/10.1177/2332858419872445

St-Amand, J., Girard, S., & Smith, J. (2017). Sense of belonging at school: Defining attributes, determinants, and sustaining strategies. *IAFOR Journal of Education, 5*(2). https://doi.org/10.22492/ije.5.2.05

Stelitano, L., Doan, S., Woo, A., Diliberti, M., Kaufman, J. H., & Henry, D. (2020). *The digital divide and COVID-19: Teachers' perceptions of inequities in students' internet access and participation in remote learning. Data note: Insights from the American Educator Panels* [Research Report No. RR-A134–3]. RAND Corporation.

Swallow, M. J., & Morrison, M. L. (2021). Intersections of micro-level contextual factors and technological pedagogical knowledge. In M. Niess & H. Gillow-Wiles (Eds.), *Handbook of research on transforming teachers' online pedagogical reasoning for engaging K-12 students in virtual learning* (pp. 170–193). IGI Global.

Thanasoulas, D. (2000). What is learner autonomy and how can it be fostered. *The Internet TESL Journal, 6*(11), 37–48.

U.S. Department of Education. (2021, June). *Education in a pandemic. Education in a pandemic: The disparate impacts of COVID-19 on America's students.* https://www2.ed.gov/about/offices/list/ocr/docs/20210608-impacts-of-covid19.pdf?tpcc=nlcapsule

Van Pate, E. (2022, May 1). *Evaluating the use and sustainability of Bitmoji classrooms within online elementary classrooms* [Doctoral dissertation]. Indiana University. https://scholarworks.iu.edu/dspace/handle/2022/27617

Verloop, N., Driel, J. V., & Meijer, P. (2001). Teacher knowledge and the knowledge base of teaching. *International Journal of Educational Research, 35*(5), 441–461.

Waxman, H. C., Huang, S. Y. L., & Padron, Y. N. (1995). Investigating the pedagogy of poverty in inner-city middle level schools. *Research in Middle Level Education, 18*(2), 1–22.

Williams, B. (2000). *Strengths of diverse urban learners.* Presentation at the American Psychology Association Convention, Washington, DC.

World Economic Forum. (2016). Chapter 1: The future of jobs and skills. *The future of jobs.* https://reports.weforum.org/future-of-jobs-2016/chapter-1-the-future-of-jobs-and-skills/?doing_wp_cron=1642630095.2573850154876708984375

14

A WHOLE NEW WORLD

Virtual Excursions for Learners From Urban Settings

Renee Whelan and Michael Salvatore

Guiding Questions:

- How have the number of virtual excursions increased science learning through interdisciplinary experiences in urban P-3 classrooms?
- How have virtual excursions increased access to exploring science beyond the classroom environment for high-needs students?
- How do we increase access for urban students to attain careers in science, technology, engineering, and mathematics?

Introduction

In the widely diverse city of Long Branch, on the central coast of New Jersey, a high-needs school district has been working to provide students, regardless of age, background, and circumstance, access to rich content through an array of pedagogical modalities. These modern, equitable virtual practices identified in the Long Branch Public Schools system can be replicated in other high-needs schools throughout the country.

Due to persistently sought grant opportunities, innovative professional development, and an increase in the availability of no-cost excursions, nearly 75 early childhood classrooms in Long Branch expanded virtual trips for their learners. Through inquiry-based pedagogy, teachers were able to expose children to various locations worldwide, exploring the physical elements of obscure regions as well as popular geographic terrains while introducing limitless future workplaces and career opportunities. The introduction of novel locations sparked an unmatched

DOI:10.4324/9781003274537-17

enthusiasm for learning and increased engagement in every classroom as educators tailored interdisciplinary learning experiences beyond each excursion.

Teaching and learning at the intermediate and secondary levels have strikingly similar characteristics to those of early learning; both require unique pedagogical content knowledge complemented by an array of digital tools and virtual experiences beyond the schoolhouse. As young curious learners mature into inquisitive teens, intermediate-level professionals in the Long Branch Public Schools have nourished their instinctive spirits with foreign curated tours, advanced medical procedures, and adventurous treks through the world's most beautiful and rugged terrains. This chapter highlights science learning through virtual excursions in PreK-12 classrooms, beginning with the youngest learners in preschool through Grade 3.

Background

The Long Branch Public Schools District, on the eastern seaboard of the New Jersey coastline, is frequently described as an urban coastal community. Each district school is located within the limits of the midsized city of Long Branch, which has approximately 40,000 residents, many of whom have migrated from Central and South America.

The district is categorized by the New Jersey Department of Education (NJDOE) as a District Factor Group (DFG) B district based on the population's socioeconomic status, including the percent of adults with no high school diploma; percent of adults with some college education; occupational status; unemployment rate; percent of individuals in poverty; and median family income. The DFG B designation (State of New Jersey Department of Education, 2000) is the second lowest in socioeconomic status, with DFGs ranging from A (lowest) to J (highest).

The 10 public schools in Long Branch served approximately 5,700 students during the 2021–2022 school year. The district's underrepresented minority (URM) enrollment exceeds 74%, with students who identify as Hispanic being the majority (58%). Three of the schools are early childhood learning centers serving children in preschool and kindergarten, three elementary schools serve children in Grades 1 through 5; in addition, there are one middle school, two high schools, and a comprehensive K-12 alternative learning academy.

The preschool program, implemented in the early learning centers, is fully funded by the State of New Jersey due to the outcome of a notable legal case on equitable school funding (*Abbott vs Burke*) and the 20-plus iterations over two decades. The *Abbott V* decision in 1998 resulted in the expansion of early learning programs in 31 of New Jersey's high-needs districts. Since that landmark decision, Long Branch Public Schools have grown to serve approximately 800 preschool-aged children annually. The district was reconfigured in 2014 so that preschool children could seamlessly transition to kindergarten in the same building, allowing for the ability to align professional development, curriculum, instructional goals, and assessment platforms between grade levels. The reorganization also provided an opportunity for families to become more familiar and comfortable with their children's schooling experiences, whereby family partnership was fostered and valued from the beginning of the educational trajectory.

All elementary programs have designated thematic magnet programs that align with learning academies at the intermediate level. The foci are performing arts, leadership, and engineering, purposefully woven into core content areas and complemented by elective courses and extracurricular activities/events.

At the secondary level, organically constructed small learning communities are identified as theme-based "schools" located on separate floors in an ultramodern five-story learning facility. The career-linked "schools" are aligned with the magnet and academy themes at the primary and intermediate levels and offer a wide array of opportunities to amplify the learning experiences, including apprenticeships and interning.

Is Science Slipping Away?

Science learning in the early childhood years has not been the priority in many classrooms due to emphasis on increasing children's literacy and mathematics achievement (Bassok et al., 2016). That is, science learning tends to be the last component in many districts' daily schedules because of accountability efforts such as the No Child Left Behind Act (2001) that target high-needs school districts (Diamond & Spillane, 2004; Marx & Harris, 2006). As a result, at times, teachers do not even get to science in the school day, especially in high-needs districts, yet teachers notice that children clearly enjoy the science content (Wexler, 2019). In a study from Berkeley Research, 40% of elementary teachers stated that they taught science for 60 minutes or less each week (Hall, 2011). Compared to poorer districts, principals in more affluent districts are more than twice as likely to have launched science initiatives in the past five years (Shields et al., 1994). This is highly unfortunate, as the early childhood years are a critical time for the development of scientific knowledge and skills, influencing performance variations among subgroups of children, and are predictive of science achievement through eighth grade (Morgan et al., 2016). Indeed, research has shown a positive relationship between time spent on science content and science achievement (Curran & Kitchin, 2019).

Rather than integrating science within subjects to increase science learning time, many teachers have followed curricula where subjects have been isolated (Kaptan & Timurlenk, 2012). When content is intentionally separated, the understanding of the subject matter is fragmented (diSessa, 2002; Sternberg, 2003). Research indicates that an interdisciplinary approach to learning is more meaningful to children and provides positive outcomes (Jensen, 1996; You, 2017). That is, integrating science creates deeper and more coherent conceptual frameworks compared to learning the subject matter in isolation (Gouvea et al., 2013. Higher-level inferences are made when more connections are made in the brain through immersion-style learning (Kelly, 2001). Science learning provides context for connections in literacy and mathematics.

In the Long Branch School District's preschool program, a comprehensive curriculum is implemented per New Jersey Department of Education guidelines. As the children enter kindergarten and elementary school, subjects are compartmentalized, with at least 90 minutes dedicated to literacy and more than 60 minutes dedicated to mathematics. When topics and subjects are isolated like this, it is difficult for young learners, especially English language learners, to deepen their learning of concepts and skills. The lack of extended time to study a topic limits building background knowledge, vocabulary and language development, and overall comprehension (Bintz, 2011).

Field trips provide opportunities for students to explore science content beyond the minimal time dedicated to teaching science within the school day as well as deepen knowledge in relation to a specific topic of study. However, in recent years, the number of field trips has declined in districts due to logistical, accountability, and funding issues. Additionally, families in lower socioeconomic households might not have the money to pay for school field trips. Children living in poverty may not have opportunities with their families to travel or experience extracurricular activities such as visiting museums, aquariums, and zoos. This creates a divide in classrooms, whereby some children have background knowledge in relation to topics discussed in class whereas others have not had outside experiences to provide them with a frame of reference.

Fortunately, virtual excursions with science-related content have increased in the last few years and can provide students more instructional science time when integrated in other subjects throughout the day. Thus, teachers are able to go more places now with their students for free virtual field trips (Devaney, 2008; Hani, 2015). Virtual excursions provide students with access to explore, investigate, and visit places around the world.

However, while many families in the United States enjoy high-quality broadband internet access, allowing for the ease of research, as well as location and topic exploration, an access/information gap is becoming increasingly evident in cities and rural communities throughout the world. Efforts are being made to address this issue through the advancement of smart parks and e-cities that provide free access to the web, but these modernizations are unlikely able to close the gap and be considered equitable learning. Web browsing in a city park or next to a historical monument can be fun under the right conditions; however, deep learning occurs in safe environments, suitable for dialogue and exploration such as school and the privacy of one's home.

Intentional Exploration in the Virtual Classroom

As schools throughout the country have invested in building a robust digital infrastructure, classroom pedagogies have become receptive to the integration of technology as an instructional tool. For instance, in Long Branch, first-grade teachers incorporated virtual field trips for their students to the rainforest. This was part of a study that stemmed from a digital storytelling initiative in early childhood classrooms. The school received iPads through a competitive technology grant from the NJDOE. (Grants have provided technological advances and access to Long Branch's P-3 children.) This particular grant provided children with access to tablets and apps to support writing through a digital platform. A group of first-grade teachers decided to focus on the rainforest based on the children's interests.

Children worked collaboratively to research the layers of the rainforest. They viewed National Geographic videos, took virtual field trips using a rainforest cam, and worked with the school librarian to find books about the rainforest. They discovered animals that lived in this habitat and had opportunities to see this by traveling virtually to rainforests in Central and South America.

The guiding question was "Why do certain animals live in different layers of the rainforest?" Students were given the choice of what kind of project they wanted to create about the animals they chose to research. They wrote digital stories about their rainforest animals. The classrooms were transformed into rainforests to display all their projects. As a culminating activity, students shared their digital stories with their parents. A brochure was created by the class that invited parents to a special viewing party. Students rehearsed and performed a short play before showing their digital stories to their special guests. Many of the Next Generation Science Standards were addressed through this study. For example, life science was naturally incorporated, as was a discussion of biomes, weather, climate change, and rainforest preservation.

The integration of science, geography, and English language arts (ELA) was seamless as children participated in shared research and writing projects. This interdisciplinary study was engaging to the students, who became explorers, researchers, and animal experts. The promotion of independence and choice fostered active learning. The children received scaffolded support from the teacher as they researched, collaborated, and wrote about their findings. The unit of study deepened children's understanding of scientific topics. Further, the interdisciplinary nature of the study reinforced vocabulary in context and integrated sustainability topics such as climate change. When topics or themes are used in the early years, there are more opportunities to apply academic vocabulary to strengthen comprehension (Neuman & Wright, 2014). The children benefited from the collaborative opportunities, simulated excursions, and multiple opportunities to use vocabulary in context.

Young learners in Long Branch had another unique opportunity when Google offered free use of its augmented reality to beta test their product (the offer was found through Google Education). An augmented reality visit was coordinated, which provided all kindergarteners in the district an opportunity to go into the deep sea and watch a wide range of fish swim next to them in the classroom. Children's faces lit up with excitement as they shouted out the names of fish that were all around them. This led to many other conversations about the ocean, sea creatures, and the connection to Long Branch beaches and the Atlantic Ocean. Teachers commented on students' high-level engagement and vocabulary development in relation to the sea. The Google visit enhanced the study of the sea and reinforced vocabulary in science. This interdisciplinary experience helped all children make connections throughout the day because teachers were intentional about using the study as a springboard for concepts learned in ELA and mathematics.

As public education has evolved in the information age, standard pedagogical elements have been modernized, especially at the intermediate and secondary levels. For example, in the Long Branch Public Schools, the traditional assemblies on topics such as antibullying, substance use/abuse, and gang awareness have evolved into digital excursions. Why hustle students into a crowded auditorium with hundreds of their peers, battling distractions, giggles, and a tremendous amount of pressure, when intimate groups can engage with world-renowned experts in a small team setting at any location in the school? After all, many students do not engage with a speaker in an auditorium. This simple digital transformation has personalized the learning experience and allows for learning to be built into traditional courses, as opposed to halting the entire school for quarterly assemblies.

Purposeful engagement is essential at all learning levels, but especially in the intermediate grades and at the secondary level as students are constantly searching for relevance in the world around them. One example of virtual excursions that made lasting impressions are those for students in science classes at Long Branch High School.

Each term, students are exposed to learning standards in biological sciences and anatomy. Leading medical experts from the neighboring hospital serve as hosts to students while performing and narrating the procedures they are carrying out. Each student is provided with an invitation to access a live surgery in the surgical center and encouraged to interact and ask questions during the procedure. Despite the graphic content, the level of questioning, focus, and participation is unmatched. Eyler (2018) coined the term *social pedagogies* for these types of experiences to describe the processes associated with student engagement with authentic audiences in an effort to enhance learning.

During this virtual excursion to the local medical center, students were not afforded the opportunity to ingest the irritating aroma of the medical room; nor were they provided with the details of the temperature in the room or the starchy feeling of the freshly laundered scrubs; however, each learner's modalities were on overload as their auditory and visual senses were tested throughout the procedure. Students and teachers still recall with great detail the tools used to perform the medical procedures and the incisions made in specific regions of the body.

One student cringed and held her hands over her ears as the doctor operated a device that sounded like a circular saw, while most of the students and educators in the room were impressed with each medical professional's patience and demeanor during the routine procedure. Curious learners got many questions answered regarding their ability to operate at such a high level under tension-filled moments, while for others, their lack of interest in the profession was confirmed as the intensity increased. In short, this digital experience safely placed students in a risky, high-stakes environment that benefited all who participated.

The opportunities afforded to urban school students through the aforementioned virtual experiences have purposefully woven various disciplines into singular lessons and created a truly interdisciplinary approach to teaching and learning. Moreover, they provide unrestricted access to lucrative career paths and renowned professionals from culturally rich backgrounds and diverse perspectives with the intention to illuminate possibilities to secondary-level students with limited networks and finite resources. Virtual excursions in public schools are meaningful, as they can mirror the initial exposure of many college apprenticeships without the risks and costs associated with higher education. Increased exposure translates to possibilities, which all children deserve.

Conclusion

Virtual excursions have a distinct purpose in urban schools beyond the allure of using digital applications and tools, which are not always available in the homes of inner-city children. As the expectations for student engagement have increased, learning organizations in high-needs settings must work to provide quality access to remote locations, as well as access to diverse professionals in both attractive and lesser-known careers. As high-needs schools attempt to diversify the teacher and administrator workforce, they can begin by working with partner districts and professional organizations in diverse settings to build a learning community that reflects the demographics of the community they serve. This purposive and inclusive act is a model for equity in action that personalizes learning experiences for all students in high-needs districts.

Personalization of learning has become the hackneyed phrase of educational mission statements and strategic plans in the 21st century. It is time for urban school officials to prioritize this social pedagogical process through virtual means in order to provide students with relevant learning that connects them to the wider world and the diverse cultures within it. Our world needs more empathy, not applications. And with a saturation of virtual excursions in educational settings, we might give our students the compassion they need and deserve to solve the problems of today and the obstacles in the future.

Tips for Advancing Virtual Excursions in Urban Schools

The following tips are designed to assist educators in planning for virtual experiences in their schools and classrooms that support science learning using an interdisciplinary approach.

- Provide time for teachers to research and plan for integration of virtual excursions based on what students are learning in class. Plan academic vocabulary connections and developmentally appropriate measurable learning outcomes.

- Provide leadership support for project-based learning or topics of study to extend and deepen learning and provide more time for inquiry-based science learning. Leadership should encourage teachers to use an interdisciplinary approach based on children's interests, current events, and topics of study to promote more science and social studies integration throughout the day (inclusive of virtual excursions).
- Develop connections among subject areas and learning standards/objectives to foster interdisciplinary learning inclusive of simulated virtual experiences. Consult with special teachers and ESL (English as a second language) teachers to extend the learning to other times of the day.
- Develop a library of free virtual excursions for the school/district. Add cultural and community excursions/explorations to the library that reflect the children and families being served.
- Apply for grants to obtain updated technology such as smartboards and virtual reality headsets.
- Refer to the document Advancing Equity in Early Childhood Education (National Association for the Education of Young Children, 2019), which highlights young children's right to equitable learning opportunities.
- Since many school programs are heavily based on literacy and mathematics, expand professional development and holistic programs to extend the preschool comprehensive approach, integrating all subject areas into all grades.
- Since virtual excursions are not integrated into many programs in early childhood education, allocate time for teachers during professional learning communities (PLCs)/grade-level meetings and/or prep time to plan how to integrate a virtual excursion into their day to enhance an area of study.
- Incorporate speakers from diverse cultures and backgrounds to broaden exposure and introduce varied perspectives on global topics.
- Introduce innovative career opportunities for high-demand positions such as computer scientists and STEM professionals.

Key Takeaways:

1. Intentionality in instructional design allows for interdisciplinarity, which enhances the retention of learned material.
2. Virtual exploration is not limited to physical destinations and allows for the inclusion of diverse teachers and industry professionals.
3. As conversations about equity ring through schools in the United States, access will always be the equalizer; therefore, supporting both the technical and adaptive infrastructure is imperative, especially for high-needs populations.

Recommended Resources

- Bordcosh, L. (2018). *Using virtual reality in ESL classroom.* www.cambridge.org/elt/blog/2018/01/17/using-virtual-reality-in-the-classroom/
- Croteau, J. (2020). *15 fascinating aquarium virtual field trips.* www.weareteachers.com/aquarium-virtual-field-trips/#:~:text=15%20Fascinating%20Aquarium%20Virtual%20Field%20Trips.%201%20Seattle,Aquarium.%20%205%20National%20Aquarium.%20%20More%20items
- Google Arts and Culture. (2022). https://artsandculture.google.com/
- Han, I. (2021). Immersive virtual field trips and elementary students' perceptions. *British Journal of Educational Technology, 52*(1), 179–195. https://doi.org/10.1111/bjet.12946
- Han, I. (2020). Immersive virtual field trips in education: A mixed-methods study on elementary students' presence and perceived learning. *British Journal of Educational Technology, 51*(2), 420–435. https://doi.org/10.1111/bjet.12842
- Incell. (2022). https://luden.io/incell/
- Nation Museum of Natural History Virtual Tours. (2022). https://naturalhistory.si.edu/visit/virtual-tour
- Sample VR and AR Lesson Plans. (2022). www.classvr.com/downloads/sample-lesson-plans/
- Sites in VR. (2022). https://play.google.com/store/apps/details?id=air.com.ercangigi.sitesin3d
- University of Toronto OISE. (2021). *Virtual reality in the classroom.* https://guides.library.utoronto.ca/c.php?g=607624&p=4494048
- VeerTv. (2017). *7 best virtual reality apps for education.* https://veer.tv/blog/7-best-virtual-reality-applications-in-education/
- Virtual Field Trips for Elementary. (2022). https://ny.pbslearningmedia.org/shared/12718/4846901/#.X4ZCzeaSmUk
- Virtual Field Trips: Take a Virtual Field Trip. (2021). https://spep.libguides.com/virtualfieldtrips
- Virtual Reality Classroom. (2022). https://nearpod.com/nearpod-vr
- Virtual Reality for Education. (2022). http://virtualrealityforeducation.com/resources/getting-started-vr-classroom/

References

Bassok, D., Latham, S., & Rorem, A. (2016). Is kindergarten the new first grade? *AERA Open, 2*(1). https://doi.org/10.1177/2332858415616358

Bintz, W. (2011). Teaching vocabulary across the curriculum. *Middle School Journal, 42*(4), 44–53.

Curran, F. C., & Kitchin, J. (2019). Early elementary science instruction: Does more time on science or science topics/skills predict science achievement in the early grades? *AERA Open, 5*(3). https://doi.org/10.1177/2332858419861081

Devaney, L. (2008). Gas prices fuel rise in virtual field trips. *Eschool News*. www.eschoolnews. com/2008/07/14/gas-prices-fuel-rise-in-virtual-field-trips/

Diamond, J. B., & Spillane, J. P. (2004). High-stakes accountability in urban elementary schools: Challenging or reproducing inequality? *Teachers College Record, 106*(6), 1145–1176.

diSessa, A. A. (2002). Why "conceptual ecology" is a good idea. In M. Limon & L. Mason (Eds.), *Reconsidering conceptual change: Issues in theory and practice* (pp. 29–60). Kluwer. https://doi.org/10.1007/0-306-47637-1_2

Eyler, J. R. (2018). *How humans learn: The science and stories behind effective college teaching.* West Virginia University Press.

Gouvea, J. S., Sawtelle, V., Geller, B. D., & Turpen, C. (2013). A framework for analyzing interdisciplinary tasks: Implications for student learning and curricular design. *CBE-Life Sciences Education, 12*(2), 187–205. https://doi.org/10.1187/cbe.12-08-0135

Hall, L. (2011). Teachers have little time to teach science, study shows. *Berkley Research*. https://vcresearch.berkeley.edu/news/teachers-have-little-time-teach-science-study-shows

Hani, M. (2015). Focus on technology: Virtual field trips: Going on a journey to learn without leaving school. *Childhood Education, 91*(3), 220–222.

Jensen, E. (1996). *Brain-based learning.* Turning Point Publishing.

Kaptan, K., & Timurlenk, O. (2012). Challenges for science education. *Procedia—Social and Behavioral Sciences, 51*, 763–771. https://doi.org/10.1016/j.sbspro.2012.08.237

Kelly, M. (2001). Integrated curriculum in the primary program. In *The primary program: Growing and learning in the heartland* (pp. 553–584). www.education.ne.gov/wp-content/uploads/2017/07/IC.pdf

Marx, R. W., & Harris, C. J. (2006). No child left behind and science education: Opportunities, challenges, and risks. *The Elementary School Journal, 106*(5), 467–477.

Morgan, P., Hillemeier, M., & Maczuga, S. (2016). Science achievement gaps begin very early, persist, and are largely explained by modifiable factors. *Educational Researcher, 45*(1), 18–35.

National Association for the Education of Young Children. (2019). *Advancing equity in early childhood education.* www.naeyc.org/sites/default/files/globally-shared/downloads/PDFs/resources/position-statements/advancingequitypositionstatement.pdf

Neuman, S., & Wright, T. (2014). Teaching vocabulary in the early childhood classroom. *American Educator*, 4–13.

Shields, P. M. (1994). *Evaluation of the National Science Foundation's statewide systemic initiatives. Program: First year report. Volume 1: Technical report.* SRI International.

State of New Jersey Department of Education. (2000). *District factor groups for school districts.* www.nj.gov/education/finance/rda/dfg.shtml#:~:text=The%20District%20Factor%20Groups%20

Sternberg, R. (2003). What is an "expert student"? *Educational Researcher, 32*, 5–9.

Wexler, N. (2019). Elementary education has gone terribly wrong. *The Atlantic*. www.theatlantic. com/magazine/archive/2019/08/the-radical-case-for-teaching-kids- stuff/592765/

You, H. S. (2017). Why teach science with an interdisciplinary approach: History, trends, and conceptual frameworks. *Journal of Education and Learning, 6*(4), 66.

15

RURAL SOCIAL STUDIES TEACHERS' POSTPANDEMIC USE OF TECHNOLOGY TOOLS

Scott W. DeWitt and Ethan Podwojski

Guiding Questions:

- What are rural social studies teachers' perceptions of the impacts of having to teach fully and/or partially remotely during the onset of the COVID-19 pandemic?
- Which strategies that they adopted or developed during remote and hybrid teaching do social studies teachers in high-needs rural schools see as having continuing value in fully in-person instruction?

Introduction

This chapter flows from a pilot interview study of four social studies teachers at rural U.S. high schools. We asked participants to describe their experiences related to the dramatic transition to remote teaching at the beginning of the COVID pandemic and the instructional strategies that they adopted during the pandemic and are continuing to use after returning to face-to-face schooling. In all cases, the teachers' schools returned to in-person instruction in the 2021–2022 school year, so responses to this aspect of the study were based on experience rather than being entirely speculative. The issues raised by these two guiding questions resonated with us because of the seeming disconnect between the existing "digital divide" that has been identified in rural schooling (Kormos & Wisdom, 2021) and the need for remote teaching that occurred due to the pandemic. Given that they were suddenly forced to deliver instruction entirely over the internet, did teachers find that aspects of that implementation had enough value to be continued when fully remote instruction was no longer required?

DOI:10.4324/9781003274537-18

High-Needs Rural Schools

The interviewed teachers work at three rural schools that we call Riverton, Plains, and Meadowland. All are located in a Midwestern U.S. state. The National Center for Education Statistics (NCES) (2022) lists the three participating school districts as Town:Distant, Rural:Distant, and Town:Remote, respectively. The schools range in size from approximately 280 students to 340 students in Grades 9 through 12. The three schools' student bodies are each more than 90% White, with no other Census racial category accounting for more than Meadowland's Hispanic student population of 4.5% (National Center for Education Statistics (NCES), 2022).

In addition to the challenges inherent in small, rural school settings, these school districts face significant economic issues. Each of the schools is Title 1 eligible and reports student mobility rates between 125% and 200% of the state average. In addition, per-pupil spending for these schools is 69% to 75% of the overall state average, despite receiving state funding of $2.2 million to $4.4 million in addition to local revenue. The federal funds provided to the school districts have alleviated some of the resource limitations that had previously hindered use of technology tools in instruction. For example, two of the three districts represented in this study used pandemic funds to provide tablets to all of their students for remote and, eventually, in-person learning.

Participants

The four social studies teachers interviewed for the project identified their settings as rural. These teachers saw those settings as generally advantageous in facing the pandemic challenges compared to their perceptions of suburban or urban school situations, primarily because of their small size and the teachers' perceptions of community cohesion.

TABLE 15.1 Community Characteristics

School and Teacher Pseudonym	Sq Miles (rounded to nearest 10) (USA.com, 2022)	Pop Density Per Sq Mi (rounded to nearest 10) (USA.com, 2022)	Student Mobility as a % of State Average (State Board of Education website)	Per-pupil Spending as a % of State Average (State Board of Education website)
Riverton [Tucker & Abby]	130	50	200	75
Plains [Sara]	110	50	125	75
Meadowland [Miles]	430	20	150	69

Note: All statistics rounded to preserve participant confidentiality.

Rural Social Studies Teachers' Postpandemic Use of Technology 211

TABLE 15.2 Teacher Information and School Pandemic Response

Teacher Pseudonym	Years Teaching	Courses Taught	School Meeting Context by Year	School Technology Context
Tucker	17	U.S. history, state history, personal finance	End of 2020: remote 2020–21: split schedule; ½ of students 2 days/week; 1 day all remote 2021–22: in person with individual students remote	1-to-1 Chromebooks prior to pandemic
Abby	14	6 preps	Same school as Tucker	
Sara	9	World history, sociology, cultural geography, U.S. history	End of 2020: remote 2020–21: in person with individual students remote 2021–22: in person with individual students remote	1-to-1 Chromebooks as a result of the pandemic
Miles	16	U.S. history, ancient history	End of 2020: remote 2020–21: in person with individual students remote	1-to-1 prior to pandemic at different school; current school used class sets but moved to 1-to-1 Chromebooks as a result of the pandemic

Participating teachers were all experienced, with 9 to 17 years in the classroom. Each taught multiple grade levels and subject areas, having as many as six different classes to prepare in a single semester. Their schools' approaches to the pandemic varied somewhat, but all were entirely remote at the onset, in the spring of 2020. Instruction the next year was either in person with an option for students to be remote or a split schedule, with half of the students coming to school two days per week and all students remote on the fifth day. Only one of the teachers had no experience with one-to-one computing prior to 2020.

Findings

The participating teachers identified several areas where they saw impacts from the remote teaching and the technology tools they had adopted to accomplish that teaching, including (a) equity, (b) student engagement, (c) student achievement, and (d) specific useful technology tools and social studies–specific applications of those tools. In several cases, the teachers saw the implementation of technology solutions to provide remote instruction as addressing issues of equity that were hidden, or at least not acknowledged, prior to the disruptions of the last several years.

Equity

An area where the teachers saw positive community results of technology adoption was increased equity. Their comments were specific to the increase in availability of technology to schools in general and to students in economically and cognitively challenging situations in particular.

The teachers saw the distribution of Chromebooks as a positive step toward providing all students access to technology tools. For the Meadowlands School District, one-to-one computing was a new initiative. All of the teachers' schools took the added step of mitigating poor or nonexistent internet connectivity at students' homes by providing hotspots. In these rural school settings, teachers perceived these actions by their school districts as significantly leveling the field for students from particularly remote areas or in economically challenged home circumstances.

For Miles, being forced to move to remote instruction also sped schools' transition to integrating more computer technology. While he admitted to still struggling with how best to do that, he also saw ways that technology can improve learning opportunities for students with specific needs, for example, by posting class notes to Google Classroom so students with IEPs have easy access both in and outside of school.

The classroom benefits of students' ubiquitous access to computer technology were less evident to Abby than the skills that the use of the technology requires. Nevertheless, she described as significant the equity benefits of regular access to and use of computers and the internet for students' future job prospects. The benefit of such access and use leads to the issue of how the teachers incorporated the available tools into remote teaching and what they continue to use.

Engagement

Remote, hybrid, and in-person class settings posed different challenges to the teachers as they negotiated teaching during the pandemic and in the aftermath.

Student engagement in remote settings is hard to monitor. Student attention in postpandemic in-person classes was uniformly viewed by participants as less focused, which the teachers ascribed to the impact of students' and parents' expectations developed during remote instruction.

Engagement in Remote Learning

Teachers expressed two major concerns related to student engagement with learning while in remote settings. First, knowing whether students were paying attention to lesson materials was more difficult than in an in-person classroom setting. A second engagement issue involved the choices these rural students made and the obligations they had outside of the schoolwork that had been part of their day-to-day lives. With the advent of remote instruction causing students to stay at home, or at least not requiring them to attend school, many students took on family responsibilities or took advantage of the opportunity to work during what had previously been standard school hours, which often led to students not completing their work or not attempting it at all. The disruption of the usual school-day time commitments contributed to some teachers and schools moving to asynchronous lessons. This change provided more flexibility for students but made it even more difficult for the teachers to determine students' level of engagement with material, and the teachers reported decreased levels of student completion of work over time during fully remote instruction.

Besides their access to instruction, other factors were also involved in students' choices about whether to complete assigned tasks. For example, Miles and Abby reported on a policy in their districts that students' grades could not be lowered based on the results of their work during the fully remote time span in the spring of 2020. Regardless, all teachers expressed the view that remote instruction led to less engaged learners. This loss of engagement had continuing impacts even on those students who returned to in-class instruction, as further discussed in what follows.

Engagement in In-Person Learning

The teachers saw a continuing impact on students' approach to learning by the remote learning caused by the pandemic. Specifically, they interpreted students' actions in their current classrooms as being negatively impacted by the technology-dependent remote learning they were required to engage in as a result of the pandemic. For them, the most notable of those negative impacts was a reduction in student–student and teacher–student interactions, which they viewed as central to their teaching role.

Student Achievement

Participating teachers' experiences in in-person classes after remote instruction caused them to perceive lower student motivation to complete tasks and lower student achievement when assignments were completed. For example, at Miles's school, 45% of students who had started as ninth graders in the fall of 2017 had dropped out by spring of 2021. Miles interpreted this unusually high percentage of dropouts as an indicator that for many students at this rural school, not having to physically go to school was interpreted as not having school at all rather than an expectation that learning would happen at home. So those students chose to do what they had otherwise expected to do when they finished their formal schooling: They went to work.

The teachers all decried the long-term impact of the pandemic on their students' achievement levels. They did not attempt to separate out how much of that impact was due to the social disruption of COVID, remote learning, or frequent changes in school schedules and policies. Rather, they focused their energies on trying to help the students who remained in school. In doing so, they sought to leverage new (to them) technology tools to improve engagement and achievement.

Useful Technology Tools

In addition to the challenges mentioned already, the teachers identified positive results of the forced implementation of digitally based instructional strategies. Their solutions to the challenges of providing high-quality instruction both during the pandemic and going forward addressed preparing and implementing instruction and student activities.

Preparing Instruction

Each of the teachers reported that their schools had adopted Google Classroom as the vehicle for remote instruction and cited Google Classroom as a key resource in their transition to distance learning. In one case, occasional use of this resource predated the pandemic, while two of the schools adopted it as a result of the need to implement entirely remote instruction. The teachers described benefits of Google Classroom in preparing lessons and collecting student work and for students in organization and access to materials.

The teachers reported that Google Classroom provided them with a way to plan and organize units and lessons more efficiently. That is, they planned multiple lessons for a specific course and saved the materials for their own and for students' use. This facilitated a more holistic approach to unit planning and provided students working remotely with opportunities to work at their own pace, or at least to have more flexibility in juggling the demands on their time.

The teachers continued to use this strategy after returning to in-person instruction, although with adaptations. For example, Tucker and Miles put lessons into Google Classroom to be available when they are away from work and have a substitute teacher or on a snow day. Abby makes more regular use of the strategy as a way to provide access to lesson materials to students who have been absent from class.

Another aspect of these teachers' adoption of new strategies as a result of the pandemic was illustrated by Miles's description of his new flexibility in the types of student work products he accepted and his excitement about the students' creativity that flexibility had helped elicit. Miles described three different ways that his students took advantage of his openness to technology to demonstrate their learning: photographs of completed projects rather than transporting large models or projects into class, video recordings in place of in-person class presentations, and recordings of student-written songs focused on historical content. These options provide access to classroom success for students who might not physically be in class as well as opportunities for students to expand their technological abilities. He also reported that this expansion of potential avenues for students to demonstrate their learning contributed to increased engagement for some students.

Participating teachers reported continuing to use the organizational and storage capacities of Google Classroom as a tool to facilitate student learning even in situations in which they are not able to be in school. But continuing application of technology tools was not limited to those circumstances. Each of the teachers has adopted instructional strategies that they first implemented during the pandemic because they see the value of those strategies for student learning.

Implementing Instruction

By combining the hardware capabilities available to her, Abby was able to include remote students in classroom activities through Google Meet—for example, by enabling remote students to see material on her interactive whiteboard. She mentioned the difficulties with the microphone picking up what students in class were saying but has adapted to that by having those students write comments so that remote students could get the benefit of other students' thoughts. Miles is implementing a similar strategy but records class rather than having students participate synchronously. He uses his laptop to record class sessions, then puts "together an email that includes the video lesson and a little bit of a summary of what we did. I send it out every day and the kids really like that. That's something that's helpful to them." These strategies provide options for students to participate in or keep current with their day-to-day classwork.

During remote instruction, Tucker and Abby sought to mitigate issues with student engagement through the use of online forums, where students would post answers to questions and then respond to classmates' answers. They continue to use online forums to promote student interaction, acknowledging that it requires more administrative attention from the teacher, as they must track responses to make sure students are, in fact, responding to others and doing so appropriately. By requiring students to respond online to others' comments, they have expanded the role of questions that would traditionally result in written responses turned in to and seen only by the teacher. This moves students' exchange of ideas beyond the classroom and outside of normal school hours, requiring students to interact with each other's ideas. Further, students who are hesitant to speak in class often find that this strategy gives them additional time to formulate responses and so facilitates their participation.

The teachers described other examples of ways in which they had adapted remote strategies to provide active learning opportunities for students after the return to in-person instruction. The tools used in those strategies are described in the "Recommended Resources" section. They include administrative tools like Go Guardian, which teachers used in class to keep track of what individual students were doing on their computers during class time. Content delivery tools included saving teacher-made videos on a private YouTube channel or teacher- or student-made videos on Loom. The teachers used Flip, Actively Learn, and Nearpod for formative evaluation and to promote student interaction in small-group settings and Noodle Tools as a scaffolding and organizational tool for research projects.

Applications Specific to Social Studies

While many of the technology tools and strategies used by these teachers are beneficial for teachers in any discipline, several provide learning opportunities specific to goals of social studies. For example, communications tools like Loom and Flip allow students to create "[p]roducts such as . . . multimedia presentations [that] offer students opportunities to represent their ideas in a variety of forms and communicate their ideas to a range of audiences" (NCSS, 2013, p. 60). The student-to-student response capabilities of Google Classroom allow students to "individually and with other students . . . critique the use of claims and evidence in arguments for credibility" (p. 61). The research and organizational program Noodle Tools provides a flexible platform for students to utilize when engaging in inquiry-focused processes as recommended in the Inquiry Design Model (Swan et al., 2018). As always, the tools themselves do not guarantee that students will meet those goals. Teachers must organize instruction and frame assignments to most effectively match the relevant technology tool to the learning goal.

Conclusion

The many shifts in policy that occurred during spring 2020 and through the 2020–2021 school year due to the pandemic required teachers to be very adaptable. That need for flexibility highlighted for these teachers a central requirement of teaching: openness to new learning. The learning curve for remote teaching required the teachers to combine their knowledge of their students, the social studies curriculum, and the computer applications available to them.

This intersection, or technological pedagogical content knowledge (TPCK; Koehler & Mishra, 2009), highlights the complexity involved in teaching during the pandemic.

The tools and strategies that formed the bases for the experiments in planning and instruction that the rural social studies teachers interviewed for this study had adopted during the pandemic were continued, adapted, or sometimes dropped as in-person schooling resumed. The retained strategies provide these teachers with improved means of connecting with students who miss class for health or other reasons. Beyond that, increased access to technology tools and skills has enhanced equity in learning for previously underserved students. In addition, teachers' integration of technology into their day-to-day instruction, even if on a less ubiquitous basis than during fully remote instruction, has provided them with a broader range of tools with which to enhance student interaction in learning activities and continue to promote student mastery of social studies learning goals.

Key Takeaways:

1. There are accessibility and engagement benefits of technology tools for students in both in-person and remote settings.
2. Technology tools learned and adopted during the pandemic can be used to enhance social studies teaching and learning.
3. The challenges of student engagement with remote learning are ongoing and can only be partly addressed with technological solutions.
4. Interactive technology tools can provide a bridge between schooling and students who are unable to attend in person, either on a short- or a long-term basis.

Recommended Resources

Each of the following programs was mentioned by teachers in the interviews as being helpful to them in delivering instruction.

- Actively Learn (http://read.actively.learn.com): A McGraw-Hill program usable with Google Classroom that allows posting assignment questions and notes with texts and videos
- Flip (https://info.flip.com/): A "video discussion app" designed for small-group interaction. Useful but prohibited in some districts due to privacy concerns.
- Go Guardian (for in class) (http://goguardian.com): A school- or district-level service that allows oversight of students' tablets/computers while in class.

- Google Classroom (http://edu.google.com): A comprehensive suite of tools to help teachers to manage materials
- Loom (http://loom.com): A program that allows users to record short videos to share with students or for students to share. The free version generally is sufficient for teacher use.
- Nearpod (http://nearpod.com): A program that allows users to make PowerPoint slides or other lesson materials interactive or use the lesson materials on the site
- Noodle Tools (http://noodletools.com): Subscription-based research management site
- Private YouTube Channel (http://youtube.com): A short how-to video on creating your own private channel may be found at www.youtube.com/watch?v=zHN3BDmOM6w.

References

Koehler, M., & Mishra, P. (2009). What is technological pedagogical content knowledge (TPACK)? *Contemporary Issues in Technology and Teacher Education, 9*(1), 60–70. www.learntechlib.org/primary/p/29544/

Kormos, E., & Wisdom, K. (2021). Rural schools and the digital divide: Technology in the learning experience. *Theory and Practice in Rural Education, 11*(1), 25–39. https://doi.org/10.3776/tpre.2021.v11n1p25-39

National Center for Education Statistics (NCES). (2022). *Home page.* U.S. Department of Education. https://nces.ed.gov/

National Council for the Social Studies (NCSS). (2013). The college, career, and civic life (C3) framework for social studies state standards: Guidance for enhancing the rigor of K-12 civics, economics, geography, and history. Author.

Swan, K., Lee, J., & Grant, S. G. (2018). Inquiry design model: Building inquiries in social studies. National Council for the Social Studies & C3 Teachers.

World Media Group, LLC. (2022). *USA.com.* https://usa.com/find-schools

CONTRIBUTORS

Heejung An, Ed.D., is a professor and director of the M.Ed. in the Curriculum & Learning Program with a concentration in STEM/STEAM education, Department of Educational Leadership and Professional Studies at the College of Education, William Paterson University. Her research interest centers on the intersection of cognition and instructional technologies, STEAM education, online teaching and learning, digital equity, and effective design and delivery of professional development and professional learning. She is the director of the Inclusive Arts Integration (https://inclusiveartsintegration.weebly.com/), funded by the Geraldine R. Dodge Foundation (2017–present). Heejung currently serves as a co-chair for the STEM Innovation SIG at the Society for Information Technology and Teacher Education (SITE), from which she received Outstanding Paper Awards in 2006 and 2021. She may be reached at anh2@wpunj.edu.

Alicia Burchell, M.Ed., is an educator and instructional coach with a focus on structured literacy and multisensory math. She earned her bachelor of science in K-6 education from Penn State University in 2009 and her Master's of Education in PK-12 reading specialist and instructional coaching from Slippery Rock University in 2017. For 12 years, Alicia taught in a variety of roles in K-5 Title 1 public schools serving a diverse population of students. These roles included general education teacher, reading/math intervention specialist, and instructional coach. Alicia is now the owner and lead tutor at her own virtual tutoring company, The Virtual Classroom. She may be reached at aburchell09@gmail.com.

Thomas Chandler, Ph.D., is the deputy director and a research scientist at the National Center for Disaster Preparedness and an adjunct associate professor at Teachers College, Columbia University. He focuses on postdisaster housing and

220 Contributors

economic recovery, community sheltering and relocation assistance, pandemic preparedness and response, and community preparedness. His work has appeared in *Disaster Medicine and Public Health Preparedness, Traumatology, Population and Environment*, and *Interactive Learning Environments*. He may be reached at tec11@ columbia.edu.

Joshua L. DeVincenzo, M.Ed., is a senior instructional designer and adjunct lecturer at Columbia Climate School's National Center for Disaster Preparedness. His focus is on developing learning experiences associated with training projects that navigate disaster preparedness, response, recovery, and resilience. Joshua has also developed and taught courses at the University of Pennsylvania, Teachers College of Columbia University, the Earth Institute Professional Learning Programs, and the Columbia School of Professional Studies. He holds a master's degree in education policy from the University of Illinois at Urbana–Champaign and is a doctoral candidate in Adult Learning and Leadership at Teachers College, Columbia University. He may be reached at jld2225@columbia.edu.

Scott W. DeWitt, Ph.D., is an associate professor and chair of educational studies at Knox College. He teaches curriculum, methods, diversity, and teacher education courses in addition to supervising student teachers. Among other venues, he has published in *Theory and Research in Social Education, The Social Studies*, and *Contemporary Issues in Technology and Teacher Education*. He also co-authored, with Melissa Marks, *Teaching Diversity: Activities to Start the Conversation* (Information Age Publishing, 2020). He was awarded the Larry Metcalf Exemplary Dissertation Award by the National Council for Social Studies. Scott served as a secondary social studies teacher for 10 years. He may be reached at swdewitt@knox.edu.

Samuel F. Fancera, Ed.D., is an assistant professor and director of the M.Ed. in Educational Leadership and School Principal Certificate programs at William Paterson University. Sam also teaches in the Doctor of Education in Leadership program and works with doctoral candidates to develop, design, and conduct their dissertation research. As a former principal who regularly used technology for professional development and learning, Sam's research is focused on how school leaders can leverage the use of social media in practice to improve school- and student-level outcomes. He invites you to connect with him on Twitter: @ SamFancera. He may be reached at fanceras@wpunj.edu.

David Fuentes, Ph.D., is interim associate dean in the College of Education and professor in the Department of Teacher Education: PreK-12 at William Paterson University. His administrative philosophy focuses on servant leadership in a constant effort to make programs as responsive as possible to student and faculty needs, desires, and vision, leading to successful practices. His research, teaching, and service have largely focused on issues related to multicultural and bilingual education, equity in K-12 schools, and understanding various school outcomes. His current research centers around teaching and learning in high-needs communities, diversity, equity, and inclusive pedagogy in teacher education and in K-12 schools, Hispanic-Serving Institutions (HSIs), and higher education. David earned his Ph.D. in curriculum and instruction from The Pennsylvania State University and is a former EL teacher from the commonwealth of Massachusetts. He may be reached at fuentesd2@wpunj.edu.

Neil Grimes, M.L.S., M.Ed., is the education and curriculum materials librarian at the David and Lorraine Cheng Library at William Paterson University. He is a former K-12 school library media specialist, high school social studies teacher, and elementary STEM teacher, having worked for 13 years in an urban school district in northeastern Pennsylvania. Neil currently serves on the American Library Association's Education and Behavioral Sciences Section (EBSS), Curriculum Materials Center Committee, and the American Library Association's Committee on Education. Additionally, he is also currently serving on two New Jersey Library Association statewide committees and is co-chairing the Committee on Professional Development. He may be reached at grimesn@wpunj.edu.

August Howerton, B.A., is a fourth-grade teacher in Kannapolis City Schools in Kannapolis, NC. She is a graduate of the elementary education program at the University of North Carolina at Charlotte and completed her honors research project on the influence of technology on engagement and achievement in mathematics. She may be reached at august.howerton@kcs.k12.nc.us.

Erik Kormos, Ph.D., is an assistant professor of educational and assistive technologies at Ashland University. His main area of interest research stems from his time as a social studies teacher in American and international urban K-12 schools. He may be reached at ekormos@ashland.edu.

Maria Lanni, M.Ed., is a kindergarten teacher in a dual-language program in the Passaic Public Schools, NJ, where she teaches in a Spanish classroom. She has an M.Ed. in curriculum and learning with a bilingual/ESL concentration. She may be reached at lannimaria27@gmail.com.

Gihan Mohamad, Ed.D., is an assistant professor at William Paterson University in the School Library Media program. She has over 20 years of experience teaching and addressing children and young adults' information needs and an earned doctorate in educational technology. Gihan has presented nationally and internationally about diversity and inclusion, educators' collaborative relationships, design thinking, and digital literacy. Her research interests and publications include educational technology, school librarianship, the collaborative relationship between teachers and librarians, Universal Design for Learning, and the role

222 Contributors

of school librarians as instructional leaders and technology integrationists. She may be reached at mohamadg@wpunj.edu.

Kimberly Moreno, Ed.D., began her career in education in 2009 as an alternate-route science teacher for Union City, NJ, where she developed the first Health Science Careers Career Technical Education (CTE) program. She served as a Career and Technical Students Organization (CTSO) advisor of Health Occupations Students of America (HOSA) and Seeking Educational Equity and Diversity (SEED) project coordinator. In 2015, Kimberly was the NJ recipient of the National Milken Educator Award. She has worked with the New Jersey Department of Education and presented on career and technical education and STEM education and served as a career cluster lead and Perkins Loan Officer through an intergovernmental loan program. Currently, Kimberly is a vice principal at Wayne Valley High School and adjunct professor at William Paterson University. She may be reached at kimberly.moreno1984@gmail.com.

Geryel Osorio-Godoy, B.A., is a graduate research assistant at the National Center for Disaster Preparedness at Columbia's Climate School. She is a graduate of Florida International University with a bachelor's degree in psychology and is currently completing a dual master's degree program in public health and urban planning at Columbia University. She has professional experience in K-12 school systems, the nonprofit sector, and independent consulting. Geryel hopes to equip organizations with more effective antiracist efforts that decolonize, deconstruct, rebuild, and empower historically excluded communities. Her work meets at the intersection of mental health, affordable housing, reproductive justice, queer liberation, healing, and joy. She may be reached at goo2110@columbia.edu.

Ethan Podwojski, B.A., is a 2020 Knox College graduate and a secondary education social studies teacher. After completing student teaching during the COVID-19 pandemic, Ethan used his experiences to better apply technology in the classroom as well as incorporate social and emotional learning into his daily lessons. He may be reached at epodski@gmail.com.

Drew Polly, Ph.D., is a professor in the elementary education program in the Cato College of Education at the University of North Carolina at Charlotte. Drew has authored or co-authored over 100 peer-reviewed articles or book chapters about teaching and learning, with a focus on mathematics education, technology integration, and teacher education. He may be reached at Drew.Polly@uncc.edu.

Ellen M. Pozzi, Ph.D., is an associate professor and the director of the School Library Media program at William Paterson University. Her research interests include library history and diversity in children's literature. She has recently contributed (with Gihan Mohamad and Laurence Gander) the chapter "Why Can't I Just Use the Classics?: Bringing Diverse Books to Teachers and Librarians" to the *Handbook of Research on Teaching Diverse Youth Literature to Pre-Service Professionals*. She may be reached at pozzie@wpunj.edu.

Nisreen Rajab, M.Ed., was born and raised in Palestine, obtaining her undergraduate degree at The Islamic University of Gaza, with a bachelor's in English language education with honors in 2012. After college, she worked as an English teacher for elementary students at the United Nations Refugees School (UNRWA) in Gaza. In 2013, she was granted a Fulbright Foreign Language Teaching Assistant (FLTA) scholarship and moved to the United States, where she worked at William Paterson University as an Arabic language professor assistant. She is a 2019 graduate of the M.Ed. in curriculum and learning program with a concentration in bilingual/ESL from William Paterson University. Nisreen has always been involved in the Palestinian and Arabic Communities in New York and North New Jersey. Between 2017 and 2019, she worked as an ESL teacher for adult refugee students at Smile for Charities, NJ. She has been the English conversation instructor at the Palestinian American Community Center since 2018. She currently works as an ESL teacher at Wayne Township Public Schools District, NJ, and she is a team member for the Learning Arts at Home project at William Paterson University. She may be reached at nisreenrajab@gmail.com.

Michael Salvatore, Ph.D., is a senior vice president at Kean University and former NJ Superintendent of the Year. Michael is working to close equity gaps through the democratization of data on Kean's campuses. He currently leads the University Planning Council and the Presidential Task Force for Research. He may be reached at Lbsuper2011@gmail.com.

Triada Samaras, M.F.A., is an adjunct professor at William Paterson University and Kean University. She is also a practicing artist. For over 20 years, Triada has been exploring the themes of identity, house/home, voice, and geography in her artwork, often in art activist and socially engaged contexts in New York City and Athens, Greece, gaining national and international recognition. Originally educated in fine art at Smith College and the Museum School of Fine Art in Massachusetts, Triada has also completed graduate work in art education interdisciplinary art at Teachers College, Columbia University, and Goddard College. She may be reached at triadasamaras@gmail.com.

Diallo Sessoms, Ph.D., is an associate professor of educational technology in the Department of Early and Elementary Education at Salisbury University. He earned a master's degree in educational psychology followed by a Ph.D. in instructional technology at the University of Virginia and has served in several positions at Salisbury University, including special assistant to the provost for academic

224 Contributors

innovation. Diallo is currently a faculty fellow at the Dave & Patsy Rommel Center, and his research is focused on makerspaces in elementary education. He recently developed and opened a makerspace for the education department at Salisbury University. He may be reached at ddsessoms@salisbury.edu.

Joe Sherman, M. Ed., has spent more than a decade as a middle grades social studies educator at Cardinal Local Schools in Northeast Ohio. His research interests include technology in the social studies classroom, teaching online readiness, and unique characteristics of middle-grades learners. He may be reached at joe.sherman@cardinalschools.org.

Woonhee Sung, Ed.D., is an assistant professor in the School of Education at the University of Texas at Tyler. Woonhee obtained her Ed.D. from Teachers College, Columbia University, in the instructional technology and media program. Her research focuses on the design, development, and implementation of technology-integrated learning environments to foster computational thinking and maker projects with programming and robotics tools in K-12 STEM fields. She may be reached at wsung@uttyler.edu.

Pei-Lin Weng, Ph.D., specializes in accessibility and usability research and is currently working as an accessibility and business development consultant at Perun Business Group. Prior to this, she was an associate professor of special education at William Paterson University. Pei-Lin earned her Ph.D. in special education from Purdue University. Before completing her doctoral degree, she worked with students with disabilities as a speech-language pathologist, an augmentative and alternative communication (AAC) consultant, and an assistive technology consultant. She may be reached at pwengtw@gmail.com.

Renee Whelan, Ed.D., is a shared instructional coach for early childhood programs and a part-time professor. She has over 25 years of experience in early childhood education, concentrating on curriculum, assessment, community partnerships, and professional learning as well as years of fiscal review and budgetary experience. Her research interests include early childhood mathematics and literacy, STEAM, sustainability, teacher leadership, one-on-one conferencing, and cognitive coaching. She may be reached at whelanr@wpunj.edu.

INDEX

Note: Page numbers in *italic* indicate a figure, and page numbers in **bold** indicate a table on the corresponding page.

3D modeling 110, 111
3D printers 106, *106*, 107, 111
21st Century Learning framework 119

AAC 174
ABCD study 19
academic curricula 169, *170*
access **158**
accessibility 28, 29, *30*, **32**, **33–34**, **35**, 173
accessibility, usability, wellness, and support (AUWS) *see* AUWS
achievement **158**
ACRL 86
action 85, 90–91
administrators: digital divide and 22–23; family support and 124; strategies and practices 31, **32–33**
Adolescent Brain Cognitive Development (ABCD) study 19
advanced placement classes 75–76
affect 9
American Rescue Plan 10
Amro, F. 19
An, H. xv, 3, 28, 29, 130
Anstead, J. 91
app evaluation 171–172
Arnove, R. F. 23

artistic development pedagogy 141–142
art media and practices 141
arts-integration pedagogy 139
arts-integration programs *see* Learning Arts at Home (LAH)
assessment: disparities in 69–70; equitable practices 70–71; multiple options frequency *89*
Assistive Technology Act Training and Technical Assistance Center 175
assistive technology (AT) 174–175, *175*
Association of College and Research Libraries (ACRL) 86
Astin, A. W. 184
AT 174–175, *175*
audacity 107
audience xxiv
augmentative and alternative communication (AAC) 174
AUWS 28, 29, *30*, **32–36**

background knowledge, of students 140
Barrett, L. 93
Bavel, J. J. V. 18
Beauchamp, G. 22
belonging 12
Berns, R. 75
Birdbrain technologies 109

226 Index

Bitmoji® 181, 183, 189, 191
Black, P. J. 71
blended learning 29–30
Bonk, C. J. x, 36
Boone, R. 172
Boy Who Harnessed the Wind, The (Kamkwaba) 111
Bozkurt, A. 20
Brown v. Board of Education 7
BUILDERS 112
Building Unique Inventions to Launch Discovery, Engagement, Reasoning, and STEM (BUILDERS) 112
Burbules, N. C. 17
Burchell, A. 179

caregivers *see* parents, guardians, and caregivers (PGCs)
CAST 84, 171
Center for Applied Special Technology (CAST) 84, 171
Chandler, T. 17, 43
Children's Museum Makerspace 101
Cho, A. 110
ClassDojo 124
classroom discussions, virtual 190
classroom management 188–189
cognitive development 18–19
CoI 184
collaboration 119
Common Core State Standards Initiative 138
Community of Inquiry (CoI) 184
connections 140, 141–142
content-neutral technologies: maker movement 101–102, 104, 105, 113; makerspaces 101–113; overview 99–100
Continuity of Operations (COOP) Planning for Education Agencies (REMS) 50
continuity-of-operations planning (COOP) 46–50, **48**
COOP 46–50, **48**
COVID-19: administrators and support staff and 22–23; digital learning and 69–70; distributive justice and 23; impact of xx–xxi, 3–4, 43–44; online learning issues and 29–30; parents, guardians, and caregivers and 21; remote literacy instruction 185, 187–190; scope of 46; *see also* pandemic planning
creativity 119
critical theory 8

CRT *see* culturally responsive teaching (CRT)
culturally responsive teaching (CRT) 132, 132–134, **133**, 136, *137*
curriculum reviews 76
Cyberschools (Jones) xii

Dabbagh, N. 19
Dave and Patsy Rommel Center for Entrepreneurship 107
Deoni, S. C. 19
design thinking 110–113
DeVincenzo, J. L. 17, 43
DeVos, B. 45–46
DeWitt, S. W. 209
digital divide: accessibility 181; administrators and support staff and 22–23; bridging 43–51; COVID-19 and 179; defined 5, 17, 120; distributive justice and 23; educators and 19–20; issues related to 13, 17–18; parents, guardians, and caregivers and 20–22; policy analysis 43–51; socioeconomic status and 70; students and 18–19; in urban schools 118
digital equity: assessment and 70–71; defined 5; problem of 5; rural schools 121; urban schools 121; whole child approach and 10–13
Digital Harbor Foundation (DHF) 100
digital leadership xxi
digital learning: for academic and functional curricula 169–170, *170*; defined 29, 168; history of 168; principles of 121–123; rapid shift 69–70; strategies and practices 31–36; for students with disabilities 168–176; terminology 168; in urban schools 118, 120–121; *see also* online learning
digital-use divide 5
direct impact **48**
disabilities, students with: academic and functional curricula 169–170; accessibility 173; app and software evaluations 171–172; assistive technology 174–175; digital learning history 168; functional curricula 169–170, *170*; funding resources 174; lending resources 175; overview 167–168; UDL and 170–171
distinctions of equity **133**
distributive justice framework 23
diversity 31

Index 227

diversity wheel *137*
do-it-yourself (DIY) ethos 101
Dorn, E. 19
Dougherty, D. 104
Dreamers (Morales) 135, 136, 138, 145–146
dual-language learners 132; *see also* English language learners (ELLs)
Duncan, A. 113

early childhood education 18, 19
Early Learning and Educational Technology Policy Brief 118–119
Eastern Shore of Maryland 99–100
Easterseals Crossroads 175
Educate to Innovate 102
educators, pandemic impact on 19–20
Educators' Toolkit 189
ELLs *see* English language learners (ELLs)
ELT (expanded learning time) 22
emergency operations plan (EOP) **48**
engagement xiv, 84, 88, 162–163, 204, 213
English language learners (ELLs) 19, 23, 124, 135, 150; *see also* dual-language learners
EOP **48**
equity: digital *see* digital equity; grading and 70–71; power of 80; in rural schools 212
equity-based mathematics 158–159, **158**, 164
Ersoy, E. 162
Ertmer, P. A. 100
Escobar, M. 112, 113
excluded curriculum 150
Executive Order 13985 4
expanded learning time (ELT) 22
expression 85, 90–91
Eyler, J. R. 204

Fancera, S. F. 54
Federal Emergency Management Agency (FEMA) 49
FEMA 49
field trips 202
Flip 216
Flipgrid 123–124
formative assessment 71, **77–79**, 80
found materials 141
four Cs framework 119
Framework for 21st Century Learning 119
Fuentes, D. 3

functional curricula 169–170, *170*
funding resources 174

Garrison, D. R. 184
Gill, B. P. 186
Gillingham, A. 190
Google Classroom® 180, 182, 214–215
Google Docs 124
Google Meet 215
Google Slides 181, 183, 189, 191
Goudeau, S. 21
grading policies 69
grading practices: benefits of equitable grading 76; best practices 73–75; categories of 72–73; COVID-19 and 73; equitable 70–71, 75–76; objectives 74; observable criteria 74–75; opportunities for success 75; recommendations 76–80; standards-based 76; zeros in 75
Grimes, N. 179
guardians *see* parents, guardians, and caregivers (PGCs)
Gutiérrez, R. 158, 164

H1N1 pandemic 44–45
Haberman, M. 186
habits 13
Hammond, Z. 133
hand signals **77**
Heppell, S. xii–xiii
Herold, B. 120
Herrmann, L. 19, 22
Higgins, K. 172
high-needs schools 6–8, 20; challenges in 100–101; online learning in 29–30; remote literacy instruction 185–187; rural 99–114, 210–212; strategies and practices 31–36; urban 118–126, 199–206
honors classes 75–76
Horowitz, R. 132
Howerton, A. 157

IDEA 85, 167, 174
identity **158**
Inclusive Arts Integration 131
INDATA 175
indirect impact **48**
Individuals with Disabilities Education Act (IDEA) 85, 167, 174
information literacy 86–87
integrated support systems 13

228 Index

interdisciplinary learning 202–205
International Society for Technology in Education (ISTE) 31
ISTE 31

Jim Crow 7
Jones, G. xi–xii, xvii

Kachel, D. E. 91
Kalogiannakis, M. 172
Kamkwaba, W. 111–112, 113
Karroum, B. 148
kindness stamp *108*
knowledge demands 136
knowledge development 12
Kormos, E. xiv, 100, 118
Küçükoglu, H. 140

LAH *see* Learning Arts at Home (LAH)
Lance, K. C. 91
language conventionality 136
Lanni, M. 130
learner autonomy xv
learner engagement 162–163
Learning Arts at Home (LAH): Arabic videos 147–149; background 131–132; book selection criteria 134, *135*; conceptual framework 132–134; English videos **142**; goals of 134; pedagogies 139–142; pilot study findings 151; qualitative measures 136–138; quantitative measures 135; reader/viewer and task measures 138; recommendations 149–151; Spanish videos 144–146; three-part model 134–138
learning ecology 8–10
learning environments 11–12, 14
learning experiences 12
learning loss 10, 19, 20
learning management system (LMS) 123
Learning Policy Institute (LPI) 10
learning principles xv–xvi
learning recovery: frameworks for 48–50; terminology **48**
learning time 22
lending resources 175
levels of meaning 136, 137
libraries, virtual 187–188
Lifelong Kindergarten 107
literacy development pedagogy 139–141
literacy instruction, remote 185–187, 190
Liu, Y. C. 132

LMS 123
Loom 216
LPI 10

Mace, R. 84
Make All America a School (Jones) xi–xii
maker movement 101–102, 104, 105, 113
makerspaces: background 102; described 103–105; design thinking, making, and learning 110–113; elementary level 111; higher levels 111–113; image of *102, 103, 104, 105, 106*; philosophy and pedagogy 109–113; tools 105–109, *105*
making connections 140, 141–142
Maryland 99, 100, 107
math action technologies 165
mathematics: activities, high-quality 164; digital learning for students with disabilities 169; equity-based 158–159, 164; recommendations and future considerations 164–165; scaffolding 164–165; support of learning 164–165; Thinking Blocks Multiplication program *160–161*, 162–164
Math Playground program *see* Thinking Blocks Multiplication program
Math Speak 169
McCoy, D. C. 18–19
McCullough, A. W. 165
Mealer, B. 113
Medicaid 174
mindsets 13
modeling, of fluent reading 140–141
Mohamad, G. 83
Morales, Y. 134, 135, 136, 138, 145
Moreno, K. xiv, 69
multicultural education **133**
multilingual arts-integration *see* arts-integration programs

NAESP 22
National Association of Elementary School Principals (NAESP) 22
National Center for Education Statistics 167, 210
National Education Technology Plan (NETP) 157
National Strategy for Pandemic Influenza 44
NETP 157
New Jersey 131–132, 199–206
No Child Left Behind Act 201
Noodle Tools 216
notebooks 188

NotSchool xii–xiii
null curriculum 150

Oksuz, C. 162
online learning: early years x–xii; factors affecting 28; in high-needs schools 29–30; *see also* digital learning
open-ended questions 140
open-source tools 107, 109
Orton-Gillingham approach 190
Orton, S. T. 190
Osorio-Godoy, G. 17
Ottenbreit-Leftwich, A. T. 100

pandemic planning: continuity-of-operations planning 46–50; historical background 44–46; long-term recovery 48–50
Papadakis, S. 172
parents, guardians, and caregivers (PGCs): digital divide and 20–22; strategies and practices 32, **35–36**
Paterson Public Schools District xxi
PBIS 189
PDL *see* professional development and learning (PDL)
Peacock, S. 184
Pease, P. x, xii
Pelz, B. 121
personalization of learning 205
picture walks 139–140
Podwojski, E. 209
policy analysis: district level 47–48, 49; Early Learning and Educational Technology Policy Brief 118–119; federal level 44–46, 50; historical background 44–46; long-term recovery 48–50
political contexts 7
polling **78**
Polly, D. 157
positive behavior interventions and supports (PBIS) 189
positive relationships 11
post-COVID learning ecology 8–10
power **158**
Pozzi, E. 83
PRC-Saltillo 175
Price-Dennis, D. 20
principles of learning xv–xvi, 10
problem-based learning approach 113
professional development and learning (PDL): obstacles 56, 57–59, 57; social

media and networking and 55–56; staff inclusion 59; Twitter and 56–62
professional learning *see* professional development and learning (PDL)
project-based learning 206
props 139

Qazi, M. 112, 113
qualitative measures 136–138
quantitative measures 135

Rajab, N. 130
Ramsey, C. A. 111
RAPID Learning Recovery Framework 48, *49*
RCRC initiative 50
read-aloud videos 131–132, 134, *135*, 136; Arabic examples of **147**, *148*; English examples of *143*; examples of **142**; Spanish examples of **144**, *145*
reader/viewer and task measures 138
Readiness and Emergency Management for School (REMS) 50
relationships, positive 11
Remind 124
remote literacy instruction 185–187
REMS 50
representation 85, 89–90
Resilient Children, Resilient Community (RCRC) initiative 50
response cards **78**
robots 109
rubrics **79**
rural schools: content-neutral technology 99–114; high-needs schools 209–217; social studies 209–217
Ruth and the Green book (Ramsey & Strauss) 111

safety 12
Salisbury University Makerlab *106*
Salvatore, M. 191
Samaras, T. 130
school equity 4–6, 13–14; *see also* school (in)equity
school (in)equity 8; *see also* school equity
school leaders 55, 56, 59, 60, 62–63
school libraries: challenges in 91–92; survey findings 88–91, 92; UDL and 85–86
science integration 201, 204
science of learning 10, 12, 14
Scratch 107

230 Index

SDL xiii
Sealey-Ruiz, Y. 20
SEL *see* social and emotional learning (SEL)
self-directed learning (SDL) xiii
Sessoms, D. 99
Sherman, J. xiv, 118
Shulman, L. S. 184
skill development 13
SMN: future value of 62; usage data 54–55
SNAP 19
social and emotional learning (SEL) 141
social development of learners 6–7
social justice education **133**
social media and networking (SMN): future value of 62; usage data 54–55; *see also* Twitter;
social networking 55
social pedagogies 204
social reproduction 8
social studies classrooms: challenges in 119–121; four Cs framework 119; strategies 121–123; teachers 120; technologies for 123–125; technology access 120–121
social studies in rural high-needs schools: applications specific to 216; community characteristics **210**; engagement 212–213; equity 212; instruction, implementing 215–216; instruction, preparing 214–215; introduction 209; school pandemic response **211**; student achievement 213–214; study findings 212–216; study participants 210–212; teacher information **211**; technology tools 214–216
sociocultural context 6–8, 9, 14
sociocultural development of learners 7
socioeconomic status 70
sociopolitical context 6–8
software evaluation 171–172
Soñadores (Morales) 134, 135, 136, 138, 145–146
Sosa Díaz, M. J. 20, 21
Soto, G. 143
Southern Black Belt 112
SparkFun 109
Special Supplemental Nutrition Program for Women, Infants, and Children (WIC) 19
standards-based grading 76
State of Indiana Division of Disability and Rehabilitative Services 175

strategies and practices for equitable digital learning: accessibility **32–33**; for administrators **32–33**; for parents **35–36**; support 33; for teachers **33–35**; usability **33**; wellness 33
Strauss, G. 111
structure 136
summative assessment 71
Sung, W. 28
Suppes, P. 100
Supplemental Nutritional Assistance Program (SNAP) 19
support 28, 29, *30*, **33**, **34–35**, **36**
support staff 22–23

Taber-Doughty, T. 172
teach-back **78–79**
teacher for visual impairment 169
teachers: in high-needs schools 120; strategies and practices **33–35**
Technological Pedagogical Content Knowledge (TPACK) 184, 187
technology as instructional tool 203
technology infusion 110
TEC-VARIETY framework xvi
Tell Me More About Ramadan (Karroum) 148–149
Thinking Blocks Multiplication program 158; learner engagement 162–163; overview *160–161*, 162; pre- and posttest data 163; process of 162; scaffolding and support 164–165; student achievement 163–164
Thomas, M. 84
Tondeur, J. 101
Too Many Tamales (Soto) 143
TPACK framework 184, 187
traditional classrooms, vs. virtual classrooms **182**
Trump administration 45
Tustin, N. 120
Twitter: acknowledging use 65; education chats 56; future value of 62–63; introducing staff 64; model use 63–64; moderating use of 65; for SDL 56–62; personal learning and 64–65; pitfalls 61–62; as preferred platform 59–62; recommendations for use 63–65, 64; staff inclusion 59; successes 60–61

UDL *see* Universal Design for Learning (UDL)
UNESCO 47

United States Department of Education (USDOE) 4

Universal Design for Learning (UDL): action 85, 90–91; background 84–87; challenges in 91–92; engagement 84, 88; explained 83–84, 84–87, 102–103; expression 85, 90–91; four Cs framework 119; guidelines 85; information literacy and 86–87; makerspaces and 102–103; principles of 88–91, 171; representation 85, 89–90; school libraries and 85–86, 88–92; students with disabilities and 170–171; study highlights 86–87

urban schools: digital learning strategies 118–126; virtual excursions 200–206

usability 28, 29, 30, **33**, **34**, **35**

U.S. Department of Education 44–45, 46, 50, 73, 118

Varela, A. 21

Venkatesh, K. 84

Ventura, J. xxi

verbal response **77**

Verloop, N. 187

videos, read-aloud 131–132

virtual binders 188

virtual classrooms: benefits of 183–185, *183*; binders 188; classroom discussions 190; classroom libraries 187–188; classroom management 188–189; creating 181–183; intentional exploration in 202–205; manipulatives 189–190; notebooks 188; vs. traditional classrooms **182**; wall displays 188

virtual excursions: background 200–201; interdisciplinary study 202–205; overview 199–200; purpose of 205; tips for 205–206

virtual manipulatives 189–190

visual impairment, teacher for 169

volatile, unpredictable, complex, and ambiguous (VUCA) conditions 22

VUCA conditions 22

wait time 77

Walker, H. 172

wall displays 188

Watkins, S. C. 110

Webb-Dempsey, J. 132

wellness 28, 29, *30*, **33**, **34**, **36**

Weng, P.-L. 167, 172

Whelan, R. 191

whole child approach 9–10, 10–13

whole-systems approach 14

WIC (Special Supplemental Nutrition Program for Women, Infants, and Children) 19

Wiley, D. 36

William, D. 71

Zaranis, N. 172

zeros in grading 75

Zones of Regulation 189